Social Science
and Utopia

HARVESTER STUDIES IN PHILOSOPHY

General Editor: Margaret A. Boden,
University of Sussex

Other titles in preparation.

Social Science and Utopia

Nineteenth-Century Models of Social Harmony

BARBARA GOODWIN

Lecturer in Political Theory, Brunel University

THE HARVESTER PRESS · SUSSEX

First published in Great Britain, 1978, by
THE HARVESTER PRESS LIMITED
Publisher: John Spiers
2 Stanford Terrace, Hassocks, Sussex

© Barbara Goodwin, 1978

British Library Cataloguing in Publication Data

Goodwin, Barbara
   Social science and utopia.
   1. Utopias — History
   I. Title
   301.34   HX806

ISBN 0-85527-791-2

Filmset by The Humble Wordsmith Limited, Tonbridge, Kent.
Printed in Great Britain by
Redwood Burn Limited, Trowbridge, Wiltshire

CONTENTS

PREFACE

THE road to utopia is devious. I set out equipped with political philosophy and a liking for literary utopias, and arrived with the conviction that utopianism is a distinctive form of social science. The consequent depiction of the early socialist and anarchist utopians as aspiring social scientists is intended to shed light on the problems of early social science and also on utopian theory as a genre.

I am grateful to Isaiah Berlin, Graeme Duncan, Philippa Foot, Jack Lively, Steven Łukes, Frank Manuel, Trevor Pateman and Charles Vereker for comments and advice, and in particular to the late John Plamenatz for his detailed criticism and help. My thanks also to St Antony's College, Oxford for its support during the research, and to my colleagues in Brunel's Department of Government for their interest and encouragement.

BARBARA GOODWIN
Brunel University,
1977

ABBREVIATIONS USED IN REFERENCES

Fourier:

Oeuvres Complètes, vols. I-XII . . . . OC I-XII
The Utopian Vision of Charles Fourier, ed. J. Beecher and
R. Bienvenu . . . . Beecher and Bienvenu

Owen:

A New View of Society . . . . NVS
Report to the County of Lanark . . . . RCL
Book of the New Moral World . . . . BNMW
Six Lectures delivered in Manchester . . . . *Six Lectures*
*A Development of the Principles and Plans
on which to establish Self-Supporting
Home Colonies* . . . . HC
*Revolution in the Kind and Practice
of the Human Race* . . . . *Revolution*
Godwin:
An Enquiry concerning Political Justice . . . . PJI-II .
(3rd edition unless stated).

Saint-Simon:

*De la Réorganisation de la Société
Européene* . . . . *Réorganisation*
*Lettre d'un Habitant de Génève à
ses Contemporains* . . . . *Lettre*
Sur la Querelle des Abeilles et des Frelons . . . . . . *Querelle*
Du Système Industriel . . . . *Système*
Catéchisme des Industriels . . . . *Catéchisme*
La Physiologie Sociale: Oeuvres Choisies,
ed. G. Gurvitch . . . . Gurvitch
Saint-Simon: Selected Political Writings,
ed. F. Markham . . . . Markham
The New World of Henri Saint-Simon,
F. Manuel . . . . *New World*

Marx & Engels:

Selected Works (Moscow, 1970), 3 vols. . . . . . . MESW I-II

CHAPTER 1

UTOPIA REVISITED

GOOD reason must be proffered for devoting new books to old utopias, the relics of political aspiration. This study is not a celebration of utopianism and the imagination, but an attempt to show the significance of certain utopias within the development of social science. Although an admittedly tendentious enterprise, it does not do injustice to the utopians concerned, or unduly distort their meaning, since all of them regarded themselves as having a social-scientific purpose. Godwin, Owen, Fourier and Saint-Simon were eminently post-Enlightenment thinkers in their view of society as a human artefact open to rational improvement, and this basic homogeneity makes a comparative study feasible. Their intention was to derive the principles of an ideal society from a scientific analysis of man: in historical perspective, their theories can also be seen to have provided remedies for the burgeoning social diseases of early capitalism, and inspiration for radicals convalescing after the disasters of the French Revolution.

An academic resurrection of these utopians has occurred in the last two decades. Saint-Simon has been acclaimed for his account of technocratic state capitalism and for his influence on Marx. Owen's bicentenary in 1971 was commemorated by social historians. Fourier's liberated sexual writings were themselves liberated from the mice in a Parisian attic and published in 1966, proving of great interest to the theoreticians of permissiveness. Godwin, always a focus of scholarly interest as an early anarchist and advanced moralist, has now been taken up by the anarchist underground. Although new publications of note have resulted from this revival, many treatments of these thinkers still concentrate on expositions of the content of the utopias: the present study concerns itself with the form and structure of the theories and their relation to a wider intellectual movement.

The common end of the utopias was the eradication of conflict, crime and misery, and the creation of social harmony, and their common means was a systematic analysis of human nature. The utopias emerge as the necessary outcome of this logical process, and are seen by their authors as models of the perfectly constructed, perfectly functioning society, not as manifestoes or fantasies. As such, the models are intrinsically preferable to imperfect societies, so that the need to realise them in the real world appears as a scientific imperative. My purpose is to examine this utopian logic, and the attempt to create a frictionless social machine through ideal methods of social control, and to assess the degree of compatibility between the scientific and the utopian endeavour.

THE MARK OF THE UTOPIAN

The elusive concept of utopia must be grasped in order to provide conditions for its application in political thought. The pun dwells equally on 'no place' and 'good place' but perjorative use of the term has focused attention on the former. Inspection of the political ideal shows that utopia is necessarily a good place, although only accidentally is it nowhere to be found. The utopian is not a fantasist but a revolutionary. How then do we identify the realistic and constructive utopian theorist? Mannheim's definition suggests that the utopian is recognised by the tendency of his beliefs, translated into action, to overthrow the existing order. This has the unsatisfactory corollaries that utopians are best recognised *ex post*, that only successful utopians can ever be identified, and that upon the realisation of utopia, it ceases to be utopia. By contrast, for Marx, the defining characteristic of the utopian is his *lack* of function, his ineffectuality, and the *a priori* impossibility of his functioning in society, because of his remoteness from material causes and historical events.[1]

The connection between the meaning and the function of utopianism is best made at a theoretical level. Political theory has its myths, justificatory and revolutionary, and utopia is one of them. It serves, in company with the Golden Age and the State of Nature, as a reference point for the development of critical theory, but also as a repository of new political paradigms and values. This mythical and speculative role of utopian theory places it outside the reach of truth-functions and other methods of verification, making it *sui generis*. We must look to the possible uses of utopia to justify these peculiarities. If a culture is to be criticised radically, by reference to alternative values outside its own ideology, a utopian model is a valuable device. When the theorist wishes to refashion society wholesale, utopia offers him a useful space, devoid of preconceived features, within which to work. In fact, the critical and the constructive constituents of utopian political theory are not really as separable as the delineation of its two functions might suggest: the negation of the present requires a formulated, particular alternative, since the theorist can only select dimensions of present reality for negation from a perspective of preferred alternative values.

But if the onslaught on society requires utopia, utopia also needs society, for the best of worlds is invariably described with reference to an inferior, imperfect world. Whether primarily critical or constructive in intention, utopianism must be historically and culturally located in the writer's social context, and is inseparable from the object that it seeks to destroy. Mannheim, too, makes this clear, arguing that utopia, while transcending contemporary social structures and thought, has essentially a historical existence and form. Again, however revolutionary the will of the writer, his utopia is indisputably contextual in the sense that 'the best' cannot be defined without some reference to what he is familiar with, since imagination is parasitic on experience. This historicity of utopia, incidentally, makes it as difficult to produce a general theory of utopia as to write a general theory of the state.

The argument so far suggests that utopia functions in

political theory as a kind of myth, catalytic to critical and revolutionary thought, which requires for this purpose certain qualities: singularity and finiteness (a plurality of utopias will not serve) and a form both historical and transcendental. But in addition to this account of utopia's function, a definition of utopianism is needed to identify utopian theorists. Some general characteristics of utopian thought and its thinker suggest themselves.

The utopian constructs a *model of an ideal society* located in the past (mythical or real), present (but situated elsewhere) or future, for critical and didactic purposes. He may intend and promote the realisation of his scheme, or may rely on its persuasive powers, but he has in any case a *serious preference* for this alternative society. Whether destructive or constructive in function, utopias are necessarily based on a *concept of the Good Life*, which features as an explicit, central ideal. Of course, most political theorists have some opinions about this but the utopian is distinguished by the radicalism and totality of his vision. Utopian accounts of the Good Life are also differentiated from most moral and religious theories of the virtuous life by their scope and subject matter: they focus not on the individual moral being, but on that more complex creature, *man-in-society*, and seek to improve both elements of this compound.

Beyond doubt, the primary characteristic of utopianism is *perfectibilism* of some kind, for the meaning of utopia has always been extended from 'good place' to 'the best place', the ideal state. But there are two strains of utopian perfectibilism: firstly, the idea that society and its institutions can be so arranged and governed as to be perfect — a somewhat mechanistic social perfectibilism. Secondly, there is the doctrine of human perfectibility, which in the utopian context means that human nature and social behaviour are considered perfectible throughout society, not merely in the individual paragon. This doctrine is nowadays associated with the Enlightenment and after, but it equally underlies Plato's projected education for the Guardians, and — although frequently eclipsed by the Christian dogma of Original Sin — is a recurrent theme of utopianism since classical antiquity. It seems logical that the two kinds of perfectibilism should run in tandem, but they also occur separately: for instance, More's eponymous Utopia relies on social engineering rather than human perfection, and he is resigned to the persistence of crime.

The transmutation of 'good' into 'perfect' has certain structural and problematic consequences. Being more exclusive than 'good', it highlights the question 'Perfect according to which criteria?' which is often answered by resort to absolutist standards. Furthermore, 'perfect' connotes a superlative state which must be considered beyond the reach or necessity of change, since there is no progressing beyond the perfect. This syntactical dictate, literally obeyed, gives many utopias a static, unreal quality, which detracts from their credibility.

In fact, a conception of utopia based merely on optimalities scarcely deserves the title of utopia. As Paretan analysis indicates, there are many optimal arrangements of society, but the criteria for identifying the *best* arrangements are so designed as to produce the unique formula which the syntax of the superlative demands. Utopians must concern themselves with the best of worlds, leaving optimalists to shuffle resources within given, real constraints. This concern, and the singularity and certainty of his goal, marks out the utopian from other reforming spirits.

The creation of a unique, final model of utopia embodying preferred ideals has often, not surprisingly, been supported by an absolutist epistemology, ever since Plato set the fashion. The nexus of absolutism and utopianism cannot be analysed in terms of cause and effect, there is merely a high correlation of these two modes of theorising. It is both necessary and justifiable that the committed utopian should believe himself to have a true conception of human good, and the most appropriate programme for attaining it. A self-proclaimed utopian scheme such as Robert Nozick describes in *Anarchy, State and Utopia*, which allows for the multiplication of possible utopias and free and frequent choice between them by inhabitants, fails all the tests of utopianism listed here, in particular that of commitment to a substantive view of good.

The utopian's single-mindedness need not generate intolerance, but it logically entails a certain course of action. Values, like moralities, are universalisable. The form of utopia, deriving from the nature of moral and social values, is equally universalising, and the utopian is duty-bound to try to universalise and realise his unique vision. He is in principle an imperialist, dedicated not to the widening of choices, but to propagandising on behalf of his own choice, validated by his own values. His monomania has to be excused in terms of his impeccably good intentions towards mankind!

Also characteristic of utopian thinking is the denial of the idea of historical continuity and development, which the invention of an alternative society implies. Of course, the concept of historical continuity and progress is relatively new, as Becker argues,[2] so that to impose retrospectively on earlier utopias the label of ahistoricity is not in any sense to condemn. It can be hypothesised that thinkers such as Fourier, Saint-Simon and Marx, who placed their ideal societies at the terminus of the train of history, were in part reflecting the current predilection for progress, and so making their ideal societies more plausible for their contemporaries. But the creation of an alternative ideal (unless dialectically conceived) necessarily remains an anti-historical activity, given received ideas of history, and its realisation would constitute a rupture of tradition. So utopia is intentionally ahistorical in this sense, although this in no way contradicts the point that utopia will and must be historically located.

What other labels can be pinned on the essential utopian? Crucially, he believes that social structures can be manipulated, and men can be persuaded or moulded, otherwise his own enterprise would be in vain. Hence, he must believe that social organisation and human behaviour are not mysterious but explicable, and that determining mechanisms can be perceived and controlled: he is thus likely to be a materialist, he may be something of a scientific determinist, but he is rarely a fatalist. Is he necessarily an optimist?

Surprisingly, both pessimists and optimists figure in the ranks of utopians, since the Good Life is conceptually accessible via a maximin policy as well as via an optimistic pursuit of absolute perfection. Plato's pessimism about the common man and Fourier's optimism about liberated man can equally form the basis for utopian construction.

A criterion of scope must be invoked to distinguish the utopian from the theorist who holds certain ideals, but has no overview or utopian scheme. A utopian characteristically presents a total social project, comprehensive in its description of social life and organisation. By contrast, the theorist who holds ideals in a fragmentary fashion, or never marshalls them into an ideal society, is no utopian.

Because his project entails commitment to concrete social proposals, and because he cannot conveniently or consistently leave areas of choice or ambivalence, the utopian typically, though not always, provides a blueprint for the future society, encompassing political and social life. This device, which borders on fantasy, is taken by many to constitute the essence of utopianism, but this is too unsubtle a condition. When the provision of a blueprint is made synonymous with utopia, it promotes a view of the utopian as a man intoxicated with fantasy. In fact, the unrealisable, 'unnecessary', intricate details of the plan are often symbolic expressions of sound theoretical points (as with Fourier's extraordinary psychological categories) and serve a didactic purpose as well as entertaining — or infuriating — the reader.

Summarising, the utopian theorist is identified as follows:

1. His *modus operandi* is to promote social criticism and change through the device of an alternative construction of society.

2. He not only argues from a vision of the Good Life (and therefore, we infer, has humane and benign intentions) but is a perfectibilist with respect to man, society or both.

3. The non-relativistic nature of 'perfect' means that the utopian prefers his utopia above all, and so his espousal of this ideal is not open-minded, but exclusive. This

results in a missionary, even messianic, outlook.

4. The utopian intentionally breaks with his own cultural and historical environment, and his scheme is ultimately located 'outside' history, although, in another sense, such a break is ultimately impossible and dysfunctional.

5. He must have a mental construction of society which admits of human intervention, and hence he conceives of society and mankind in a way which could broadly be described as mechanistic and scientific. (This stipulation clearly raises problems: does it rule out Marx's historical determinism? Does it rule out Spencer's evolutionary utopianism? I think it clearly and properly rules out the latter, but can include a non-fatalistic determinist's explanation of social development.)

But the dry bones of this definition need flesh. The hallmarks of utopian thought are a creative, innovatory imagination, and aspiration which reaches beyond the familiar towards the potential and the ideal; there is also the breadth of vision which sees social life as a totality, to be reconstructed as such. Such qualities give utopias their perpetual fascination. The early socialist and anarchist utopias which are the focus of this study combine perceptive social analysis, optimistic perfectibilism and imaginative detail in a blend of particular charm.

THE DISTINCTIVE FLAVOUR OF NINETEENTH-CENTURY UTOPIANISM

Predictably, this general and abstract account of utopianism stripped of historical location and accidental characteristics must be shelved in favour of a 'special theory' derived from analysis of the early nineteenth-century utopians. Their thought will be used to illuminate certain structural necessities for the creation of a perfect society, and the connection of certain ideals with utopian aspiration. Utopia's *necessary* form will be shown to be that of a self-sufficient, integrated, conflict-free social system which can serve as an ideal-type for social analysts and social reformers whose dominant value is harmony. The relationship between utopianism and a nascent social science which wavered between description, prescription and metaphysics will also be examined, as will the exchange of premises and methods between the scientific and the visionary enterprises which gave to each a unique and original character.

These interrelated themes of the study merit further explanation. Among the writers there is an acute awareness of their innovatory methodology, which testifies to their historical role as the midwives of sociology. Saint-Simon called his method 'social physiology', Owen '*the* social science', and Fourier 'social (or celestial) mechanics': all were striving to achieve an empirical social science in the mould of the natural sciences of their day, the necessity for which had been an obsession among the *philosophes*. Their arguments proceed from first assumptions concerning human nature, which are 'empirically' established, by observation and anecdotage, to accounts of the corresponding organisation of society, and then to the establishment of guiding values. Godwin was no aspiring sociologist, but he nevertheless provided a philosophical model of the deductive order of argument on which early sociology was to be based: he argues from 'The Power of Man in his Social Capacity' to 'Principles of Society', then to 'Principles of Government'. And he believed that an aetiology of morality and rationality could be given.

Into these theories are infused numerous values and aspirational postulates about the destiny of mankind, which made their end-products — by our modern definition — not sociological but utopian. But it was in keeping with their view of moral truth as empirically ascertainable, to take such liberties with the objective, scientific approach. Suffice it to say, all these utopians believed their method of analysis to be rational, empirical, scientific, and firmly grounded in reality; their projected utopias were merely the next step in the deductive process. The scientificity of this procedure is assessed in Chapter 8.

The chief determinant of the structure of this study is the

investigation of social harmony, the postulated goal of these utopias. The magic of the harmonious ideal derives from the Enlightenment's post-Newtonian analysis of the universe as an interlocking whole, which rendered men and society as subject to causal laws as are natural objects, and so pointed to the hope of universal harmony, and the need for a social science. The ideal stimulated efforts in the fields of morality, economics and politics to reconcile men's private interests with the public good. In particular, Mandeville, Smith, Bentham and Rousseau offered various theoretical reconciliations. The utopians endeavoured to achieve reconciliation in their institutions.

It cannot be part of the *general* definition of utopia that it should be a peaceful and conflict-free society: pessimistic utopias aim at most at the containment of conflict and deviance, and aggression may even be thought to have a certain social value.[3] But these four utopias set out to design societies in which conflict would become an impossibility. Their analysis of social conflict may now be thought superficial, but they propose plausible methods of conflict elimination. The transcendent vision of social harmony is to be realised by harnessing the human capacity for improvement and perfection, but also by creating ideal methods of social control. Chapters 4 and 5 explore these mechanisms, and find that harmony should be a structural part of any utopia worth the name. In pursuit of harmony the utopians had to confront and resolve perpetual social problems such as the reconciliation of total planning with individual freedom. In fact, they solved many such traditional paradoxes by a conceptual revisionism which honours the essence of the ideal while discarding its accidental or conventional attributes. Chapters 6 and 7 examine their innovatory treatment of social values.

The mode of administering a harmonious society depends primarily on how the relationship between individuals and society is perceived, and the analysis retraces the utopians' path, proceeding from an account of human nature to a 'deduced' description of ideal social organisation, a sequence which they claimed to be scientific. What follows, then, is both a reflection and an investigation of the utopians' social logic.

The special theory of utopia which emerges mirrors the intellectual preoccupations and aspirations of the *philosophes* and their successors, and the socio-economic circumstances of the decades after 1789. These utopians were materialists, naturalists, perfectibilists and neo-Newtonians: they believed in material causes of social events, believed that society and men were natural objects to be studied by methods analogous to those of the natural sciences, believed in human perfectibility, and longed to unearth a principle of universal harmony operating in society with the efficiency and totality of Newtonian attraction. These intellectual commitments, plus the critical empirical scrutiny of society and the rejection of metaphysical explanations, combined to produce a special brand of scientific utopia, or utopian social science.

The contemplation of these utopias leads inexorably to that perpetual dilemma of politics: can conflict be eliminated or must it be institutionalised as in a democracy? This engenders further questions. Are the causes of social conflict economic, political or psychological? Is conflict healthy and functional, or destructive? Any theoretical model of society must answer these critical questions, and the utopian committed to harmony needs a convincing story. The utopias will therefore also be evaluated as models of conflict resolution.

The polarity between nineteenth-century utopianism and its major rival, the classical theory of liberal democracy, merits analysis. The two kinds of theory are antithetical because they are structured according to contradictory myths and opposing assumptions: for example, democracy's myths of contract, consent and free choice contrast with the utopians' view of government as necessarily based on coercian and the subversion of human nature. Central to the antithesis is the treatment of social conflict, which democratic theorists viewed with resignation, or even with approval. In fact, liberal democratic theory was the shadowy combatant, the quasi-radical model, against which socialist and anarchist utopianism of this period defined itself, and evolved. Democrats are open-minded (empty-headed), utopians are committed (dogmatic), utopianism is totalitarian, democracy is vacuously libertarian: the reciprocal insults, and contrasts, are prolific. The polarity of democratic values and utopian ideals is elaborated in Chapter 7.

The central concerns of this work have now been described, although in dealing with theorists such as these it is impossible always to keep to the script. Utopians are, by nature, busybodies. Their all-embracing vision touches on most of the problems vexing social and political theorists and their limitless confidence leads them to develop serious solutions even to minor problems. Undoubtedly, these asides can be as provoking and revealing as the main text itself, and so occasional diversions and excursions are justified.

References
1. See K. Mannheim, *Ideology and Utopia*, trans L. Wirth and E. Shils, (Routledge, 1935), Ch.3 especially. Marx's views, expounded in the *Communist Manifesto* and elsewhere, are elaborated by Engels in *Socialism: Utopian and Scientific*.
2. *The Heavenly City of the Eighteenth-Century Philosopher* (Yale U.P., 1932).
3. See, e.g., K. Widmer, 'Libertarian Reflections on Human Aggression', *The Personalist* LIII (1972).

CHAPTER 2

SOCIAL MALADIES AND UTOPIAN REMEDIES

THE OLD IMMORAL WORLD

Civilisation is a social plague on the planet, and vices are just as necessary to it as is a virus to disease.[1]

Utopias with serious social intent are not merely spun out of fantasy, but emerge from a critique of existing inperfections. In their time, the utopians were best known and admired for their polemics, those scathing social criticisms of which Marx and Engels said 'They attack every principle of existing society. Hence they are full of the most valuable materials for the enlightenment of the working class'.[2] Analysis of this negative aspect of the utopians' theories is an essential preliminary which reveals the shared critical basis that supports their utopian constructs.

It is unnecessary here to establish the well-foundedness of the utopians' attacks on the social evils prevalent in England and France during and after the Napoleonic wars, but it must be remembered that in 1800 France, although only partly industrialised, with most manufacture still taking place in small *ateliers*, shared many of the economic-based evils of the more advanced country because of the embargoes and financial disruptions of the Napoleonic wars. However, the French utopians' social discontent also reflects persisting bitterness at the idealistic Revolution's decline into chaos and terror, and the later disillusionment at the Restoration of the Bourbons.

Four categories of criticism are common to these utopians: (a) the critique of private property, (b) the economic analysis, which is not co-extensive with (a), (c) the analysis of the roots of social conflict, and (d) the moralistic critique of

current, more-or-less capitalist, ideology. The most mordant
and witty social critic is, by far, Fourier, who presents his
critique of so-called Civilisation (contemporary society) in
the form of a musical scale: there are 'seven limbic scourges',
namely, laziness, trickery, oppression, carnage, climatic
excesses, spite and dogmatic obscurity, with their dominant
note, universal duplicity. (This is a modest précis of the 144
symptomatic Civilised evils which he notes elsewhere.) His
scathing account of commerce, sexual hypocrisy and philosophical obscurantism evoked praise from Engels.
Commerce is his *bête noire*, with its fraudulent bankruptcies,
smuggling, usury and speculation, parasitic lawyers,
cheating tradesmen and the vicious habit of hoarding. But
these evils are inseparably annexed to the productive forms
of Civilisation, just as selfishness and deceit are bound up
with the institution of marriage. Fourier does not analyse
such phenomena causally, but regards them as simultaneously occurring and inseparable. The cure therefore is
the simultaneous destruction of the institutions and their co-
existent evils.

Among the peculiarities of capitalist production is the fact
that the poor are no better off working than idle, due to the
vagaries of demand and supply. Over-production itself
produces a 'plethoric crisis' like that of 1826. The economic
system, fragmented into isolated producers and retailers,
generates wasteful duplication and allows many to live
parasitically. The universal hatred of work in Civilisation is,
for Fourier, the most serious indictment of the system, and
he analyses the phenomenon of alienated labour in psychological and social, rather than economic, terms. The
extent of 'civilised' mankind's aberrance from its true
destiny is marked by the socially destructive forms which
natural human passions take. Love, for example, is channel-
led rigidly into monogamous marriage, with numerous
noxious side effects — deceit, quarrels, boredom, adultery,
exclusiveness and the economically disastrous fragmentation
of natural work groups.

Fourier's diagnosis of the problems of society ranges from
the eschatological to the politically acute. In terms of his own

cosmology, he argues that man is at discord with the 'four movements' of nature, and that the universe is threatened by encroaching 'incoherence' which disrupts the all-important Order of the Series.[3] More mundanely, he argues that Civilisation falsely places the well-being of the individual in opposition to the well-being of the people as a whole, because of the competitive morality of the times. He later assails the *laissez-faire* ethic, showing that the freedom for all which it supposedly safeguards rapidly becomes a free-for-all. He castigates private property: freedom to accumulate makes the propertied individual a tyrant over his fellows. Freedom without economic independence is formal and useless, Fourier argues. 'You praise the fine name of Free Man, and the inalienable rights of the citizen to the pauper; and he has neither the liberty to work . . . nor the right to demand access to that work on which his subsistence depends.'[4]

Fourier attributes the horrors of the French Revolution to the doctrines of the *philosophes* and frequently condemns Civilisation's moral-philosophical tradition. As Walter Benjamin asserts, his critique and his utopia are 'derived both from the amorality of the market society, and from the false morality mustered to serve it'.[5] He does, in fact, proceed beyond consciousness and attack root causes. At the phenomenological level, all the evils of civilisation are interdependent, as Fourier shows, diagnosing that they are essentially caused by the subversion of human nature, and can be remedied by liberating the passions. Ultimately, we are left with a puzzle: Civilisation is clearly an unnatural yet self-sustaining system, but Fourier gives no satisfactory explanation of the *origins* of this deplorable state and its genius for survival, or of the subversion of the passions.

Godwin's social criticism appears in the subdued guise of philosophical argument, which makes his total radicalism the more surprising. Stimulated by conservative reactions to the French Revolution, especially Burke's, he wrote *Political Justice* in its defence, but this is far more than an ephemeral polemical work. Retrospectively styled 'anarchistic', it contains cogent critiques of the law, private property, government and the self-aggrandising nation-state.

The basic premiss is that government is an absolute evil, being, in fact, merely 'regulated force' which demands compliance and enslaves the minds of its subjects, abrogating their independent judgement and propagating ignorance — for Godwin, two of the worst crimes. Human weaknesses are converted into inveterate vices by being politically institutionalised, especially the love of distinction which is legitimised by the laws of property accumulation. Godwin defines justice as the distribution of goods to those who can best benefit from them; the contemporary situation of extremes of poverty and luxury epitomises injustice. The rich cannot utilise their superfluous wealth whereas 'the most industrious and active member of society is frequently with great difficulty able to keep his family from starving'.[6] Injustice is reinforced by the legal system, the instrument of the wealthy, as his novel *Caleb Williams* asserts. This verges on an analysis of state as the instrument of class oppression, but Goodwin expressly denies the possibility of class awareness, the weight of oppression on the poor being too great.

He is the implacable enemy of human suffering, and his analysis directs him to first causes: social institutions and the flaws in human nature. His individualism and intellectualism also lead him to detect evil where no *suffering* is incurred, as in a national education system, and so, although his analysis is a self-consistent whole, it sometimes appears to have a tendentious motive, and little relevance to contemporary misery.

Owen was radical enough to offend his contemporaries unforgiveably, yet fashion now calls him a paternalist, and argues, following Marx, that his condescending efforts hindered the development of spontaneous workers' movements.[7] Certainly, he believed that he could pacify and convert both employers and workers simultaneously, and the tone of his social criticism strongly indicates that he was always trimming. Blustery rhetoric surrounds his most serious and valid criticisms, which may have disguised from Owen himself the revolutionary nature of the conclusions which derive from his argument. While advocating experi-

mental communities, he failed to see that his remedies logically required nation-wide application, and a metamorphosis
of the institution of government, which he never directly
attacked. This myopia, and Owen's own lack of intellectual
expertise, give his criticism a fundamental incoherence,
despite its verbal vigour.

Owen loves classification no less than Fourier, and his
categorisation of civilised evils includes inferior production,
inferior minds, unemployment, ignorance, crime, waste and
the loss of capacities among the poor because of bad
training. His heartfelt condemnation of the conditions of
factory employment, of which he had first-hand experience,
was made concrete in his campaigns against child labour,
hazardous conditions, and against the unjust rewards of
labour. His *Report to the County of Lanark*, (1820), offered
specific remedies for unemployment, which he diagnosed as
the chief cause of crime.

Owen describes the noxious consequences of that 'Trinity
of most monstrous evils', private property, irrational
religion and marriage. Property hardens the heart, is
divisive, destroys ideas of justice and produces selfishness
and isolating individualism. Somehow Owen manages to
voice such opinions without ever questioning the *right* of the
rich to their possessions, and even argues that the poor
would not wish to deprive the rich of their property, but only
to better their own state. He lambasted religion as savagely
as he dared, and in consequence lost much support after an
atheistic speech in 1817. He loathed the mystification and
ignorance which it perpetuated, and he bitterly attacks the
stranglehold which the Church kept on the 'natural'
relations between the sexes. Marriage makes adults 'ignorant
and viciously selfish' and produces ill-educated, spoiled
children.[8]

There are embyronic indictments of the total social
system. Owen condemns the existing 'classification' of
society into rich and poor and proposes a 'natural' classification, based on age and occupation. He too condemns the
productive system in which the wealthy consume, 'some of
them most wastefully, the wealth produced by the over-

exhausted labour of the working class', while the health and the lives of the poor are destroyed in producing these luxuries.

At the ideological level, Owen condemns the prevailing ethos of individualism and competition. Once innovatory, now reactionary, these doctrines prevent natural compassion and co-operation. But his fundamental criticism is a philosophical one: the erroneous doctrine of freewill which pervades society, and is incarnate in law, propagates atrocious inconsistencies and absurdities. Although Owen rehearses Godwin's ideas frequently, this is not simply the Hume-Godwin account of free-will and necessity reiterated, for Owen develops his own account of how the human character is formed by society: all social evils arise from laws and conventions which presume that men can be as they are bidden to be, despite their conditioning. Any doctrine which justifies itself by claiming that everyone has equal opportunity — *laissez-faire*, for example — rests on the deceptive fallacy that men can escape their origins. But social institutions are invariably erected on fallacious assumptions of freewill, responsibility and equal opportunity (little wonder Owen's favourite adjective is 'irrational') and in consequence radical demolition is the only solution.

At first sight, Saint-Simon's complaints against society are those of a calvinistic capitalist. He deplores the wastefulness of France's productive system and especially objects to the wars which disturb 'industrial tranquillity'. He is eager to abolish the 'drones' so that the bees can get down to business. Idleness, he holds, is more than a social vice, it is a moral disease, a pathological state. Saint-Simon also resents the spendthrift administration run by noblemen and bourgeois for their own benefit, and yearns for the rule of the industrialists, whose selfless purpose will be economic expansion. This catalogue clearly indicates his *idées fixes,* from which, however, radical solutions proceed.

Society suffers various rifts: there is the economic division between the productive bees and the drones, the bees (96% of the population) including both managers and employees. There is also the political division between the haves and have-nots: 'I ask the reader to reflect on this observation: the haves govern the have-nots, not because they own property; they own property and govern because, collectively, they are superior in enlightenment to the have-nots.'[9] But this distinction is no longer appropriate because among those without political power there is now an enlightened band of scientists, artists and liberals who should take precedence over the propertied rulers. Saint-Simon had no conception of the possibility of any conflict other than that of interests, which he delineated, nor was he primarily concerned with economic deprivation except insofar as it causes lower productivity and greater idleness, although he later became concerned with poverty.

The diagnostic element in Saint-Simon's thought is the theory of history which he invokes to explain the process of change. The time is out of joint, because in the 'spiritual' or ideological sphere of society, metaphysical and religious doctrines have been replaced by positive, scientific theories, but no corresponding movement has yet triumphed at the social level. Society is still in the grip of feudal and military organisation, but takeover by the inevitable positivist industrial-liberal regime is imminent. Such arguments show that Saint-Simon's general analysis of society was both historical and structural. He alone of these utopians treats society with regard to its evolution, and not as a purely contemporary and static phenomenon whose evils can be eradicated instantaneously. This historical perspective gives his proposed solutions a credibility and weight which the others lack.

Diagram 1 represents the various different levels at which the utopians criticise society and reflects the structures underlying their social analysis, and their final location of the causes of all social phenomena in the nature of man. The analysis begins with the tangible symptoms of social disease — vice, poverty, misery — abstractly described as social conflict and inequality.

The institution of private property is diagnosed as the manifest direct cause of these gross inequalities, but the search for causes then proceeds to a secondary and a tertiary

Diagram I *The Structure of the Utopians' Criticism*

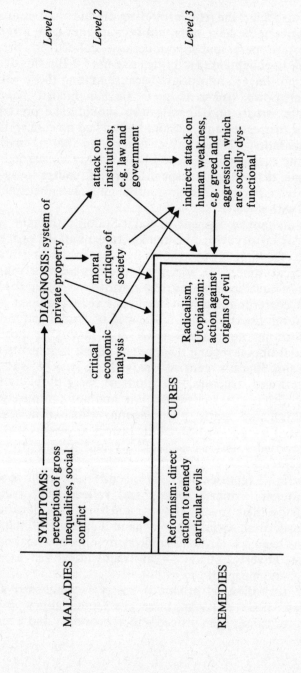

level, via such necessary questions as: is the accumulation of property attributable to the legal-governmental system? Or to the productive system? Or to an underlying ethic which sanctions acquisition? Or to ineradicable human greed? The procedure seems, within a certain theoretical framework of social analysis, to be necessary and deductive.

The utopians' radical criticisms can now be analysed in terms of the elements of the diagram. Private property is not the chief cause of social conflict and unhappiness, although it is the most manifest, being uppermost in their levels of investigation and explanation. They find other aspects more interesting, particularly ideological factors — for example, those philosophical or ideological fallacies, such as the notion of freewill, embodied in the very structure of social organisation. Their approach to private property is insufficiently analytical: there is little need to prove that a property system and social inequalities are causally connected, but more need to distinguish what may legitimately be counted as necessary private property, and what is superfluous, and results in inequalities and exploitation.

Godwin alone attempts this, with the help of a utilitarian norm. He argues that (i) I have an *absolute* right to all goods which, when attributed to me, will create an optimum distribution for all, ie. will maximise happiness, and (ii) I have a *qualified* right ('empire over') to the fruits of my own labour, unless someone else has a superior claim under (i); (iii) I have *no right whatsoever* to property in the labour of others, since such property directly contravenes the principles sanctioning the second type of property.[10] This third principle suggests an incipient understanding of exploitation. Content with fewer philosophical preliminaries, Owen and Fourier condemn the corrupt and inhumane results of the system, but Saint-Simon seems to condemn it only partially, for he intends to remove inequality through superabundance and a redistribution according to talent, perhaps with a measure of state ownership. However, his disciples soon made the abolition of private property one of their tenets. Owen's labour theory of value approaches the problems of capital accumulation, property and exploitation, but his attacks on property turn more on its corrupting effects on men than on its role in the process of exploitation.

The critique of private property leads directly to other levels of analysis. For Godwin, the property system originates in and is sanctioned by the legal system, which legitimises the love of distinction that is part of human nature: thus he postulates a direct link between human nature and social organisation. For Owen and Fourier the *laissez-faire* doctrine is one important factor which promotes the accumulation of wealth, and arguing this they move from Level 1 to Level 2 of explanation. But the argument that private property is necessarily connected to a particular form of economic and productive organisation is not developed by the utopians.

Nevertheless, there is awareness among the utopians that not all is well with the capitalist system. The paradox of capitalism, the existence of great wealth in tandem with great poverty, is stated although the necessary and reciprocal nature of the relationship disclosed by Marx remains unperceived. The paradox, for Godwin and Fourier, is that the hardest workers are the most abjectly poor, which was without a doubt *contingently* true in their time.[11] Another facet of the paradox is the fact that workers are invariably producing goods which they cannot themselves consume, as Fourier explains. 'The French peasant sells his wheat in order to eat cheap barley bread; he sells his good wine and keeps only the worst for himself.'[12] Saint-Simon too complains 'Present-day society is in truth the world turned upside down' for the same reasons: the poor are compelled to give to the rich.

The utopians often identify the contradictions of incipient capitalism with misdirection of the economy and under-utilisation of resources, implying that an improvement in productive methods alone would provide enough for all, or even create a situation of abundance in which inequalities would be trifling. Thus, their economic solution to the problem is arrived at through regulating consumption, and making the necessities of life readily available. The alternative of calculating a just distribution of existing commodities from first principles is not broached except by Godwin, nor is the solution seen primarily in terms of changing the productive process, though this will be made more pleasant, and the system of payment more just. The emphasis on consumption accords with the utopians' concern for happiness *qua* fulfilment of needs, though inevitably, compared with Marx, they appear to have mislaid pieces of the economic jigsaw. But, in fairness to them, none of the major pieces were missing — it was in the matter of arrangement and connection that they faltered.

Evidently, the utopians inclined more to a sociological analysis than an economic one. They showed a common hostility to legal institutions because all known laws seemed to oppose human desires and inclinations. Indeed, 'the laws of men are the causes of crimes', and property laws cause both crime and poverty. The hostility to law logically extends to the institution of government, as the perpetrator of bad laws. A note of scepticism about the democratic solutions proposed by contemporary reformers pervades the utopians' analyses, which reveal critical attitudes to liberty and rights, magical catchwords of the French Revolution. The utopians attack central institutions such as religion and marriage, as well as political structures, and in their utopias they abandon or transform these and, in effect, government.

An understanding of the nature of social conflict is a necessary prelude to any prescription for a harmonious utopia. Fourier and Saint-Simon saw extreme manifestations of class conflict in the Revolution, and both regard it as catastrophic, albeit symptomatic of legitimate grievances. England too, it is often claimed, was near to revolution during the period 1790-1830, and class conflict was never far below the surface. Yet none of these writers analysed conflict in terms of a conscious and overt confrontation between rich and poor. By far the outstanding conflict for them was that between individuals and inflexible, inhumane institutions — hence their resolve to radicalise all social institutions. The confrontation between rich and poor is described as contingent, not as the necessary expression of the irreducibly opposed interests of each class in the economic and social

process. Owen and Saint-Simon did not even think it necessary to dispossess the wealthy in order to achieve a
harmonious society. Comparison with the rival marxist
analysis of the necessary nature of class conflict under
capitalism naturally obtrudes itself here. Certainly, Godwin
and the early socialists did not reveal an extensive understanding of the phenomenon, but, as Engels conceded, the
real class conflict was only just taking shape in 1800.[13] In
fact, the concept of the proletariat was sufficiently indistinct
for it to be treated by Saint-Simon as the ally of managers
and employers, and the unity of the classes is a common
aspiration among the utopians.

What has been telescopically described as a 'moral
critique' of society must now be expanded. The utopians
criticise society moralistically; they also make onslaughts on
current social morality and ideology. The moralist's
analysis, uppermost for Godwin, Owen and Fourier, dwells
on the hypocrisy, insincerity, confusion and outright lies
which contemporary society propagates. Their faith in
absolute truth sharpens their pens for this battle. The
remnants of metaphysical doctrines, and religion in
particular, receive a parting kick.

In their critiques of social beliefs the utopians approached
the notion of ideology, and unearthed the fallacious philosophical principles on which contemporary ideology, and
hence social organisation, rested. Owen and Fourier refute
the *laissez-faire* ideology which represents the negation of
benevolence for Owen, and the subversive manifestation of
ambition and cabalism for Fourier. They propagate defiant
counter-doctrines of co-operation and the identity of
interests, and unanimously attack unbridled 'egoism' (the
doctrine of self-interest underlying the liberal-individualist-
democratic-capitalist ideological complex) as socially
wicked. They engage in philosophical dispute with the proponents of free-will doctrines, invoking determinist and
environmentalist ideas to rebut these. These theoretical
polemics are evidence that the utopians attributed a central
role to the prevalent forms of social consciousness, and
intended to transform these too. But institutions are neces-

sarily their primary focus, for these can be created by decree; the changing of consciousness is bound up with the notion of human perfectibility and is, they accept, a developmental process which cannot be instantly effected.

The remedies proposed reflect the order of the diagnoses. The evils of private property are to be removed by the establishment of egalitarian distributive principles, and by negation of the competitive and exploitative elements of society. Institutions which perpetuate injustice and inequality will be abolished. The invidious *laissez-faire* ideal will be replaced by doctrines of co-operation and benevolence. Even underlying human weakness is eradicable, because of the perfectible nature of man. The utopias constitute a reversal of everything most detested in society.

In both the superficial and the more profound analysis, the utopians found the world to be in a 'degrading, conflicting, wretched state of violence, uncharitable feeling, crimes and unnecessary suffering'.[14] Their critique has suffered by comparison with Marx's more restrained and *soi-disant* scientific analysis, and those concerned with the structures which subtend social phenomena may condemn the utopians for the attention paid to ripples on the surface. But their analysis took place at many levels, and it would be a mistake to underestimate the influence of these social critics, and the strength of their diagnosis, which made them utopians rather than reformers. The utopias which were never realised constituted a fertile source of critical and constructive ideas for more worldly reformers, and a pattern for future radical thinkers.

NEW WORLDS

This skeletal account of four fleshy theories is limited to the elements relevant to the analysis: fuller expositions are plentiful, as the bibliography indicates.

THE PHILOSOPHER AS UTOPIAN — GODWIN

I love to contemplate the yet unextended powers and capabilities of our nature, and to believe that they will one day be unfolded to the infinite advantage and happiness of the inhabitants of the globe.[15]

Arch-advocate of perfectibilism, Godwin saw utopia as the logical deduction from his moral system. His *magnum opus, Political Justice*, resembles the conventional political treatise but diverges into radical aspiration. A professed disciple of the sensationalist and environmentalist philosophies of Locke, Condillac, Hume and Holbach, he argued that since institutions permeate and mould men's personal behaviour, the philosopher must take 'the more comprehensive view', becoming a political theorist like Rousseau.

Having made the *tabula rasa* assumption, Godwin develops a deterministic theory of human motivation, postulating a 'fixed and certain relation' between motives and their results. We do not choose to act from motives: they have a 'necessary influence', and those reflecting the truth are intrinsically preferable, and necessarily prevail. This constitutes a refutation of freewill which Godwin identifies with capriciousness and arbitrary choice. 'So far as we act with liberty, so far as we are independent of motives, our conduct is as independent of morality as it is of reason.' By contrast, a determinism based on the causal influence of 'motives' makes possible the prediction of action, and morality itself.[16]

Reason is omnipresent and omnipotent: on this assertion rests Godwin's whole system, and his hopes. Happily, 'the thinking principle is susceptible of unlimited improvement'. Even the wild resolutions of the drunkard or murderer are 'formed upon the suggestion of the rational faculty', although passion has outweighed prudence in the process. Reason directs our voluntary actions and 'the perfection of the human character consists in approaching as nearly as possible to the perfectly voluntary state' through the elimination of the 'imperfectly voluntary actions' caused by prejudice and habit. In the perfectly voluntary state, 'private judgement', which Godwin idealises, is triumphant.[17]

In support of his argument, Godwin establishes the ascendancy of reason over passion and defies the romanticism of the late Enlightenment. He rebuts the traditional notion that man's faculties are in a state of civil war. 'We are no longer at liberty to consider man as divided between two independent principles, or to imagine that his inclinations are in any case inaccessible through the medium of his reason.'[18] Thus, the optimism which the environmentalist account of human nature generates by its rejection of innate wickedness is reinforced by Godwin's proclamation of the perfectibility of reason. The inference of human perfectibility follows:

> Sound reasoning and truth, when adequately communicated, must always be victorious over error: Sound reasoning and truth are capable of being so communicated: Truth is omnipotent: The vices and moral weakness of man are not invincible: Man is perfectible, or in other words susceptible of perpetual improvement.[19]

Two pre-occupations shape Godwin's arguments throughout *Political Justice:* his commitment to truth and his individualism. He supposes that we instinctively recognise the truth, and that this embraces the moral code. The scepticism with which modern philosophy treats such notions as 'moral truth' may not be appropriate here for Godwin, like Condorcet, canvassed the possibility of gaining moral knowledge through calculation, and making a scientific morality.[20] The keystone of his individualism is his commitment to private judgement, which connotes personal integrity, dignity and autonomy: 'as I act contrary to the unbiassed dictates of my own judgement, by so much I abdicate the most valuable part of the character of man'. The social application of this doctrine leads, inevitably, to contradictions.

> Natural independence, a freedom from all constraint, except that of reasons and inducements presented to the understanding, is of the greatest importance to the welfare and improvement of mind. *Moral independence, on the contrary, is always injurious.*[21]

Given that Godwin has previously described the province of morality as unlimited, in accordance with his determinist view that all actions interconnect, and with his utilitarianism which judges actions by their consequences, it appears that private judgement is, paradoxically, severely circumscribed, if not trivialised. Its function is merely to make the individual acquiesce in public morality — though the

postulate of an absolute moral code suggests that the reasonable individual's judgement would by definition coincide
with that of his fellows.

Contradictory elements appear elsewhere, as in the
assertion that '. . . each man is but the part of a great system,
and all that he has, is so much wealth to be put to the account
of the general stock',[22] a principle which undermines the case
for individual autonomy. Suicide is wrong because it
impoverishes the common stock; furthermore, although
individuals and society have no *rights*, '. . . there is no situation of their lives which has not its corresponding *duties*'.[23]
Manifestly, Godwin's determinism is open to an anti-
individualistic interpretation: since all human actions affect
the general welfare, we must consult the interests of others at
all times, and the province of morality is indeed unlimited.
This dichotomy of views illustrates the divergence between
Godwin the moral philosopher and Godwin the polemical
social theorist; it also corresponds to the distinction which he
makes between government and society. He felt that while
we have no obligations or duties .to government, we
emphatically have moral obligations to our fellows, the
members of society.

In his critique of social institutions Godwin is eminently
individualistic. He condemns national education which
abrogates private judgement and is the tool of government.
Of obedience to government, he argues '. . . where I make
the voluntary surrender of my understanding, and commit
my conscience to another's keeping . . . I annihilate my
individuality as a man'.[24] The most surprising facet of his
anarchistic individualism is the rejection of co-operative
principles because of the danger of subordination of the
individual. Yet the reiterated proposal that reciprocal moral
control should replace law is clearly an evocation of the co-
operative spirit. Godwin's hyper-individualism in the
political sphere assorts strangely with his condemnation of
the isolated egoist and advocacy of collectivism in the moral
sphere. There is also a constant, unresolved tension between
Godwin's utilitarianism which commandeers virtue, reason
and benevolence in the service of happiness, and his

moralistic assertions that these are good in themselves. The attribution of intrinsic moral worth to individuals conflicts with other principles and causes Godwin to debate whether in a fire he should save Archbishop Fénélon, his valet or his own mother. The problem is insoluble to someone with Godwin's diverse attachments to egalitarian individualism, utilitarianism and ideas of moral desert. The obvious solution, an ordering of moral principles, he nowhere attempts.

In delineating his ideal society, Godwin takes happiness as his central theme. 'The true object of moral and political disquisition, is pleasure or happiness.'[25] Despite his strong intellectual preference for 'higher' pleasures, he calls *all* pleasures *absolutely* good. Morality now appears subservient, though potent: 'virtue is upon no other account valuable, than as it is the instrument of the most exquisite pleasure'. A series of independent village communities, 'parishes', grouped in a loose federation, will replace the national entity and government, the legal system and the penal code, will disappear. The habitual vices of nations, self-aggrandisement and domination, will vanish. Order and cohesion within these apparently anarchistic parishes is maintained by a benevolent and watchful morality, operating in an atmosphere free of acrimony. Godwin always applauded honesty, sincerity and openness, and saw no value in any other mode of conduct; these virtues, and the moral faculty, are the basis of his utopia.

There is little indication of how Godwin saw the economic structure of his community, beyond the abolition of unjustifiable private property. Each individual will perform a modicum of useful work, with the aid of machinery, instead of a fraction of the population toiling endlessly, and necessary labour will be '. . . of the lightest kind . . . the reverse of a misfortune'. Monro's suggestion that this indicates a society of craftsmen is belied by Godwin's express hope that labour will diminish to a daily half-hour.[26] The parish is clearly to be an ascetic society in which leisure and self-development are valued above possession and consumption, and whose supreme values are reason and knowledge. Relationships will be sustained by an appreciation of moral worth, not by contract. Little more can be gleaned of the details of this utopia, for it is to the improved character of its members that Godwin's attention is directed. Greater understanding, sincerity and virtue will foster the improvement of the intellect and progress towards the impartial benevolence which Godwin defines as justice. The propagation of knowledge and truth, a collective achievement, must be conjoined with individual reason and private judgement for society to progress, and so it appears that the burden of improvement rests jointly on men and society. But Godwin chooses to emphasise individual effort and development, which is a declaration of his ultimate value.

THE RATIONAL SYSTEM OF ROBERT OWEN

A rational government will attend solely to the happiness of the governed; to attain which it will ascertain what human nature is.[27]

In a paradigmly scientific argument, as he thought, Owen argued from facts about human nature to 'the first principles of the science of man', thence to the conditions requisite for human happiness; finally he prescribed a general constitution for government and a universal code of laws. He moved from a statement of 'the ductile and passive nature of man' to the famous conclusion that 'any general character, from the best to the worst, from the most ignorant to the most enlightened, may be given to any community, even to the world at large, by the application of the proper means'.[28] Owen adopted without proof various eighteenth-century axioms about man's rational capacity and self-interest, believing that such facts would gain general credence through assertion alone.

By acknowledging purely formal characteristics to be the only hereditary data, Owen maximises, and probably overstates, human adaptability: '. . . children can be trained to acquire any language, sentiments, belief, or any bodily habits and manners, not contrary to human nature'. The essential indeterminacy of Owen's analysis is manifested in the dictum that human nature is 'universally plastic': consequently, his analysis *per se* does not determine what form of

society would be ideal. In fact, Owen's theory chiefly functions as a prop for the argument that society is responsible
for social evil, that reward and punishment are unjust and
misdirected mechanisms, and that education is the keystone
of the new society. However, the formalistic account of
human nature is supplemented by a description of the
material and moral conditions for happiness, which clearly
reflects contemporary pre-occupations and negates contemporary miseries, and so is *not* a deduction from the
analysis of human nature.

Owen's innovatory prescription for happiness (which all
citizens were to be taught at the age of two) has an
apparently moral formulation: 'individual happiness can be
increased and extended only in proportion as [man] actively
endeavours to increase and extend the happiness of all
around him'. This passage might suggest that the individual
would eventually find his greatest happiness in unselfishly
desiring others' good for their own sakes, but we must distinguish Owen's instinctively humane hope that 'the matured
man shall be compelled to feel considerable horror at
accidentally injuring the limb of the smallest insect' from his
declaredly amoral approach to social organisation and his
willingness to harness self-interest for social ends. He argues
that moral terms are purely relative, and that his desire to
give each man 'a superior constitution' is an amoral aspiration. Hence his own non-moral explication of the happiness
precept: 'individualism . . . must now give way to the
principle of *union*, or of benevolence, or, as really it is,
enlightened selfishness'.[29] So the interdependence of happiness doctrine translates as an identity of interests doctrine
which constitutes the theoretical foundation for Owen's
advocacy of co-operation. Altruism is a socially useful
capacity, not a moral virtue, in this creed.

An arch-determinist, Owen follows Godwin in lambasting
the fallacious notions of freewill and responsibility and their
institutional embodiments. But Owen abandons morality altogether, whereas Godwin makes morality and determinism
symbiotic. Yet their positions can be reconciled: Godwin
relies on 'necessary' moral motives, while Owen wishes to in-

doctrinate truths (in fact, moral precepts) which will causally determine action — which also suggests that he had some understanding of the extent and effectiveness of conditioning.

The determinist doctrine substantiates Owen's attack on punishment and his analysis of the relativistic and ideological nature of moral belief. Good and bad 'have ever been the creation of the prejudices and imaginations of the human mind, according to the education which it has received'.[30] Thanks to Owen's environmentalism 'there is no conceivable foundation for private displeasure or public enmity', and the humane and scientific outlook which supersedes morality 'will produce commiseration and pity for those individuals who possess either habits or sentiments which appear . . . to be destructive of their own comfort, pleasure, or happiness'.[31] The determinist premiss, together with the *tabula rasa*, is used to prove that human perfection is attainable collectively through enlightened universal education such as Owen attempted at New Lanark. Individual limitations would be minimised in the aggregate and each individual would achieve his own degree of perfection by the development of all his faculties. Charity, kindness and tolerance are the virtues which Owen most idealised.

The analysis of 'character formation', or education, was disputed by Fourier, who wrote 'Your desire in these settlements is to change men, to modify their characters; yet what is *really* needed is to find the machinery by which their vices may be put to good use'.[32] Owen in turn challenged Fourier's assumption of fixed characteristics. A universally plastic entity could not be changed or modified: the appropriate process was 'formation'. Arbitration between them, and evaluation of both theories rests on the solution to the still tantalising nature-nurture equation.

Owen's utopian blueprint at first appeared in various reformist guises, for the famous Villages of Co-operation (alias 'quadrangular paradises', alias 'paupers' parallelograms') were proposed as a remedy for acute unemployment after 1815. Later, in *Home Colonies* (1841) a more apocalyptic Owen represented these self-supporting enclaves as the transitional stage preceding an ideal society composed of hundreds of such interdependent communities linked by railways. The 'home colonies', based on co-operation, would provide communal living, eating and recreation buildings for 2,000 people and ensure that every member was 'fully supplied with the necessaries and comforts of life'. Agriculture would predominate, with some manufacture, and work would be allocated on the basis of preference, with each man learning several trades. The labour standard of value (which influenced Hodgskin and Gray) was to determine payment though most distribution would be according to need. Scientific inventions would 'render manual labour only a healthy and agreeable exercise' and provide men, and especially women, with 'sufficient leisure for mental improvement and rational enjoyment'. Ultimately, 'scientific aid' would produce the abundance of wealth which would facilitate the construction of ideal communities, pleasure parks and landscaped scenery.

Owen advocated democratic government, by election or rotation, for the colonies although he was by inclination a benevolent paternalist. Serious misconduct would be judged by 'arbitrators' but reciprocal correction would otherwise be adequate. New members would subscribe to the Rule Book, thus making a declaration of solidarity with the co-operative principle, and actively assuming a social obligation.

Although in the colonies only the 'natural' classification of men, by age and capacity, would persist, Owen countenanced a class stratification in the intermediate communities, optimistically claiming that this would unite the classes through mutual goodwill. Indeed, in several respects Owen conserved old evils in his new moral world. A rational religion appears in his later messianic writing, with Owen as high priest, and conservatism is most manifest in his pronouncements on purpose-built education. Children should be taught the facts relevant to 'the rank of life in which they are likely to be placed'.[33] On some interpretations, this would perpetuate a class society. Furthermore, Owen frequently seems to treat the individual as subordinate to his work, an account which evokes the utilitarian view of the individual as part of the common stock, and the biblical vision of man as the toiler. Work is not, for Owen, a major source of satisfaction: that lies in the consumption of commodities justly distributed. Ultimately, he failed to combat the capitalist work-and-consumption ethic, but incorporated it wholesale in his utopia. Nevertheless, many social evils were to be abolished in his utopia — private property, false standards of value, the Church, the legal and penal systems, and above all poverty — and in these respects Owen's radicalism far outreached his conservatism.

Overall, Owen's analysis lacks dimensions and rests on simple, linear deduction. All other elements are subordinated to the dominant environmentalist thesis. He reduces all social and historical forces to the ideology which forms men's characters, then argues that an external force in league with Truth (he regards himself as such) can supervene, abolish the irrational ideology, and the past with it, and create a new world. Such proposals have a disconcerting a-historicity and insubstantiality, typical of the autodidact's pursuit of his *idée fixe*. Although Owen the philosopher was in many ways inadequate, his active life in the labour movement contained compensating dimensions, which this account has perforce ignored. Such activities were based on, and exemplified, his philosophies, especially those of education and co-operation, and they revealed Owen as a realist, a social reformer and a utopian of substance.

SAINT-SIMON'S INDUSTRIAL EDEN

The Golden Age of the human race is by no means behind us, it is in front, it lies in the perfection of the social order.[34]

The Age of Iron is Saint-Simon's Golden Age, an epoch marked by such peace and plenty as technology alone can produce. Happily, the realisation of such a state is both inevitable and imminent, as his theory of history proves. This dialectical theory locates as the source of human progress the alternating correspondence and disjunction of human knowledge and social institutions, in 'organic' and 'critical' epochs. The autonomous development of knowledge and science activates institutional change. Organic epochs, such as the Middle Ages, are characterised by social integration and cohesion, but critical periods such as the post-Revolutionary years, are marked by social malfunctioning and, finally, disintegration. Each crisis is succeeded by greater social perfection, 'hence it is part of human nature to improve the political order indefinitely'.[35] One measure of perfection is the replacement of coercive forms of government by less onerous methods of control, and another is the state of knowledge: these are 'scientific', non-evaluative criteria. Knowledge itself proceeds from the religious mode to the metaphysical, then to the empirical — from conjectural to positive — and will culminate in positive philosophy. Saint-Simon himself endeavoured to create 'social physiology', a universal science comprehending human nature, classes and society as a whole.

Knowledge and control are directly connected.

> So long as the majority of individuals remained in a state of ignorance and improvidence . . . it was necessary for the minority to be organised on military lines, to obtain a monopoly of legislation, and so to keep all power to itself, in order to hold the majority in tutelage and subject the nation to strong discipline.[36]

This characterisation of the feudal-military-metaphysical period suggests that not only academic knowledge, but skill and self-control, advance social progress. Self-knowledge enhances the capacities of individuals and classes: 'the first thing that the *industriels* have to do . . . is to acquire a clear awareness of their power, their resources and their political capacity'.[37]

In Saint-Simon's own time the feudal epoch was disintegrating, soon to be replaced by an organic industrial-liberal-scientific regime. *Domination* (master-servant, landlord-serf) was the prevailing mode of social relations in the feudal epoch, also characterised by the extensive mutual dependence of individuals. The industrial era, by contrast, is permeated by the spirit of *co-operation*; workers combine with employers to subdue Nature, and interpersonal dependency and domination disappear. Each individual depends on the work and prosperity of *all* in this integrated economy. 'The government of men will be replaced by the administration of things.' Industrial society thus depersonalises men's relations yet integrates them more thoroughly into the social whole.

The theory of history determines the nature of Saint-Simon's utopia, which has the virtue of being historically inevitable, and the dialectical product of all previous societies, rather than the result of historical rupture. 'The industrial system is that towards which mankind has always reached; this industrial system will be the final system.'[38] But the account of the process of change seems both too idealist and too mechanistic. The ghost in the machine is the historical development of class capacities, a key concept also in the social physiology. Saint-Simon asserts that a combination of hereditary characteristics with various social environments produces classes of men marked out by particular 'capacities', a term connoting a hybrid of talent, inclination, aptitude and skill, which he contrasts with the more primitive 'powers' of the feudal epoch. A new class of independent peasants and artisans has developed, with an 'industrial capacity'; simultaneously a new concept of industrial property emerged, based on work rather than land and law. This class is ruled by ideas and respects work and social order; only minimal government is needed to guarantee peace and order. The class's new capacities revolutionise social relations which cease to rest on subservience and domination. 'In a co-operative system, where all men have a capacity and an investment, there is true association, and no other inequality exists except the differences in capacity and investment', which are functional and necessary.[39]

Saint-Simon views human nature as creative and active. 'Happiness, for Man, is first to act, then to enjoy.' There are certain functional physiological traits which divide men into three classes: *industriels* (producers), *savants* (scientists) and artists, each with specific social roles. These form the natural basis of social organisation and human satisfaction. Saint-Simon asserts that his is not a utopian scheme because it is realisable, and is based on observed human nature.[40] In his industrial society, producers predominate and idlers are eliminated. The producers form a homogeneous class, but are subdivided into *chefs d'industrie* with administrative capacities — managers who also govern — and workers. Between these groups there is extensive social mobility and identity of interests, so this natural selection of leaders is acceptable.

Industry, for Saint-Simon, 'embraces all kinds of useful work, theory and application, intellectual and manual work', and industrial society will increase industrial production to the point of superabundance. But Saint-Simon was not a prophet of the consumer society merely, for production was the crucial activity, and he was credited with inventing the first version of socialism's most famous distributive principle: from each according to his capacity, to each according to his achievements. Industrial society will provide both physical and spiritual contentment, the latter comprising the development of intelligence, appreciation of the fine arts, understanding of natural laws and 'universal benevolence'. Government is to consist of a tricameral parliament composed of scientists, artists and *industriels*, and three scientific academies. Other details of the industrial Eden are not elaborated, although a rare passage of description evokes a countryside full of pleasure parks, inns and wandering minstrels.

Industrial society, tranquil, co-operative and prosperous, also has a unique moral character. 'An extensive and enlightened industrial society is essentially moral', and 'no society is possible without common moral ideas'.[41] So Saint-Simon proposed the adoption of a positive 'terrestrial morality', which at first only amounted to a do-as-you-would-be-done-by principle. But by 1821 he was arguing that the decay of feudal morality had led to rampant egoism which must be combatted by philanthropy, and his *New Christianity* (1825) regenerated the principle of brotherly love. 'Religion must direct society towards the great end of the most rapid possible amelioration of the condition of the poorest class.' These increasingly altruistic versions of morality are the only explicit means of social control proposed, but the industrial society also idealises co-operation and benevolence. Democratic values, despised by Saint-Simon, have no place there, and indeed the manifest inegalitarianism which he propounded may pose a threat to his own system.

The peace of industrial society is achieved not only by morality but by a redirection of aggression, through science and technology, towards nature. The exercise of inter-personal power is no longer the focal point of men's lives. 'In the final analysis, the chief desire of almost all individuals is not to have an effect on men, but on nature.'[42] Man's indestructible love of domination turns towards natural phenomena, but the conquest of nature can only be accomplished by co-operation.

Saint-Simon has been many things to many men. Current fashion makes him an advocate of state capitalism, more of a prophet than a utopian. His practical influence can be traced concretely through canals, bridges and credit companies. In his unsystematic theorising appear recognis-able embryos of Marx's central ideas. He ignored the problems of class conflict and property, yet made a significant contribution to socialist thought. Saint-Simon made the working class emerge as a social class, Leroy claims,[43] a class-in-itself which had previously been con-sidered a disunited collection of paupers. He asserted their right to work, and their crucial role in the industrial process, an important step on the road to economic socialism. He also added a necessary historical dimension to the environmenta-list view of human nature, while his new methodology for a universal social science bore fruit in Comte's great system.

FOURIER'S HARMONIC UTOPIA

'Happiness is to have many passions, and many ways of satisfying them'[44]

The commentator cannot convey the quality of joyous hedonism in Fourier's detailed and prolific writing, or begin to explain the cosmic framework from which his theory emerges. But a sound psychological microtheory can be extracted from the whole which forms the basis for his analysis of social organisation. Human nature consists of twelve natural 'passions' (a term best understood as 'instincts') whose combination varies between individuals, giving each a different temperament and unique potential. The sin of Civilisation is to 'repress, mutilate and de-nature the passions and Nature, instead of studying their goal'.[45] But the frustrated sexual passion will revive, like an ulcer too soon healed, and so Civilisation's days are numbered. Then utopia, which he calls 'Harmony', will be achieved through the liberation and indulgence of all the passions.

The twelve human passions are grouped in the following way:

1. *The five sensuous passions.*
2. *The four affective passions* of *friendship*, *love*, *familism* and *ambition*, a co-operative passion,[46] which govern relationships with others and the formation of groups.
3. *The distributive passions* which produce inner harmony. The *cabalistic* denotes the passion for intrigue and group loyalty, the *butterfly* passion dictates the need for variety, and the *composite* passion requires an admixture of physical and spiritual pleasures.

The thirteenth passion, *unityism* or *harmonism*, integrates and harmonises the delights generated by the others, and aims at 'association' or unity. This meta-passion is the positive corollary of Fourier's fear of disintegration on a cosmic scale. Each individual possesses thirteen passions, but some are dormant, some dominant in each. Furthermore, in a repressive society the passions are manifested 'subversively': in Civilisation, cabalism turns to rivalry, and familism is travestied in the selfish and exclusive nuclear family. But in Harmony, the passions will be liberated, refined and perfected; e.g. vision will develop an aesthetic awareness. For Fourier, then, the 'higher pleasures' need not be cultivated, for they are immanent in the organs of sense and the instincts themselves.

Despite the neologisms and strange taxonomy, Fourier's theory of the passions gives a comprehensive account of the possibilities of man's relations to others and to the external world. The sensuous passions which crave gratification govern our relations with natural and social objects. The affective passions comprehend the whole range of relationships between human beings: what relationships — except those of indifference — are not based on friendship, love, family or co-operation? Meanwhile, the satisfaction of the distributive passions sets us in harmony with ourselves. Thus, the principle of passionate attraction embraces all possible modes of behaviour, as the surrealist Breton acknowledged. 'Your old chest of oak is still good. All is contained if not contented in its twelve drawers.'[47]

Fourier has been criticised for the omission of morality, metaphysics and intellect from his schema. The exclusion of morality is deliberate because 'morality teaches man to be at war with himself, to resist, repress and despise his passions'.[48] Morality is merely civilised ideology, not the proof of a natural moral faculty. The ideal society supersedes such devices, for in Harmony the passions themselves regulate the behaviour which in Civilisation morality inhibited with such difficulty. It is perhaps Fourier's negative attitude to the intellect which is considered unforgivable. The manipulation of concepts, self-reflection and the locating of self in space and time are paradigmly intellectual activities. But Harmony has no history, and individuals are instinctively integrated, so that such intellectual exercises would be spurious. In any case, the composite passion has a spiritual and reflective element. Although he appears to underestimate the influence of reason and intellect, Fourier in fact transposes elements of these into the various passions, so that they function instinctively, and do not hold the special position, in opposition to passion, which philosophers allocated them. Such an interpretation spares us the conclusion that Harmonians will be content yet mindless.

The micro-level theory of passions is directly universalisable as a macro-theory of organisation. Fourier distinguishes 810 temperaments (combinations of passions), 405 male, 405 female, which can be classified according to the number of dominant passions that an individual has. An 'omnigyne' such as Fourier himself, with eight dominant passions, is a rare and forceful, if not modest, character. The 810 characters together form the 'communal soul' whose composition is exactly predictable according to Fourier's mathematical-cum-musical series (which appears arbitrary to the uninitiated). The ideal community of 1,610 souls inhabits a 'phalanstery', a self-supporting community living in palatial buildings set in spacious and fertile grounds. The world-wide network of phalansteries forms an amicable and co-operative federation.

The three main activities of the phalansterians are working, eating and sex. Fourier's concept of 'attractive work' overturns the conventional utopian ideal of leisure. Work in the phalanstery utilises the individual's passions, and has all the connotations of play. 'Attractive work does not cause physical pain or mental distress; for the worker it is an amusement, a free exercise of his faculties.'[49] The rigid division of labour is replaced by multiple specialisation. Work is performed by groups of eight, small enough to engender ties of love and friendship. Individuals volunteer for work to which they are attracted and 'each individual serves the interest of the rest while simply following his own inclinations'. This happy arrangement determines the whole form of society. Each individual belongs to twenty or more groups, and has multiple loyalties and ties of friendship. 'The absorption of group rivalries by individual friendships' is the result. Since phalansterians change jobs every two hours the passion for variety is satisfied, and another bonus is that when workmates fall in love their pleasure is re-doubled.[50] It is no surprise that Harmony enjoys high productivity and abundance.

But 'Harmony cannot tolerate any general community of goods',[51] and so inequalities of wealth remain, but every member is guaranteed a generous 'social minimum' and can benefit from the patronage of his wealthier fellows. In any case, the satisfaction gained through productive activity exceeds the pleasure of consumption.

Fourier's lack of reserve on sexual matters obliged his editors to apologise for his crude genius, and caused his disciples to suppress the manuscript now published as *Le Nouveau Monde Amoureux*, which enthusiastically describes every kind of sexual pleasure in an erotic phalanstery. Freud has argued that 'one of culture's principal endeavours is to cement men and women together into larger units', a process which the sexual link disrupts by producing fragmented, self-contained pairs.[52] Fourier's view is diametrically opposed: only the perverted institution of monogamous marriage has this fatal effect. Properly organised, the release of sexual energy *increases* social cohesion. Harmony favours collective sexual activity and the minimisation of private life, but Fourier also maintains the individual's absolute right to sexual idiosyncrasy — in Harmony, someone can be found to share the wierdest fetish. The public eating festivals for satisfaction of the gastronomic passion similarly constitute a collectivisation of a conventionally private activity which augments both individual pleasure and social solidarity. The phalansterian is, in fact, integrated through work groups, age groups, sex groups, eating groups and many more. For those who would take their pleasure singly, it is a nightmare, but Fourier argues that Nature directs us to form series. His complex organisation is not incompatible with true freedom, which lies in the liberation of the passions; *false* freedom consists of formal rights imposed on the economically destitute.

Certainly, Fourier saw the risks of liberating the passions, and admitted that individual self-abandon can only lead to trouble — it must be a collective enterprise. Fourier's account of human nature is individualistic but he describes flesh-and-blood individuals, instinctive and idiosyncratic. To admit such diversity requires a pluralistic approach to society, or else a holistic theory which embraces everything: the latter is Fourier's method. His social calculus only works for the whole. His 'theory' of history is merely a superstructure unrelated to the social analysis, and so will not be elaborated here.

The breadth of versatility of Fourier's work is especially

surprising in view of his lack of education. He may well be imitating Restif's erotic fantasies and Rousseau's hatred of civilisation, but the quiddity of his theory is such that it cannot be dissolved into influences. No doubt he drew on the common pool of fashionable quasi-scientific ideas, but the individuality of his system lies in his methodological assumption that a perfect society can be devised which reflects the complex structure of human psychology and utilises recalcitrant instincts for social purposes. His execution of this design is as instructive as it is entertaining.

References
1. Beecher and Bienvenu, p. 162. The sub-title phrase is from Owen's *Lectures on the Marriages of the Priesthood of the Old Immoral World* (Leeds, 1840).
2. *Communist Manifesto*, MESW, Vol. 1, p. 135.
3. OC, X, p. 43 and OC, I, p. 55. For *Cosmologie*, see OC, XII.
4. OC, III, p. 136. See also OC, XIII, p. 624, and Beecher and Bienvenu, p. 160.
5. W. Benjamin, *Charles Baudelaire*, trans. H. Zohn (New Left Books, 1973), p. 159.
6. PJ (1st edn.), II, p. 794.
7. An argument favoured by E. P. Thompson and A. L. Morton. See bibliography.
8. See *Six Lectures*, pp. 29, 108, for these criticisms, and also *Revolution*, p. 83 ff, p. 111.
9. Markham, p. 4.
10. PJ, Bk. VIII, Ch. ii. See especially pp. 432-35.
11. See E. P. Thompson, *The Making of the English Working Class*, (Gollancz, 1963), Ch. IX. The extreme example was the position of skilled handworkers such as the weavers who, to compete with machine production, endured ever longer working hours for constantly diminishing pay.
12. Beecher and Bienvenu, p. 128. It is important to remember that the utopians, socialist economists, Proudhon, Marx, et al., are elaborating and formalising the working class's own awareness of the paradox. Co-operative journals of the time raised similar objections.
13. F. Engels, *Socialism: Utopian and Scientific*, MESW, Vol. 3, p. 119.
14. R. Owen, Supplement to *Revolution*, p. 10.
15. 'Thoughts occasioned by the perusal of Dr Parr's Spital Sermon' (Pamphlet: London, 1801), p. 48.
16. For the arguments on motivation, see PJ I, pp. 380-3, also PJ I, p. 69,

and PJ (1st edn.) I, p. 319.

17. PJ I, pp. 61-2. See also PJ I, p. 68, for comments on rationality.

18. PJ I, pp. 79-80.

19. PJ I, p. 86.

20. I read this into his remarks in PJ I, pp. 91-2.

21. PJ II, pp. 495-6. My emphasis. 'Independence' is synonymous with deviance here.

22. PJ I, p. 139. This view has modern adherents such as Lord Devlin who argues in *The Enforcement of Morals* (Oxford U.P., 1959) that individual deviance impoverishes the common stock.

23. PJ I, p. 164. My emphasis. Godwin denies that there is a correspondence between rights and duties.

24. PJ I, p. 232.

25. PJ I, p. xxiii. The following remarks on virtue are also from this 'Summary of Principles', but see also PJ I, pp. 308, 444-7.

26. D. H. Monro, *Godwin's Moral Philosophy* (Oxford U.P., 1953), p. 156. PJ (1st edn.), II, p. 329, deals with work.

27. *Revolution*, p. 58.

28. Title page of NVS, and again, NVS, p. 101. Much of the following exposition is taken from NVS. See especially pp. 102-4, 174.

29. HC, p. 30.

30. BNMW, p. 74.

31. NVS, pp. 110-1.

32. H. Desroches, 'Images and Echoes of Owenism in nineteenth-century France', in *Robert Owen*, ed. S. Pollard and J. Salt (Macmillan, 1971), p.

33. NVS, p. 144. Butt writes 'His emphasis on "useful" knowledge is quintessentially the view of the business community and of the state.' J. Butt, *Robert Owen* (David & Charles, 1971), p. 13.

34. *Réorganisation*, p.218.

35. *L'Organisateur*, pp. 31-2. The theory of history is best expounded in this work.

36. Markham, p. 76.

37. *Système*. p. 50.

38. *Système*, p. 166. It has been suggested that Saint-Simon merely invented historical laws to prove that what he hoped would happen. See W. L. Simon, 'History for Utopia: Saint-Simon and the Idea of Progress' in *J. History of Ideas* XVII (1956), pp. 311-31. There seems no justification for dismissing Saint-Simon's theory so lightly: would Simon have said the same of Marx?

39. *L'Organisateur*, p. 151.

40. *Ibid.*, pp. 63-4.

41. *L'Industrie*, t.i., p. 42, and t.ii, p. 32.

42. *L'Organisateur*, pp. 126-7, 149, 195.

43. M. Leroy, *Histoire des Idées Sociales en France* (Paris, 1950), Vol. II, p. 232.

44. OC I, p. 92.

45. OC VII, p. 404.

46. Morrell translated the term as 'sectism'. It seems to be an affection for one's confederates in any group. For a detailed account of the passions see *The Passions of the Human Soul* (London, 1850), trans. J. R. Morrell.

47. A. Breton, *Ode to Fourier*, trans. K. White (Cape Goliard, 1969).

48. OC VI, p. 25. See also the passage in C. Pellarin's *Life of Charles Fourier* (New York, 1848), p. 155, which begins 'Never do I cite a moral fact except to criticise it'.

49. OC III, p. 182. C.f. Unattractive work: the worker is 'without gaiety, without appetite for his work, without indirect enthusiasm'. OC VI, p. 92.

50. OC X, pp. 85, 127.

51. Beecher and Bienvenu, p. 249. See OC VI, p. 62, on the social minimum.

52. S. Freud, *Civilisation and its Discontents*, trans. J. Rivière, (Hogarth, 1930), p. 72.

CHAPTER 3

THE HUMAN INGREDIENT

THE eighteenth century was, Gay writes, 'a psychological age, an age when philosophy had turned from metaphysics to epistemology, when men's motives were being scrutinised with new vigour and new methods'. The dominant epistemological and psychological theories of the time engendered two antithetical views of human nature: as Hollis argues in *Models of Man*, Plastic Man was opposed to Autonomous Man (and both differed from the Ideal Christian). The input of each kind of individual to society would differ, as would the demands he made of society, so the choice of model was crucial in the formation of a social theory. The utopians were aware of the dichotomy which confronted them: all espoused the environmentalist philosophy which entails the model of Plastic Man because this also sanctions the possibility of radical change, but they were reluctant to forgo the creative and active powers of Autonomous Man, and so imposed some of his virtues on the other. For the most part, they made use of the increasingly problematical categories of philosophical psychology which were the residue of the Enlightenment, without analysing these or giving them empirical content.[1]

It is analytic that society must somehow accomodate human nature in its arrangements and that the ideal society, with goals of happiness and harmony, must make special efforts to match its organisation to its understanding of men. The logic of the utopians' argument is that social functioning and control rest on the utilisation of certain tractable human qualities. Their selection of postulates about human nature which are to serve as the basis of their social theory is therefore by no means accidental. It follows that socially useless or dangerous qualities remain in the shade, while creative and sociable elements are thrown into bright relief. The utopians' conviction that the environment makes man did not prevent them from being methodological individualists in their explanations of the mechanics of society.

The notion of human nature as something which can be characterised in a historical vacuum is highly suspect, and the utopians were aware of this, as their environmentalism shows. The major distinction which needs to be made here is that between the various categories of statements and postulates which the utopians make about human nature:

1. *Statements about behaviour patterns.* Such empirical statements are the foundation of most other statements about human nature.

2. *Motives for action.* The term 'motive' here comprehends emotions, feelings, impulses, drives, and what Godwin calls 'dispositions' and Fourier calls 'passions'.

3. *Capacities.* The terminology most favoured by the utopians, since 'capacity' normally refers to an infinite potentiality. Clearly, capacities may or may not be developed or educed.

4. *Malleability.* This is the joker in the pack, since it implies that no such fixed, identifiable entity exists. Owen's whole argument rests on 'plasticity'.

5. *Needs.* Statements about needs must also be made, for successful need-satisfaction is essential to utopia.

6. *Evaluative qualities.* E.g. human perfectibility. These refer to something beyond the behaviour-based explanation of human nature, and are often teleological, deriving from perceptions of the destiny of man.

The relationship between some of these categories is incestuous, but they must be distinguished because each kind of statement designates human qualities with particular social implications and functions: motives can be controlled and conditioned, capacities can be developed, plastic can be moulded, needs must be satisfied.

For utopian purposes, capacities are most significant, because the defining mark of a capacity is its potential for expansion and development. Capacities thus have a greater range of application than situation-specific characteristics such as motives and emotions, which resemble conditioned responses to stimuli. By contrast, to act according to a capacity seems to involve a conscious rule-following process, which must in some way be learned, and then is infinitely applicable. Competence in language is a paradigm capacity, and reason, morality and intelligence also exemplify the rule-following model. Capacities are typified by reflective and creative processes and are socially constructive. Rationality and the moral sense can be harnessed in the service of self-control and, hence, social control.

Needs by contrast, when unsatisfied, threaten the social system, and are exhaustive: that is, their satisfaction is likely to terminate the demands which they make on the political system, and to lead to social equilibrium but also perhaps to torpor. 'Gastronomic utopias' such as the Land of Cockayne, which focus solely on need satisfaction, are antagonistic to any achievement-oriented activities. Needs represent the demands which create stress within the system, whereas capacities are the inputs, whose functions in the social system differ in quality and direction. A third element of human nature omnipresent in the analysis of the utopians is the 'motive' of self-interest, the centrifugal force constantly at work in the social system, which tends to dissolve society into its individual components.

The following sections analyse four attributes — the moral sense, reason, malleability and perfectibility — and the social functions which the utopians allocated to these. The final section examines how they treated needs and the maverick motive of self-interest.

THE TRIUMPH OF REASON

Rationality is the crucial assumption of social science, for it allows the investigator to posit consistency in human action and conformity to certain norms. Nevertheless, the meaning given to rationality is usually minimal, centring on goal maximisation. The utopians postulated rationality, but for them 'reason' connotes not a behavioural, but an open-ended, creative attribute, often explicitly linked to natural morality. Despite their romantic leanings, they appropriated the unromantic concept of reason ubiquitous in the early Enlightenment, regarding it as an inexorable mental motor, propelling man towards truth and perfection. The concept denotes man's capacity for rational thought, but also his susceptibility to truth and his ability to accumulate and apply knowledge. Reason as an ever-ready mode of processing experiences suits well with the idea of perfectibility as an indefinitely-expanding process.

Godwin argues that 'reason . . . is calculated to regulate our conduct . . . It is to the improvement of reason therefore, that we are to look for the improvement of our social conditions. Reason depends for its clearness and strength upon the cultivation of knowledge'.[2] Even the malefactor parodies reason to justify his irrational actions, but the reasonable man is 'accessible to reason' and bases his actions on sound knowledge and logic. The interdependence of reason, knowledge and happiness is also expounded by Owen.

> When the knowledge which man receives shall be extended to its utmost limit, and true without any mixture of error, then he may and will enjoy the happiness of which his nature will be capable . . . man has no other means of discovering what is false, except by his faculty of reason, or power of acquiring and comparing ideas which he receives.[3]

Saint-Simon's emphasis on the leading role of knowledge and its application is intimately connected with ideas of reason, and the new capacities which he heralds are in part new ways of reasoning, which bring men's ideas and actions into accord with the industrial ideology. Finally, Fourier, deploring 'l'égarement de la raison', equates reason with instinct — what instinct demands is reasonable — and actually generates a new and unique form of reasoning, the analogy. Irrationality, for the utopians, means reasoning perverted by prejudice, passion or superstition, or actions based on such mis-reasoning. Godwin's 'imperfectly voluntary' action may also be called irrational.

Two kinds of rationality seem to be involved in all intentional action: firstly, that mental reasoning process which centres on the ability to manipulate language and logic. Secondly, there is what will here be referred to as 'purposive rationality'. This is the application of reasoning to empirical action, which requires the ability to suit means to ends. The prime social application of purposive rationality is each individual's endeavour to organise his life so as to satisfy his desires and to make his behaviour compatible with his belief system; Godwin's 'private judgement' denotes this ability. Although successful purposive reasoning evidently relies on correct logical reasoning, means-ends statements are ultimately contingent, so that purposive rationality produces propositions with empirical content which may be verified but are not necessarily true.[4] It provides imperatives, like the 'practical syllogism' scorned by logicians. The utopians conflate the two kinds of rationality in one imprecise category, 'reason', which they hold to combine inseparably the certainties of logic with the flexibility and empirical reference of purposive rationality.

Logical rationality alone does not embody the qualities required for reason to play a critical and improving role. The capacity to reason formally rests largely on the manipulation of language, and once the logical process has been internalised, the individual's logical powers cannot be further improved. As to its critical capacity, logical rationality can scarcely be an independent force for progress, because it cannot go beyond the information received. Its negative critical function is to act as a censor, rejecting information which does not conform to logical standards, or which contradicts prior knowledge.

Since logical rationality alone does not constitute an abrasive and progressive force, the active element must be located in purposive rationality. Godwin's definition of rational action illuminates the special qualities which the utopians attributed to purposive reason. He says that we should be prepared to justify actions with sound, relevant arguments. For Godwin, the standard by which the soundness and relevance of the justification is to be assessed, is the *objective truth* about the nature of the relations between objects, and between motives and objects, which he deems to be constant. He would maintain that perfected purposive rationality reflects an existing order in the external world which is empirically knowable. Indeed, all the utopians assume that a necessary structure relates objects in the social and natural worlds, from which all statements about causal connections necessarily proceed and, hence, all purposively rational arguments. From his perception of this structure, each utopian constructs a belief system to incorporate these absolute truths and his utopia rests on, and encompasses, these beliefs.

But social science now recognises many different connections between phenomena, which are generated by differing frameworks of thought, variously called paradigms, belief or value systems, and ideologies. Any such system will supply a logic which connects actions with purposes and purposes with beliefs, and these logics may conflict with one another. This contrasts with the utopians' promotion of one social science and their deference to one Truth. The relativism and functionalism of much social science in this century would, conversely, be anathema to the utopians. By assuming the singularity and immediacy of truth and the uniqueness of causal connections, and so imposing a uniform structure on the world, the utopians establish reason as an unambiguous force. It resides in the empirical-scientific workshop, a critical tool which all men can operate, which fashions absolute connections between objective truths.

However, the preceding arguments undermine this conception of rationality and the constructions placed upon it. Logical rationality alone could not bring about human improvement, and purposive rationality is dependent on chosen belief structures. From this perspective, the utopians are seen to have accepted implicitly an ideological role, and taken steps to inculcate the 'right' rationality, although they presented this quasi-scientifically. Goodwin and Owen added to the corpus of factual knowledge the prescriptions which they called 'moral truths', such as Owen's maxim that the happiness of all individuals is interconnected. Saint-Simon 'derived' truths about work, peace and order from the structure of industrial society. Clearly such truths are not scientific: what appears as deduction is in fact propaganda.

In summary, reason's boasted independent critical function must be discounted. But the utopians' attachment to reason as the supreme human faculty may alternatively be justified by reason's function as an agent of social cohesion. Reason bears an essentially socialising character. The experience of sensation is private and no-one has to satisfy criteria concerning the nature of his perceptions in order to be called sensuous. But the workings of individual reason are laid bare to scrutiny through communication and action, so that rationality connotes the solution of problems according to publicly acknowledged criteria. The French 'raison' combines the notion of rationality and rightness in this way. The workings of an individual's reason are confirmed or refuted by the test of public exposure, and the aberrant reasoner is branded as irrational, while the aberrant sensualist is usually left in peace. Reason is the structure of communicated thought, whereby men discuss and modify each others' views and actions.

Godwin's injunction that we should always be ready to justify our actions refers partly to its objective function, the public justification of attitudes and actions. In Godwin's utopia, men question each other about their reasons for action, and correct unreasoned and unreasonable actions without acrimony. In a community with shared knowledge and a uniform belief system, the arbiter of reason would be constituted by the majority of reasonable men. Godwin and Owen emphasize the universal content of rationality and the public context in which it operates and, hence, the potential which it holds for creating a unanimous utopia. Ideally, it leads to the elimination of conflict through discussion.

The utopians' views of rationality are bound up with their conceptual conflation 'true knowledge'. The dual role of early social science as teacher and preacher is manifested in this confusion. For them, the term 'knowledge' comprises the scientific understanding of natural objects and of man, treated as an object for observation and theorising. Although the utopians, in particular Saint-Simon,[5] value the beneficial advances of the natural sciences, their major interest is in promoting the development of the human and social sciences. They claimed that social-scientific knowledge made a direct appeal to reason and the moral sense, and so hastened progress towards utopia.

The scientific perspective on man transformed what had formerly been moral philosophy into a branch of the positive science of man, and scientific methods such as calculus were applied to the moral sciences, which were thus made 'rational' so that the mere revelation of moral knowledge would revolutionise human behaviour.

The privileged relationship which men are said to have with truth accounts for the improving power which the utopians attributed to knowledge. Sometimes the reverence of the utopians for the abstract idea of truth approaches that of the seventeenth century: truth is omnipotent, absolute, no individual can resist the power of truth. But the deference has a strictly utilitarian justification. Godwin argues 'the direct and only road to a knowledge of man and of human nature, and to the attainment of happiness, is through the development of truth'.[6] Fourier is even less reverent: 'there is nothing good about truth itself, it is only good relatively, according to its results'. But the power of *his* revealed truth could overthrow Civilisation in two years.[7] Truth is credited with an independent, active force, and the method of achieving utopia favoured by these four is to rely upon the spontaneous recognition of truth by human reason without further intervention. This outlook had a debilitating effect on their activities, making individual efforts for the realisation of utopia seem redundant. As Engels observed, the struggle is transferred to the plane of consciousness.

But the basis for the exalted position of truth is slender. Certainly, truth has a special connection with mankind, being a function of language: truth is a human invention.[8] But the utopians try to interpret this tautology to demonstrate that all men must be truth-loving, and maintain the

Socratic position that men cannot knowingly eschew truth or right.

However, this view of truth might have another dimension. Men have perhaps a tacit, latent understanding of certain truths about society which leads them to acquiesce readily when truths which correspond with this inner knowledge are made explicit. It is not that men possess innate ideas, but that their articulacy lags behind their understanding. Similar arguments have been used to explain why descriptive popular sociology enjoys such success: it voices widely shared but unexpressed feelings and assumptions about life.[9] So Owen's argument that there exist truths about life to which all men will accede may have a foundation in human consciousness, although all such truths are ultimately ideological.

This hypothesis suggests another role for the utopians. Given that they lived in societies where the majority of men were uneducated, their function could be regarded as parallel to that of the prophet in primitive societies. The utopian not only seeks converts but, more precisely, articulates on behalf of the people, showing men their own minds. The overt messianism of Owen and Fourier, and their faith that truth would out, supports this reading of the utopian function.

The utopians regard scientific knowledge and objective truth as *dei ex machinis*; they scarcely explore the connections between knowledge, consciousness and change. They overestimate men's capacity to act on general truths which conflict with particular truths about their interests. The real problem, which they fail to confront, is to establish a hierarchy among a diversity of truths with conflicting implications, or to unify this plurality in a higher truth. Unfortunately, the rationality-knowledge-truth nexus which is at the heart of the utopians' theories, and which justifies their own theorising, disintegrates when their optimistic accounts of rationality and absolutist epistemologies come under scrutiny. The rationality assumption is a weak link in these theories because too much is pinned on it — a mistake avoided in the more formalistic assumptions of later social scientists.

MORALITY WITHOUT VIRTUE

The notion of a universal, secular, natural moral sensibility was a favourite with the *philosophes* and, not surprisingly, morality plays a leading role in the construction and maintenance of these utopias. Godwin, Owen and Saint-Simon agree on the universality and the progressive qualities of the moral sense; Fourier alone dissents, arguing that it is a temporary burden imposed on men by Civilisation, which has no real foundation in the passions which are a law unto themselves. The utopians consider the moral aspects of human nature only insofaras they are functional in the operation of morality as a social force, and subjective elements of morality, such as personal virtue, are omitted.

A suitable definition of morality on which to base the following discussion is as follows: a code of categorical prescriptions, enforceable by conscience, not by coercion, which usually directs human behaviour towards actions which are at least harmless to other individuals, and at best beneficial to them.[10] Different concepts and definitions of morality obtain, and the code may be elaborated by rules of thumb, but all share the minimum structure defined above. Man's 'moral faculty' denotes his ability to understand, react to and follow the prescriptions of such a code, and may also be used broadly to refer to his propensity to respond in particular ways to a moral language and terms with moral content, without commitment to a particular code.

Two standard hypotheses may be offered to explain the origin of the moral faculty, and to determine whether it is a necessary or contingent feature of human nature. Firstly, it may be postulated, as by Godwin, that men are naturally inclined to act morally even if social circumstances often thwart this inclination. This natural goodness view rests on a premiss of natural sympathy or compassion and seems to assume an absolute, fundamental, universal moral code. Alternatively, it may be argued that men are inherently receptive to moral language, and capable of being moved by moral motives, but that they must still be taught a definition of good, and the principles of a particular morality. This argument dictates a relativist approach to morality, such as

Owen and Saint-Simon took: specific moral codes are the means by which specific societies manipulate the moral potential of individuals. Alternatively, it could be maintained that man is naturally *amoral*, since the assumption of 'inherent receptiveness' is unverifiable, and that of natural goodness is so *a fortiori*. The very fact that morality has to be taught indicates that it is an ideology like other ideologies, requiring no special faculty except credulity. Such is Fourier's contention. Each entails a different structuring of society and different socialising and controlling devices, and these connections will now be considered.

The archetypal natural goodness postulate is Rousseau's, whose imaginary reconstruction (as misinterpreted by his contemporaries) of the lives of savages, extolled 'the peacefulness of their passions and their ignorance of vices'.[11] Since they had, Rousseau asserts, no idea of goodness, they could not properly be credited with a moral virtue.

This postulate needs considerable adaptation if it is to be applied to civilised man, and Godwin indeed transforms it thoroughly by making natural goodness the characteristic of intelligent, civilised man, who understands moral terms through his rationality.[12] He intellectualised the moral sense, making it a *desire* to do good, coupled with a *knowledge* of right and wrong, which is spontaneous. Individuals need no help in perceiving what is immoral. 'All real crimes that can be supposed to be the fit objects of judicial animadversion, are capable of being discerned without the teaching of law.'[13] This assertion later serves as the basis for two revolutionary social prescriptions — the abolition of property, and of the legal system. It is impossible that we should *choose* to do evil; civilised man's failure to maintain higher moral standards is merely due to lack of knowledge, defective reason and, above all, to imperfect institutions.

Morality, then is natural and untutored; reason is the servant of morality, and the two combine to determine the perfectly voluntary and just action. How else could man's perfectibility be measured but by his progress towards moral perfection? Indicative of Godwin's optimism is his suggestion for a social order based on mutual moral scrutiny and advice, which illustrates his expressly instrumental view of morality and virtue. Godwin presents a fairly consistent utilitarian structure, although his emphasis on benevolence, justice and desert as independent, absolute values, menaces the utilitarian position.

A knockdown argument for natural goodness which has no connection with man's inner moral capacity is offered, *en passant*, by Owen and Fourier. Man is good, they argue, because his faculties and passions were divinely created. Of course, this was mere camouflage for their real meaning, that man's instincts are good because they are natural (and Original Sin is so much baloney), an argument which involved the impolitic step across the threshold into atheism. Significantly, anyone who postulates that man was created good must invoke that villain, the environment, to square this hypothesis with reality. Helvétius made this a standard form of argument and all the utopians use it, explaining man's moral dilapidation by the viciousness of society. Natural goodness will blossom, once evil institutions are abolished.

Owen's *tabula rasa* approach to human nature excludes any idea of intrinsic natural goodness: the Divine Blessing is merely an optional extra. He does, however, speak of the moral faculty as a basic endowment conducive to happiness, but he concentrates on the intellect and knowledge, and disclaims the use of moral terms. Yet human beings naturally incline towards the principles of Owen's humanitarian morality, for their reason will perceive the truth of such principles. The cure for the moral neutrality, which is the corollary of malleability, is the implanting of moral principles in the minds of children. Ambivalent about the use of moral mechanisms, Owen maintains — unconvincingly — that his education process merely teaches rationality.

Saint-Simon, too, sees morality as externally imposed and instrumental in social organisation. His theory clearly foreshadows the Marxian view of morality as ideology, for the social system is said to generate morality, which may affect men directly or through the historical determination of man's nature. For Saint-Simon, the industrial society is 'essentially moral' — and he approves of that terrestrial morality, which amounts to self-interest rightly pursued, in a society so unified in its structure that all interests are satisfied by the same outcome. This redefinition of liberated economic interests as morality fell short of Durkheim's definition of morality and was, for him, a central flaw of the argument.[14] But for Saint-Simon, then, as for Owen, morality is to be predicated not of individuals but of particular historical communities. What is needed is a well-behaved community *in aggregate*: no special personal virtues are required. Of course, the notion of a personal moral capacity is essential even for this aggregative approach, but Owen and Saint-Simon emphasize that the propagation of a particular morality is primarily effected through education and social institutions.

The hypothesis of amorality is often espoused, as by Fourier, to detract from the established position of a particular morality. Can such an argument be seriously advanced, given the prevalence of moral belief and the evidence of moral behaviour in society? Fourier solves this contradiction by making morality a contingent property of some historical states, imported into the realm of language and action because of its social function. So Fourier argues that morality is no more than an inessential, temporary sensibility imposed on human nature and fated to disappear in Harmony, where the workings of passionate attraction would render morality superfluous, since desires can be fulfilled without detriment to others. The self-control which morality entails is as detestable as any external form of control and equally injurious to the spontaneous operation of the passions. Certainly, obligations will exist in Harmony, but these will be constituted without reference to morality.

Accounts of the psychological genesis of the moral sense within the structure of the individual personality confirm many of Owen's arguments and point to necessary modifications of Godwin's perspective, and Fourier's. Moral responsiveness is found to originate in early conditioning and communication within the family: various patterns of childrearing produce various moral characters of which the 'altruistic autonomous' is judged to be the best adjusted to our liberal society. Our patterns of moral response are determined from an early age, and scarcely alterable thereafter, although we may later come to acknowledge or reject rationally the *content* of particular moral codes.[15] The conclusion is that we are, willy-nilly, participants in a moral meta-game, that structured game of moral responses (guilt', altruism, etc.) which can be played according to different moral codes. Social observation strengthens the case for the ubiquity of the moral sense. Such arguments destroy the basis for the hypothesis of amorality, for no-one can escape at least partial socialisation into moral attitudes.

The psychologist views the moral structure of any society, and the content of its morality, as something external to the individual, a non-experiential ideology, which he must internalise. This interpretation throws doubt upon the validity of Godwin's idea of the individual's creative moral capacity, but bears out the views of Owen and Saint-Simon. It entails a different role for morality, and different relations between morality and human improvement, since moral competence rests on the deep structure of morality, rooted in the individual personality, while performance rests on familiarity with the preferred moral code. The possibilities for improving performance are circumscribed unless a method is found of increasing competence, that is, the nature of the basic moral responses evoked by the original conditioning. This would require the control by society of children at an early age, such as Owen advocates.

Such evidence at least suggests that social theorists may justifiably make assumptions about the moral capacity, however conjectural its structure and origin may be. The assumption of a moral capacity has two functions in the theories of Godwin, Owen and Saint-Simon: it enables them firstly to employ morality as a central and economical device for social control, and secondly to designate moral progress a constituent of human perfectibility. Man's moral perfectibility is largely understood by the utopians as his ability to make ever greater contributions to the general welfare. Given this emphasis, the utopians' view of moral progress is predictably community-directed. The development of morality would eradicate anti-social acts and perfect socially useful virtues, but the private pleasures of moral development are untasted in these utopias, because socially insignificant. This perception of morality as primarily a social instrument upholds the relativist view of morality and detracts from the moral absolutism to which Godwin sometimes adheres.

THE PLASTIC SUBSTANCE

Any social determinist theory entails that human nature shall be regarded as somewhat fluid and changeable. A determinist account such as Godwin's, while making men's characters subject to external factors, leaves open the possibility of self-control and self-determination, because the moral and rational faculties at least are constant. Owen, however, makes an extreme assumption of malleability: he asserts that men's characters and opinions are *entirely* moulded by outside forces. Although this characterisation of human nature as malleable is one-dimensional, being transparently a postulate built on little philosophical evidence and designed to justify his theory of education, the resulting social theory has a radically new focus.

Malleability is a second-order human characteristic, vacuous in itself, but setting parameters for the manifestations of first-order characteristics. The concept affords no information about individual consciousness and capacities, and from this idea alone we cannot determine which direction human improvement should follow. So the utopian who regards his human subject matter as completely plastic finds himself in consequence responsible for education, conditioning and the selection of values for his ideal society, and in a dangerously authoritative position.

The advantages of human malleability for the social reformer are persuasively expounded by Owen and Saint-Simon. For Saint-Simon, man's plastic nature is demonstrated by the different, socially-determined capacities which typify various classes at certain historical periods. Historical progress has given contemporary man certain characteristics, and he plans merely to utilise these in his industrial utopia. By contrast, it is the possibility of actively determining character which makes malleability so significant for Owen. Each man's knowledge and action-guiding principles unwittingly reflect the opinions of his teachers and ancestors, but since the learning mechanism operates at the level of consciousness, he can be presented with rational doctrines, and thereby be cleansed of prejudice. This is how Owen envisages the ideal process of character formation, and although he uses evocative terms like 'ductility' and 'plasticity', his meaning is *educability*.

Human beings can *collectively* be moulded in any way; Owen is not promising to outlaw natural inequalities or congenital delinquency. He leaves unanswered questions such as whether education can alter the 'original proportions' of the individual character, and whether human instincts and desires can themselves be moulded, as well as their behavioural manifestations.[16] He trisects original human nature into the physical, the mental and the moral, of which the last two interact and are malleable; essentially, he reduces the hereditary element to a minimum. Freud, Piaget and others have suggested that the process of character development, which includes the environmental element, also has fixed structures which might from the perspective of the utopian, be as intractable as the hereditary elements: such accounts cast doubt on Owen's simple stratification of human nature.

There are serious objections of postulating human malleability as the foundation stone for utopia. Firstly, no determinate definition of human good or perfection can be inferred from malleability, so the utopian himself chooses which human faculties to nurture, which to suppress. The dangerous indeterminacy of this situation and the consequent helplessness of those undergoing manipulation by conditioning is exemplified in the writings of B. F. Skinner. 'The problem, in short, is not to design a way of life which will be liked by men *as they are now* but a way of life which will be liked by those who live in it.' That is, if conditioning techniques are as far-reaching and humanity as plastic as Skinner believes, existing human inclinations, desires and values need not be taken into consideration in the designing of an ideal society. Furthermore, a man who judges a culture or society by his own liking or disliking is 'immoral' for 'he sets himself up as a standard of human nature'.[17] Skinner denies such upstart standards and substitutes his own! In general, the dismissal of men's feelings about society as contingent and modifiable creates a void which the planners, educators or psychologists must fill. The danger of a utopian dictatorship is always immanent — yet the utopian can operate in no other way. There follows a second objection to a society devised to exploit individual malleability for social benefit: no individual should habitually exert power over another man, for this endangers his independence and dignity, making him a means to another's end. But Owen's argument entails that society should be divided between active and passive agents, the educators and the educated, the mould and the plastic substance.

A third danger lurks in making plasticity the point of departure for utopia: this could lead to espousal of the view attributed to the later Saint-Simonians and Social Darwinists, that the goal of the exercise is 'evolution', the better adaptation of man to the existing social system, a view which as a corollary reduces human desires to a secondary consideration. These dangers are incipient in Owen's proposals and those of Saint-Simon. Such an approach is anti-utopian in its abandonment of the general theme of utopias — the reconstruction of society for man's convenience.

These objections show malleability to be an unsatisfactory premiss for utopia building. It is methodologically inadequate, being indeterminate and labile. In general it is also true that malleability, plasticity and even adaptability are essentially passive attributes, less useful in forming a society of equal and independent men than the creative characteristics of reason and morality.[18] Practical objections also abound: if human nature is a blank sheet for the philosophers, it is a blank cheque for the educators. Education and conditioning are themselves regrettably protean and can be turned to good or evil ends. These strictures do not discredit Owen's benevolent intentions, but we may question whether his system embodied safeguards to prevent character formation from becoming human exploitation.

HUMAN PERFECTIBILITY

> Every perfection that human beings are competent to conceive, human beings . . . are competent to attain.[19]

Human perfectibility is the dynamo which propels society towards perfection, but as a philosophical idea it suffers from numerous imperfections and conceptual difficulties. Perfectibility is an active and creative attribute, directed towards achievement, rather than to the receipt of satisfaction. Among the creative capacities, perfectibility is that capacity which is concerned entirely with the improvement of other capacities. It is a 'meta-capacity', for unless defined with reference to something else, the term is empty: it is parallel to (and essential to) the concept of harmony, denoting an ordering or realisation of subordinate elements. The notion is itself a construct which rests upon man's ability to measure improvement in accordance with norms. Any definition of perfectibility implies an evaluation of human purposes through the choice of these standards. Furthermore, the notion usually reflects a teleological impulse, a desire on the part of the thinker to legislate on the destiny of mankind. Despite these conceptual difficulties, the Enlightenment's interest in psychology and optimism about perfectibility made it analytic that thereafter utopia should also be 'eupsychia'.

None of the utopians was so naïve as to see perfection as a definable, fixed goal. Godwin's definition of perfectibility is 'the faculty of being continually made better and receiving perpetual improvement', while for Owen it denoted the possibility of giving every man a 'superior constitution'. The probability of attaining absolute perfection is handled gingerly, except by Fourier whose precise descriptions of the perfect man are undeniably absurd.

Perfectibility must first be distinguished from progressiveness. 'Progress' can be used neutrally, as when Godwin writes 'man is in a state of perpetual progress. He must grow *better or worse*, either correct his habits or confirm them', but its usage is rarely so impartial. The utopians' normal use of the term indicates improvement, and is normative, approbatory, and often specifically moral. Turgot's description of material progress in his Four Stages theory, and Condorcet's sketch of the progress of the human spirit towards knowledge and freedom influenced their concept of progress. Saint-Simon is a direct successor in his dialectical fusion of material and spiritual progress; Godwin detects constant, linear progression in the accumulating wealth of human achievement. Later, progress was identified with material or technological improvements, but when the utopians spoke of scientific progress, they frequently meant an advance in the understanding, not the mastery, of nature, which is a predicate of the intellect, not the will. The dynamic nature of progress is such that increasing knowledge will re-fashion the goals of previous periods, and the concept is ultimately relative and interpretative. But the utopians define the goals absolutely and delineate their static, final societies in apparent ignorance of these shifting sands.

By contrast, perfection at first appears to refer to a particular, absolute end, and so to be freed from this problem by its superlative nature. But we must be able to frame criteria by which we can recognise the perfect state. In simple and circumscribed situations there may be a watertight standard of perfection, but with objects as complex as human beings, located in equally complex and structured environments, the use of the term requires both a selective and a speculative approach.

Perfection is not a scientific concept but an ethical one, so its importation into would-be scientific theories detracts from their objectivity and verifiability. In Owen's case, the attempt to establish a self-evident definition of human perfection leads to inconsistencies because no conclusions about what constitutes perfection derive from his central premiss that human nature is plastic. His definition of perfection (full exercise of all human faculties) is therefore imposed, not derived. All definitions of human perfection evidently rest on an underlying evaluative framework, and teleology may intrude, posing further problems. But the utopians, in their attempts to emulate the sciences, claim to base their criteria on *facts* about human nature, which makes it possible to scrutinise their notions of perfection. Nevertheless, their selection procedure is normative. The influence of the Enlightenment is evident in the choices of Godwin, Owen and Saint-Simon, who all rest their hopes on the improvement of man's moral and rational capacities.

When a term like 'perfection' is made substantive in order to function in a social theory, its content should be made specific — but the search for precision raises many speculative questions and difficulties. In the case of moral perfection may not the elimination of morally undesirable qualities entail the disappearance of some useful ones, thus detracting from social perfection? May not the benevolence of the perfect altruist sap the independence of his fellows?[21] Can ideal moral behaviour be defined outside specific contexts? The answers can only be conjectural.

Such problems may be skirted if moral perfection is translated from the language of motives into that of action, as in Owen's first socialising principle: 'He [the schoolchild] is never to injure his playfellows, but on the contrary he is to contribute all in his power to make them happy'.[22] Godwin too defines the ideal *action* — perfectly voluntary and perfectly benevolent. Certainly, a behavioural definition of perfection simplifies the matter, but it can only cover a narrow range of human actions. In any case, the perfection of behaviour according to rules is not what was intended by any of these utopians.

Fourier alone attempts a precise description of perfection, the perfection of the twelve passions. Once the 'ultra-aetherial' eye has evolved, the visual passion is perfected, and so on. Each passion contains its own possibility of perfection, and the fully-perfected Harmonian is a man whose every passion is refined. Thus, the need for selection does not arise. But for Fourier, human perfection, although a source of individual delight, is not socially useful, for progress to Harmony takes place, not by the perfection of the passions, but by their transformation from subversive to direct manifestations. So Fourier's perfectibilism is an afterthought, not an integral part of the mechanism of change.

Another question which arises is whether the utopian's perfectibilism is constituted on an egalitarian or inegalitarian basis. Is perfectibility to refer to those characteristics common to all men, which can, despite individual variations, be equally improved for them all? Or should it mean the greatest possible improvement of each man's idiosyncratic collection of attributes? Before a harmonious solution can be reached, a theoretical answer must be provided to these questions.

The concept of perfection is not logically related to that of equality, so the matter is open. The egalitarian utopian is likely to opt for human perfection in those areas in which men could in principle be made equal. It would not be practical, functional or fair to advocate perfection of physical strength or appearance, since natural inequalities in these areas are almost ineradicable. Happily, those attributes which are most useful socially are those in which some measure of equality seems feasible.

The universal, egalitarian perfectibilist stand is exemplified by Godwin, who sees reason and morality as available to all men, equally capable of being perfected in any individual. 'The points in which human beings resemble are infinitely more considerable than those in which they differ.'[23] Indeed, society could not function without a universal, equal distribution of moral conviction, honesty and goodwill, for the mutual surveillance principle depends on this. But his whole structure is at risk if men do not in fact have equal potential to develop in these directions, and there remain moral backsliders and poor reasoners.

Owen circumvents the inherent difficulties of the egalitarian position by admitting that different men have different capacities, and that some will still be inferior when equally perfect, i.e. when their own potential is fulfilled. But these individual differences are unimportant, as perfection is a characteristic of the aggregate. Simple, uniform societies like those of Owen and Godwin cannot contain diversity, being designed on the assumption of a common human nature. They wish to maintain that men are alike in ways relevant to social behaviour, so that a common standard of perfection can be formulated, but their functional generalisations camouflage real human diversity which may threaten their systems in reality.

The inegalitarian approach, on the other hand, in no way detracts from the concept of perfection and a harmonious society, but enhances its realism. Fourier and Saint-Simon accentuate the ways in which men differ and are unequal, arguing that unequal capacities can and should be perfected according to their own particular potentialities. Perfection, *qua* 'perfection to an equal degree', can contain a multitude of diversity. The perfectibilism of inegalitarians subtends a different image of society from that of the egalitarians. A pluralistic society such as Fourier describes thrives on variety and inequality, and would be disrupted were all men to attempt to perfect the same skills and passions. Equalisation and uniformity would be similarly disastrous for Saint-Simon's stratified industrial society.

The importance of human perfectibility as a contributory factor to social harmony is self-evident; now, the road from human to social perfection must be delineated. Clearly, some capacities tend towards a perfection best predicated of society, for example, an increase in human knowledge, which although it rests on the achievements of individuals, depends even more on society's providing the material conditions in which discoveries can be made, and knowledge advanced. In this sense, of course, social perfection is more than a mere aggregate of individual perfections, and cannot be located exclusively in groups or individuals. Saint-Simon's perfectibilism, like that of Condorecet, rests largely on the hypothesis that the improved knowledge and technology of a scientific elite will raise the whole of society nearer to mental and moral perfection.

Knowledge is clearly central to the construction of a perfect society, yet the utopians assume a *necessary* connection between scientific knowledge, progress and perfection which is patently spurious, since the extension of scientific knowledge in no way entails an understanding of how to apply the knowledge for human benefit, or the will so to do. Lurking behind these optimistic assertions is an argument which derived from the eighteenth-century naturalism and romanticism with which these utopians were imbued: that the natural order, when properly understood by men, will no longer appear to oppose and threaten them and will harmonise with the human order. The utopians' predictions of superabundance imply that Nature will be domesticated in the service of mankind, and their other arguments are in similar vein. Fourier develops a flamboyant version of the fallacy, extending the idea of natural harmony to a metaphysical theory of cosmic unity: once social harmony is established, nature will produce anti-lions, anti-whales and a whole menagerie of domesticated beasts which will perform tasks to which man's strength is unequal.[24] Furthermore, the newly harmonious earth will emit benign vapours and receive those of other planets, to its benefit. From our perspective the anthropocentric view of the universe which the utopians, as children of their time, held, can be seen to be groundless theoretically and fallible empirically.

No amount of analysis can entirely illuminate what the utopians meant by perfection, for they are imprecise. But, to recapitulate, perfectibility, the capacity to achieve perfection, is a second-order term, without content in itself; the individual optimist himself supplies the criteria. It may prove especially hard to define human perfection when it is projected into a totally different utopian society where circumstances could alter our view of what qualities are socially or personally desirable. The unfolding, incremental nature of the concept as Godwin defines it certainly entails changing criteria: perfection must grow by stages, the criteria of measurement being always superior to those of a previous stage. Human perfection is seen largely as a means to social perfection. The lack of interest in individual perfection beyond what is socially functional is a serious limitation of these theories but no doubt a necessary one, since assumptions and conditions cannot be endlessly multiplied, especially in would-be scientific theories.

One problem in combining an absolutist epistemology with a perfectibilist theory is that a dynamic view of human nature undermines the reputedly stable factual foundations of knowledge about men. Can Owen's definition of truth which 'remains one and the same under every view and comparison' embrace knowledge about the 'plastic quality'. of human beings? Yet it is pre-requisite of his social theory that there should be a corpus of assumptions about human nature and behaviour on which the theory builds. Only Fourier tries to solve the problem of epistemological dynamics by planning a society in which human improvement and social innovation together form a baffling spiral of change.

The utopians flash perfection as a passport to utopia, overlooking the problems intrinsic to the notion, because the function of perfection in these theories is partly to persuade the reader to suspend disbelief. How could a society as anarchistic as Godwin's be made to work? Because men become morally perfect, renouncing pride and spite. Why will the industrial society be free of conflict? Because the desire to dominate gives way to the love of work, peace and co-operation. The practical usefulness of the concept in radical theories, as a general justification for free-ranging aspiration, is undeniable, but the process of filling this conceptual shell with special meanings generates the problems which have been described — but by no means solved!

NEED AND GREED

The utopians' analysis of human nature rests on the selection of highly sociable and functional qualities, and their perfectibilism operates on these as an intensifying device. The connection between these creative capacities and the attainment of social harmony is close. Intrinsic to the notions of rationality and morality is the idea of standards universally agreed and sanctioned which contribute to solidarity and cohesion. But an exclusive concentration on these amiable characteristics produces an optimistically unbalanced picture of humanity. As a corrective, we must investigate how the utopians proposed to hold in check potentially disruptive aspects of human nature, namely, the individual needs which constitute a perpetual drain on society's limited resources, and which necessitate priorities of distribution that set up social tensions: also, self-interest with its divisive tendencies — in short, need and greed. Philosophical psychology identifies these as two constituents of human nature which set limits to the form which an ideal society can take, and threaten its inner harmony.

Classical and medieval utopias have dwelt on the superabundant satisfaction of material needs — the latter in defiance of the Christian dogma which branded this as mere worldliness and indulgence. The assumption that human needs are satiable endowed these fantasies with a tranquil, static and determinate quality. The opposing assumption, that man is an infinite consumer and appropriator, greedy and insatiable, supported the liberal ideas of perpetual progress and the image of an indefinitely expanding — and far from tranquil — capitalism.[25] A contrastingly ascetic vision was developed by other utopians — More and the eighteenth-century 'communists' Mably and Morelly, whose societies sanctioned moderate consumption but placed a far higher value on good citizenship and social contribution. The nineteenth-century utopians moved towards a more balanced view of consumption, but the social imperatives which are constituted by needs are, for them, overshadowed by the more exalted and constructive role of the capacities.

Misery in an imperfect society is usually the result of unsatisfied needs and frustrated wants, and although the mere satisfaction of needs may not be sufficient to constitute happiness, it is at least a necessary condition. However, the notion of need is problematic and some of the difficulties will now be mentioned. The best procedure will be to set out the major controversies in the area, and a suggested model, then to measure the utopians' theories against these, since they do not deal explicitly with need.

A behavioural definition of need has been offered by Bay: a need is 'any *behaviour tendency* whose continual denial or frustration leads to pathological responses'.[26] Such a definition leads us to the bare bones of human need, but is basic in the extreme, and inadequate for model-building. As always, the behavioural approach excludes mental elements, which are central to the formation of the desires which civilised society construes as being as important as biological needs. A wider definition comprehending conscious needs might be as follows: 'those actively felt wants or impulses, and rationally chosen aims, which are universal or common to a substantial group of people, and which generally give rise to dissatisfaction/unhappiness if unfulfilled, or pleasure if fulfilled'. This conveniently eliminates capricious desires, which we would not wish to become the objects of public policy, and the emphasis on universality excludes idiosyncratic desires which no general plan could cater for, while 'serious' wants are subsumed under needs. We may not always need what we want, or want what we need, but we are unlikely to consider a society utopian unless we get what we *really* want.

In the utopian context it is crucial to emphasize the subjectively-felt aspect of need, the connection with desire, since the satisfaction of conscious need is a primary condition for happiness. But utopia can even go beyond providing adequate satisfaction of needs which are felt and expressed. Although the concept of an unconscious need is surrounded by difficulties it can be hypothesised that the satisfaction of unformulated needs, unperceived desires and unarticulated interests *can* be a source of pleasure — and this supererogatory delight may indeed be the hallmark of the utopian effort to augment happiness. Furthermore, utopia may itself generate new needs through the provision of various facilities, just as capitalism is generally agreed to have established the needs which dictate a high level of consumption and its own expansion. Such implanted need will be 'aspirational' since the utopian will seek to stimulate needs which he considers beneficial to individuals and to society.

The question of which needs are basic has always been problematic: many distinctions have been made concerning types of need, of which the chief ones are those between arti-

ficial and real (or natural) needs, and between false and true
needs. Despite these usages, it is well-nigh impossible to
apply these distinctions empirically and to distinguish legitimate from illegitimate needs in real life. Rousseau, who
called socially-generated needs artificial, conceded that they
could be as necessary as the natural kind. 'It is by no means a
light undertaking to distinguish properly between what is
original and what is artificial in the nature of man.'[27]
Marcuse, critic of those needs generated by capitalist society,
defines minimum unconditional needs, but fails to show any
qualitative difference between true and false needs in the way
that they are felt, or to prove that false needs can be ignored
without causing *real* misery.[28] (By contrast, B. F. Skinner
argues that nearly all 'basic' human needs could be conditioned away.) Similarly, the needs caused by relative deprivation cannot be disregarded merely because they are based on
false expectations or mistaken reference groups: utopia has
to eliminate the social structure which distorts expectations,
but has at first to pander to established expectations to avoid
creating unhappiness. Evidently, the process of sifting true
from false needs is highly evaluative.

But even if we could infallibly establish which needs are
false and which real, would it be desirable to consider the
false needs inferior? It can be argued that *all* satisfied needs
add to the total of happiness, and all should therefore be
satisfied without distinction; the more needs there are, the
greater the potential for human happiness. Such an
argument could especially be applied to the development of
cultural needs. The utopian would be wise to follow a quasi-
utilitarian policy, maximising needs and pleasures, except in
the case of needs propagated by unjustified social envy or
'inhumane' needs whose satisfaction harmed other individuals.[29]

It follows that the utopian must formulate a policy
towards need on the following lines:—

1. Satisfaction of absolute needs, fixing the minimum as
    high as society can afford.[30]
2. Elimination of relative deprivation — through egali-

tarian satisfactions or pluralistic devices making comparison impossible.

3. Selection of which above-minimum needs are to be catered for.
4. Establishment of aspirational needs, e.g. cultural needs, etc.
5. Setting of a maximum, to prevent an unseemly cult of affluence or ostentation.

These policies are exemplified in the work of the utopians: Fourier and Owen guarantee a social minimum (1); Fourier and Saint-Simon create social stratifications which make reference across groups impossible (2), while Owen and Godwin establish egalitarian standards of consumption; all the utopians dwell on the necessities of (3) and (4) — this is their chief task; Godwin also explicitly sets a maximum with his sumptuary laws, and Owen stresses moderation (5) though for Fourier no genuine passion can lead to excess. Although this again raises the spectre of manipulators and manipulated, the manipulation of needs in this way is acceptable and desirable if both means and end are approved. Some manipulation seems harmless enough, viz. Fourier's proposal to *train* men to eat five meals a day and four snacks!

No analysis of need as such appears in the works of these utopians; it is as if they presumed agreement on what constitutes need, and the desirability of satisfying it. Their views are, however, implicit in their accounts of what constitutes satisfaction. Every member of Owen's Home Colonies will be 'fully supplied with the necessaries and comforts of life', but despite his premiss of malleability, he regards needs in utopia as permanent, capable of being satisfied by a once-for-all prescription: most utopian blueprints err in this way. Godwin assumes that his anarchistic villages will provide adequate material satisfactions, and he is more concerned with mental fulfilment. Saint-Simon and Fourier pay great attention to material needs, for each is confident that he has found a method of production capable of multiplying consumer goods and generating abundance. Indeed, Saint-

Simon and his followers regarded commodities almost as a panacea. Nevertheless, the utopians' conceptions of need are less sophisticated than their analysis of capacities.

Fourier, however, develops an advanced analysis of need through his theory of the passions. Each passion, in effect, generates a need. For example, the satisfaction of the butterfly passion is necessary for creative activity. A monotonous task is at worst harmful to the individual's personality, and alienating, and, at least, counter-productive. 'Familism' is best regarded as a kind of tribal kinship feeling, for he insists that it is not linked to blood relations but to wider groups and adoptive relations. This passion also can be interpreted as an expression of need, the need to establish certain roots, fixed relationships, human links with past and future.[31] The satisfaction of the passionate needs which Fourier defines is synonymous with the organisation of society itself, without the intervention of an intermediate distribution process. By contrast, in many supposedly utopian societies some needs are suppressed in pursuit of a goal (the reality principle) and mediated satisfaction is distributed only after some delay.

Even if the situation depicted by Fourier is organisationally impossible, it suggests the necessity of uniting the processes of production and satisfaction so as to avoid alienation which may result from their separation and to satisfy a multiplicity of needs simultaneously. The conversion of work into play is an ideal solution to this problem of work and need, first proposed by Schiller and conceived of independently by Fourier.[32] Another solution is that of Saint-Simon who hopes, by solving the problem of production and creating abundance, to dissociate work from the satisfaction of need, with liberating results. His followers took the argument to its conclusion: from each according to his capacity, to each according to his needs.

Although needs represent an input or demand on the social system, they will also constitute the justification of the proposed utopia since the satisfaction of human wants underlies all possibilities of happiness and utopia aims above all to achieve the wellbeing of its members. Clearly, no society could concentrate on the development of capacities at the expense of satisfying needs, or vice versa, since these attributes are so intimately connected. Although the utopians devote little space to the discussion of needs, need satisfaction is of prime importance in their societies, and they imagine themselves to be scientifically deducing the conditions for satisfaction, so that resources may be used with maximum efficiency. In short, the utopians do not depict new lands of Cockayne: they are in control of the sorts and degrees of need satisfaction which will exist in Utopia, and they not only insist on moderation, but also deploy the means of satisfaction in ways which will reinforce social control and cohesion.

The arguments so far in this section will have antagonised those who hold that talk of 'real needs', evocation of 'unconscious desires' and the promotion of 'aspirational needs' are inherently totalitarian. So at this juncture it must be re-emphasized that the utopian's task is to improve or perfect society, not to tidy it like a housewifely reformer. Only by hypothesising different forms, conditions and areas of satisfaction can the utopian hope to achieve any prescription for improvement other than 'more of the same'. In the experimental concoction of utopian theory it is permissible to speculate that the representative, historically-located individual — fallible, socialised, prejudiced as he is — is not the final arbiter of what constitutes human needs. It is not this speculation, but the attempt to impose his ideas on an unwilling populus that makes the utopian into a totalitarian. The speculation may be innocent and even scientific in intention. However, those who find talk of real needs presumptuous will never forgive the hubris of utopians.

A calm acceptance of the inevitability of self-interested action characterised the thought of the Enlightenment and *laissez-faire* liberalism, and lifted the moral stigma previously attached to self-interest.[33] Likewise, the utopians accepted self-interest as the mainspring of human action, and even welcomed the infusion of this ubiquitous energy into human affairs, despite its associated disadvantages. 'There was . . . to Saint-Simon nothing deplorable in the fact that progress was dependent upon such passions [as self-

interest and self-love].'[34] Indeed, competition and individualism had originally provided the dynamism for
industrial and scientific progress. When the utopians
deprecate untamed self-interest as a social evil, they cost it in
terms of detriment to society, rather than as a moral vice,
and use morally neutral terms such as 'egoism' and
'individualism'. But given this liberal approach to a human
characteristic once decried as the source of all evil, the
utopians still had to devise a formula for the taming of self-
interest, to circumvent the social disruptiveness, divisiveness
and intractability of the self-interested impulse.

Self-interest is more than survival-oriented selfishness; it is
a psychological-cum-moral concept denoting a cluster of
constant, self-directed attitudes. It connotes the performative principle deriving from self-love, and implies not
merely the pursuit of one's own interests for the satisfaction
of personal needs, but their pursuit in a way detrimental to
others, whereas self-love entails merely a preference for self,
without necessarily bad consequences for others.

The standard solution of the problem of self-interest is the
substitution of an altruistic morality, which must supplant
self-interest as a motive. Godwin seeks to prove that altruism
pays off even for the egoist. 'No man reaps so copious a
harvest of pleasure as he who thinks only of pleasures of
other men.'[35] He argues that benevolence is as valid a motive
as self-love, and quite separate. Although 'the good of our
neighbour . . . is originally pursued for the sake of its advantage to ourselves', this eventually becomes a secondary good
because 'we are able in imagination to go out of ourselves'
and because we naturally convert the means to good into an
end-in-itself. Men's lives are interdependent, so each man
has a duty and inclination to increase the happiness of
others. Owen also teaches that 'the universal, selfish, or
individual feeling, of our animal existence, may be so
directed as to derive its chief gratification from contributing
to the pleasure and happiness of others', and that 'happiness
of self . . . can only be attained by conduct that must
promote the happiness of the community'.[36] He and Godwin
believe that we will eventually, and ideally, desire the happi-

ness of others for *their* sakes — an advance on the weaker characterisation of altruism as selfishness with the sting drawn.

Saint-Simon describes morality as a knowledge of the rules combining private and general interests, and Fourier's thirteenth passion, unityism, dictates that each individual, while following only his own interest, must unconsciously serve the interests of the mass. Thus the utopians espouse versions of altruism with much of the moral content removed, based strictly on social necessity: this is to be propagated by educating men as to their real, interconnected interests, not by exhorting them to virtuous action for its own sake. More interesting is Owen's materialist account of selfishness, which he believes to be the result of the struggle for scarce commodities and survival. In his villages of co-operation 'all the natural wants of human nature may be abundantly supplied, and the principle of selfishness . . . will cease to exist, for want of an adequate motive to produce it'.[37] Saint-Simon and Fourier, describing their cornucopian utopias, predict similar effects.

Most realistic and innovatory, and most in keeping with the demoralised morality of utopia, is the argument of Owen and Saint-Simon that the *form* in which self-interest manifests itself is to be changed by the propagation of a new ethic which will put an end to the exaltation of self-interest. 'Individualism . . . must now give way to the principle of *union*, or of benevolence, or, as really it is, enlightened selfishness.' Philanthropy must accompany this, but the co-operative ethic will achieve the transformation throughout society.[38] The origins of socialist morality appear here in the liberal concept of enlightened self-interest. Fourier too supports the co-operative ethic, but not in order to divert the forces of self-interest — a term which, being no part of his non-moralistic psychology, is meaningless for him. Men who act at the behest of their passions are not acting out of self-interest, and after the destruction of civilisation, where passions conflict, the social mechanism will harmonise the acts of each with all, *spontaneously*.

The utopians attempt to tame or enlighten self-interest

practically by destroying the conditions in which it thrives; they also try to eliminate the repercussions of self-interest at the conceptual level by elaborating their own versions of the famous 'identity of interests' doctrine. This fallible argument turns on an authoritative redefinition of 'interest' which makes my interest that of my neighbour and *vice versa*. However, a more unified and co-ordinated society such as utopia might make this true.

The utopians consider man as essentially a social animal, and a premiss of natural sociability underlies all their other postulates. They describe his other attributes in such a way as to minimise those potentially threatening to social life, and to extol the eminently sociable characteristics of rationality, morality and perfectibility. Although interested by the mental and moral capacities, they treat these according to their social functions, rather than with regard to the individual development which such qualities can stimulate. If individuals focused their energies on their own development and inner life, these would be egoistically and introspectively channeled away from the social activity necessary to utopia, and might unbalance the social mechanism. This would also produce a greater diversity of tastes and talents than utopia could contain. The utopians — except Fourier — were understandably anxious to standardise forms of social behaviour as a basis for organisation.

Yet it seems strange that the utopians should have so concentrated on the objective and public aspects of individual activity, while their contemporaries, such as Hegel, were analysing the subjective development and unfolding of the individual in relation to society. But in fact the idea of self-fulfilment appears in the accounts of perfectibility, and takes these utopias beyond the level of material satisfaction. In the early socialists' works there are also elements of a theory of self-creation through work and man's relation to nature, foreshadowing that of Marx, echoing that of Hegel.

The common, unifying basis of these utopians' accounts of human nature, and their optimism, is the environmentalist determinist approach, which allows them to depart from earlier views of human nature as a fixed, and indelibly blemished, entity. But throughout this chapter it has been contended that the more flexible, environmentally determined or perfectible human nature is considered to be, the less possible it is to *derive* social standards directly from the concept, as the utopians claim to do. Anything can be inscribed on the blank sheet. The utopians do not (as they hoped) evade the responsibility of fixing standards by escaping into a realm of 'absolute' human qualities such as rationality, and appealing to their favourite — but partial — arbiter, absolute truth. In their search for standards they believed that they were being scientific when in fact they were building ideologies. The selection of human characteristics and definitions of human purpose are evaluative, and the creation of a utopian structure on such a basis is an ideological enterprise, and not merely a deductive or social-scientific process.

References
1. P. Gay, *The Enlightenment*, Vol. 1 (Weidenfeld & Nicholson, 1967), p. 408. M. Hollis, *Models of Man* (Cambridge U.P., 1977), passim.
2. PJ I, p. xxvi.
3. NVS pp. 152-3.
4. Many more refinements can be introduced into the concept of purposive rationality. See, e.g., S. Lukes, 'Some Problems about Rationality' in B. Wilson (ed.) *Rationality* (Blackwell, 1970), p. 208, who lists four more precise definitions of rationality applied to action, which include a Parsonian definition of efficient action, and the idea of promotion of the agent's long-term ends.
5. F. Manuel is informative on the scientific background to Saint-Simon's theory. See *The New World of Henri Saint-Simon*, (Harvard U.P., 1956), chs. 10 & 21. Also Ch. 8 below.
6. See Godwin, PJ I, p. 86-92 (my italics); Owen, NVS, p. 155; BNMW, p. 15.
7. OC X, p. 138. Also p. 136.
8. See Godwin, PJ I, p. 53n. The relationship is also sketched in the 1st edn. I, p. 319.
9. Argued by F. Cioffi in 'Information, Contemplation and Social Life' in *The Proper Study* (Macmillan, 1970), Royal Institute of Philosophy Lectures, 1969-70.
10. C.f. Godwin's definition in PJ I, p. 158-9, which seems adequate. It is reasonable to suppose that some degree of altruism is part of the meaning of morality.

11. J-J. Rousseau, *Discourse on the Origins of Equality,* (Everyman, 1913), especially p. 180.

12. Despite the transformation of ideas, Rousseau influenced Godwin, who notes that Rousseau was the first to teach that governments are the source of human vice (PJ II, p. 129n) and also erroneously calls Rousseau 'an advocate of the savage state'. See also A. O. Lovejoy, 'The supposed primitivism of Rousseau's Discourse on Inequality' in *Essays in the History of Ideas* (John Hopkins, 1948).

13. PJ I, pp. 61, 314. This would be reassuring if we believed that all men were upright.

14. É. Durkheim, *Socialism and Saint-Simon* (Antioch Press, 1958), p. 197-202.

15. See the critical summary in D. Wright, *The Psychology of Moral Behaviour*, (Penguin, 1971). Wright notes that 'though conventions and customs vary widely from one society to another, basic moral principles apparently do not'. (p. 13) Anthropologists also argue that the moral sense is universal and that moral attitudes are directed at similar objects and situations among all races. Such moral attitudes would be manifestations of certain universal behaviour principles relating to needs, values, ego processes and defence mechanisms. See M. E. Spiro, 'Human nature in its psychological dimensions', *American Anthropologist*, Vol. 56 (1954), pp. 19-30. He argues that the similarities are rooted in the personality at a very basic level.

16. See Appendix, Note I.

17. These arguments appear in *Contingencies of Reinforcement* (Appleton-Century, 1969), Ch. 2.

18. See L. T. Sargent, 'Human Nature and the Radical Vision' in J. Pennock and J. Chapman (eds.) *Human Nature in Politics* (New York U.P., 1977).

19. Godwin, PJ I, p. 93.

20. PJ (1st edn.) I, p. 169-70. My italics.

21. This was Herbert Spencer's argument in defence of limiting altruism. See *The Data of Ethics* (London, 1879), pp. 251-2. 'With the progress of adaptation each becomes so constituted that he cannot be helped without in some way arresting a pleasurable activity'. Lorenz also argues for the interdependence of 'good' and 'bad' human instincts.

22. NVS, p. 134.

23. PJ I, p. 240.

24. E. Bloch, in *Freiheit und Ordnung* (Frankfurt, 1969), claims a prophetic status for Fourier on account of these fantasies: the anti-whale is the steamboat, the anti-lion a locomotive or car, and the 'aetherial fluid', which men will imbibe through a new organ of sense, represents radio waves (pp. 8-9). Fourier's inventions were less ecologically troublesome than the modern equivalents.

25. C. B. Macpherson describes the development of such notions in *The Political Theory of Possesive Individualism* (Oxford U.P., 1962) and *Democratic Theory* (Oxford U.P., 1973).

26. C. Bay, 'Needs, wants and political legitimacy', *Canadian Journal of Political Science*, Vol. I (1968), p. 242. See also the criticism of this approach by W. E. Connolly, 'On "Interests" in politics', in *Politics and Society*, Vol. 2 (1972), p. 471 especially. His condemnation of the narrowness of this definition corresponds to my arguments.

27. *Discourse*, pp. 154-5.

28. See especially *Essay on Liberation* (Penguin, 1969) for Marcuse's attack on the needs developed in bourgeois society.

29. For example, Sade's argument that all imperative sexual wants should be instantly gratified would be rebutted by this condition. See F. Manuel & F. Manuel (eds.), *French Utopias* (Free Press, 1966), p. 226 ff.

30. 'The level of so-called absolute need can just as well be fixed at one level as another'. W. G. Runciman, *Relative Deprivation and Social Justice* (Penguin, 1972), p. 105.

31. The familist instinct seems to require that the individual should be surrounded by people fulfilling various roles, i.e. acting towards him as mother, brother, etc., rather than individuals tied to him by consanguinity; therefore, a role-generating 'family' group of any convenient size, even if it were artificially constituted, could perform this function for each individual, as the comparative success of fostering systems shows.

32. See F. Schiller, *Letters on the Aesthetic Education of Man*, trans. E. Wilkinson and L. Willoughby (Clarendon Press, 1967), especially Letter 15 on the centrality of play to human nature and enjoyment.

33. L. G. Crocker, *The Age of Crisis* (John Hopkins, 1959) usefully summarises this process. See chs. 9-10.

34. Manuel, *New World*, p. 166.

35. PJ I, p. 448. See also PJ I, p. 425-7.

36. *Six Lectures*, p. 72, and NVS, p. 103. Also pp. 106, 145, 155, etc. The idea that the sight of others' unhappiness mars one's own pleasure is clearly derived from the doctrine of natural compassion, probably Rousseau's version. See also PJ I, p. 443-4.

37. RCL, p. 257.

38. HC, p. 30. See also *Système*, p. 21.

CHAPTER 4

CONTROL IN UTOPIA

THE survival of a social system in its particular form depends on the successful resolution or suppression of the conflicts of interest which generally arise where there is a plurality of desires that limited resources cannot satisfy. The resulting conflicts are manifested in various forms: conflicts between individuals' particular interests, between individual and institutional interests, between class interests. The proposed solution is consequent upon the manner in which the problem is conceptualised, and the liberal analysis differs from that of the marxist, or the anarchist. Various solutions seem, commonsensically, to inhere in the structure of the problem: the antagonistic pursuit of interests (by one social grouping) may be defined as deviant (by a more powerful grouping) and suppressed. Alternatively, those in power may modify or redirect those interests likely to cause social conflict, or eliminate them entirely. For example, the liberal solution, the received doctrine against which the utopians reacted, proclaimed the solution to be a *legal* delineation of the areas in which individuals were free to pursue their interests, over which a minimal state was to preside as arbiter.

Formulations and resolutions of the problem of social conflict can be restated in terms of social control, which refers not to the safety-net which catches deviants but to the processes which order society by reconciling interests and actions. The establishment of such procedures is central to the model-building in which the utopians were engaged. The structuring of their organisations and choice of control devices follow the scientific pattern of their argument in that they derive from the elements of human nature which the utopians considered socially functional. Control is conventionally considered the task of government, but since they minimise or abolish government agencies, their instruments of control must be sought elsewhere.

Since the need for social control is predicated on the assumption of a conflict of interests, a few words must be said about 'interests'. It is assumed here that an individual's interests are the total of felt needs and desires which he will make some active attempt to satisfy — for it is in the area of *action* that conflicts of interest requiring control arise. This behavioural definition rules out some of the refinements of understanding of the concept which, for example, Barry elaborates,[1] but is adequate to indicate the kinds of activities that a utopian society must at least reconcile and at best foster in order to promote the happiness of its members. (I also assume — as do the utopians — that social deviance is an expression of conflicts of interest and disharmony, not merely a statistically predictable event of interest mainly to criminologists.) The kinds of 'interest' of which the individual is himself unaware, and does not actively pursue, are from this standpoint irrelevant to control and are relegated to the field of constructive social policy and planning.

It must be remembered that the term 'conflict of interests' can refer to disputes between individuals or individuals' disagreements with public policy. Often the utopians do not distinguish between these different sources of social disruption; in general, their controls aim to reconcile individuals since the state will no longer be a meaningful entity. A conflict of interests may result from directly antagonistic interests or from the pursuit of mutually indifferent interests with conflicting consequences: the utopians circumvent both problems by their assumption that interests are *naturally cooperative* — but, following their usual policy of overdetermination, they also introduce methods of control to ensure that this assumption comes true.

The first section of this chapter briefly reviews and evaluates the spectrum of methods of control at a theoretical level. The second examines the utopians' critiques of the conventional instruments of control, critiques which prepare the ground for their own revolutionary proposals. Finally, the controls which the utopians proposed to employ are examined, in their terms; a conceptualisation of their function in the terms of this analysis follows in Chapter 5.

A SCHEMA OF CONTROL

The modes of attempted control over deviance reflect a society's predominant theories and assumptions about the causes of deviance and are rooted in basic ideas about human nature.[2]

It is now a familiar argument that non-legal methods and modes of socialisation contribute to the maintenance of order: control does not begin and end with the processes of law and punishment. Control, although at its most manifest when prohibitive, has a more convert and positive effect in promoting and envouraging constructive social behaviour. All methods of control partake of this dual nature, although some are naturally more prohibitive than positive, and *vice versa*. As the quotation above suggests, all efficient methods of social control are dependent on the successful harnessing of man's faculties: physical control makes use of his vulnerability to pain, while other controls manipulate the intellect, and psychological control aims to dominate man through his psyche. Inbred attitudes such as fear, guilt, gratitude are invoked as devices of control. The controlling agent selects methods which reflect his view of men's natural aptitudes and weaknesses.

Eight paradigm forms of control can be distinguished:—

1. *Coercion*. An extravagant use of force, directly related to the controller's immediate purpose. Law and coercion are often mutually exclusive. Coercion is uneconomical and exceptional, best characterised by its certainty of result, inefficiency of resources, and overtness.

2. *Terror*. The use of exemplarily (perhaps randomly) applied violence. The terrorising action may not be obviously connected with the desired behaviour, but is intended to exert psychological pressure on those who are *not* yet victims to be obedient. Terror is

economical, *ex ante*, overt, and exploits the mechanisms of fear.

3. *Legal Punishment*. A circumscribed use of coercion to prevent future actions of a criminal kind. Force is applied according to principles openly stated in law: only deviants are punished. *Ex ante* threats of punishment prevent deviance, so there is economy of force and resources. Both intelligence and physical vulnerability are utilised.

4. *Education, or Rational Instruction*. Factual information and reason together secure socially desirable conduct. This relies on the intellect. There is an ideological element. The resulting mechanism is self-control, operating at the level of awareness, through the intelligence.

5. *Morality*. This also utilises men's intelligence, but operates chiefly through men's conditionability and enforcement by conscience, which is part of a psychological mechanism. The precepts of morality tend to be ideological, not factual. However, it is distinguished here from indoctrination (7) because it makes an appeal to systematic reasoning. Morality is paradigmly self-control, but activated by a (covert) external controller.

6. *Inducements*. Although not usually categorised as a mode of control — perhaps because non-aversive, and even pleasurable — the offering of rewards, honours and other inducements must be included here. Inducements appeal to rational self-interest: a decision must be taken whether to accept and obey. Inducements are indicative of external control, but choice lies with the individual.

7. *Indoctrination*. The teaching of prescriptions and imperatives. This method relies on intellect, but denies its function, i.e. the exercise of critical reason. Indoctrination demands *belief* and may take place through unperceived socialisation processes. Indoctrination tends to produce self-control without understanding.

8. *Psychological Conditioning*. The implantation of sub-

conscious behaviour patterns designed to eliminate crime and encourage socially useful acts. This circumvents rationality, e.g. Pavlovian and Skinnerian conditioning. The result is externally-controlled self-inhibition, and the individual has no comprehension of the purposes of the control.

9. *Total Conditioning.* This comprehends extensive psychological and physical manipulation, the latter operating through methods such as genetic engineering, personality-changing drugs, electric shock therapy, prefrontal lobotomy and all the other methods beloved of writers of twentieth-century dystopias.

Although these methods can be distinguished in principle, in practice they merge and overlap considerably, as control is usually achieved through a mixture of physical, intellectual and psychological devices. Ridicule brings into play all these elements. Social control invariably depends on a combination of methods. Punishment is supplemented by moral socialisation, so that the rate of deviance is manageable, and the blanket term 'socialisation' itself embraces several kinds of control — education, indoctrination, morality and conditioning.

The suspiciously clear-cut distinctions made here make it possible to examine systematically the utopians' approaches to control. The ideal types of control are presented diagrammatically in Diagram 2, grouped according to their salient characteristics on a continuum. Methods (1) — (3) are aversive and aim to harmonise *actions* with social policies, and guarantee obedience. Their physically coercive basis indicates that their goal is not conformity of opinion but of *behaviour*, although terror may produce mental submission as well. All are overt. By contrast, education, inducements, morality and (to a small degree) indoctrination seek to achieve voluntary agreement with social policies, and to harmonise *interests* and *opinions*: orderly behaviour should follow as a matter of course. Methods which involve conditioning circumvent the thought processes and produce an uncomprehending harmony of *actions* and *beliefs*. These

Diagram 2: *A continuum of control*

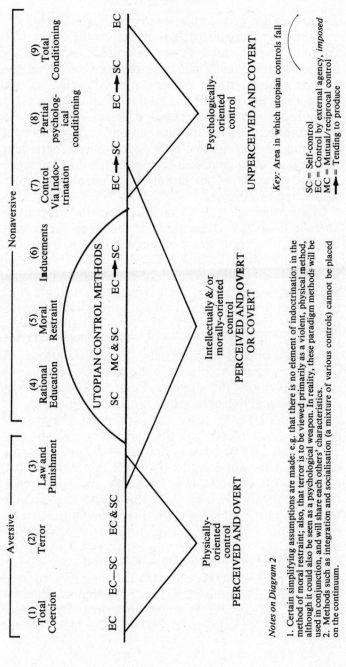

Notes on Diagram 2

1. Certain simplifying assumptions are made: e.g. that there is no element of indoctrination in the method of moral restraint; also, that terror is to be viewed primarily as a violent, physical method, although it could also be seen as a psychological weapon. In reality, these paradigm methods will be used in conjunction, and will share each others' characteristics.

2. Methods such as integration and socialisation (a mixture of various controls) cannot be placed on the continuum.

methods employ covert and nonaversive techniques.

The controls are also differentiated by the degree to which they are implemented by an external controlling agency: those methods which maximise the element of self-control are most condign to a utopian organisation of society, promoting, as they do, the pleasures of self-mastery, and minimising aversive interference from without. In many ways, inducements are the ideal non-aversive instruments for obtaining conformity to utopia's conventions, particularly as their use actually generates happiness for the recipients. The idea of pleasure as an incentive to sociable behaviour is elaborated by Fourier.

One further control device important for utopians is not assimilable to any of the methods shown on the continuum: conflicts of interest can be eliminated by the construction of a fully-integrated, organic society, in which individuals are allotted fixed roles. The totally integrated, role-playing individual would accept the norms implicit in his role, and have no opportunity to harbour anti-social desires. The essence of control would be the social structure itself. The organic, divinely ordered society of early medieval Christendom constituted such a system, as did traditional Hindu society, organised according to the principles of dharma and caste; and among the utopians, Fourier's society exemplifies *par excellence* control by integration.

How shall we evaluate the ideality of these modes of control? Each offers benefits and, to complicate matters, evaluations may be made according to different criteria. For example, Diagram 3 depicts possible relationships between methods of control and variables such as happiness, freedom, egalitarianism, efficiency and the respect for human dignity. Such a graphical representation circumvents the laborious explanations of such relationships usually necessary.

Any utopian must make the kind of evaluations represented in the diagram when deciding how to order his society. The relationship between happiness, control and freedom, for example, is crucial to utopia. The subjectively felt happiness of individuals rests on many factors, especially

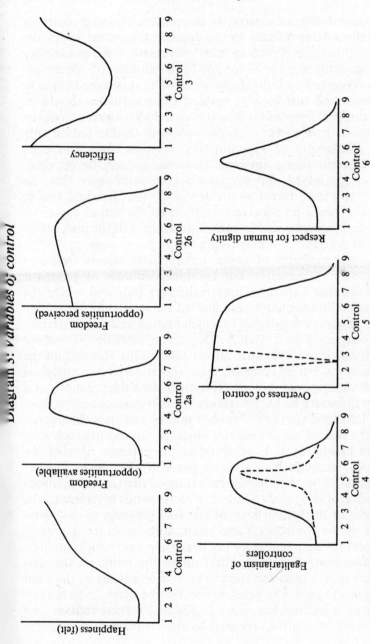

Diagram 5: variables of control

1. The horizontal axis is the continuum of control from Diagram 2, marked by numbers.
2. The rating of the methods of control against variables is ordinal.
3. The dotted lines indicate some alternative interpretations of the relationships; e.g., terror could be an overt or covert weapon (Fig. 5), and the methods in the centre of the continuum could be operated by egalitarians or an elite (see Fig. 4).
4. Definitions of the variables: *Egalitarianism* is measured by the ratio of those in control to those in subjection, or controlled. The larger the ratio, it is assumed, the more egalitarian the method. The graph which measured *elitism* would be the inverse of Fig. 4. *Efficiency* is the effectiveness of the control in producing that behaviour desired by the controllers. *Human Dignity* is considered to rest on a view of man as autonomous, rational and intelligent. Therefore, methods which respect human dignity are those which acknoledge man's unique intellectual and psychological qualities and do not abuse them for the purpose of control.

the satisfaction of desires. In the context of social control it usually relates directly to the degree of freedom which the control permits. Freedom itself may relate to the availability of opportunities for action, or to the number of opportunities perceived by individuals, even when they are not free to follow them all. Ideally, both of these variables should be maximised. Freedom is also connected with awareness of the controls themselves, since overt controls tend to reduce only the availability of opportunities, whereas covert controls, while maintaining apparent freedom, reduce the opportunities (perceived and available) more insidiously (2a). So there is a third factor — the degree of 'felt' freedom which, since it bears no necessary relation to the actual degree of freedom, may be said to constitute a world of illusion, about whose delights most liberals are highly puritanical.

In the majority of cases, unhappiness results from the existence of perceived but forbidden courses of action: it follows that happiness may readily be procured where the perceived opportunities are limited but available. Happiness also relates to the degree to which human nature and dignity are respected in a society. Degrading methods of control such as torture will cause misery both to the victims and the spectators; but by contrast, men who undergo psychological conditioning may not perceive their own degradation, and may therefore be happy. Hence the correspondence between the left-hand parts of Figures 1 and 6, and their divergence on the right. Only the outside observer can censure such anodyne happiness as is achieved at the extreme right of the graph, although it is a vexed question whether he has the right to do so. The happiness rating of the various methods of control (1-9) shown in Fig. 1 corresponds inversely to the degree of the second kind of freedom (2b) and to the overtness of the controls (5) and relates directly to the degree of respect for human dignity (by which are meant such qualities as autonomy and rationality) up to the point on the axis which marks indoctrination. This indeterminacy of the final evaluation makes it necessary to invoke other criteria than that of subjective happiness to produce a final verdict. The methods of control favoured by the utopians cluster in the middle of the continuum (5-7) as Diagram 2 shows, and it can be argued that this is because of the nature of utopia. This argument will be examined, with the aid of some dystopian counter-examples.

The widely-held belief in the sanctity of life and human dignity are sufficient grounds for the general abhorrence of controls such as coercion. Such methods produce an excess of pain, fear and unhappiness, and could never feature in utopia. But the regulated use of coercion in the form of punishment has fewer disadvantages: indeed, law and punishment in many respects constitute the ideal system of control since they maximise choice and the possibility of rational planning by individuals. However, the utopians attack their theoretical foundations and hope to avoid social deviance by the use of prophylactic methods. In any case, their knowledge of the uniquely right way to live renders the latitude and choice which the law permits unnecessary.

The methods at the right of the continuum, indoctrination and conditioning, were not analysed until the twentieth century; then, they were swiftly branded as manipulative and totalitarian. Indoctrination is here defined as the persuasive, anti-rational use of propositions, concepts and language,[3] an all-pervasive conditioning of the intellect. Language is fundamental to the operation of the intelligence which is in turn vital to the direction of the individual's social activities. In the nightmare of *Nineteen Eighty-Four*, foolproof indoctrination perpetuates total devotion to the Party by a multitude of intrusive methods. Since the Party stands for an unjustifiable, self-interested élite and a mass of absurd and contradictory doctrines, the reason of the Party member has to be beguiled into acceptance of these incongruities. 'An elaborate training, undergone in childhood and grouping itself round the Newspeak words *crimestop*, *blackwhite* and *doublethink*, makes him unwilling and unable to think too deeply on any subject whatever.'[4] The compression of Newspeak terms also conceals contradictions and false assumptions, undermining language-based logic. In Zamyatin's *We*, the pattern for *Nineteen Eighty-Four*, the manipulation of language and thought changes 'I' into 'We', promoting selflessness and collective solidarity. Indoctrination's primary function is to disguise what the autonomous individual might consider to be his interests, in order to direct his behaviour to other ends, or substitute different interests, such as those of the community or of the ruling class. A purpose-built ideology is essential to indoctrination: reluctance — and inability — to think outside a given ideological pattern signifies its success.

But it may be maintained that psychological conditioning is more insidious and irreparably harmful than indoctrination. B. F. Skinner's utopia, *Walden Two*, (dystopia to his critics) exemplifies the use of psychological conditioning at the subrational level. In the Walden community, the contingencies of reinforcement are so manipulated that obedient social behaviour results. The 'ethical training' of the children by Skinnerian conditioning is completed by the age of six, and adults are entirely self-controlled, totally socialised. The most famous exemplar of total conditioning is Aldous Huxley's *Brave New World* in which genetic engineering and pre-natal regulation determine the characteristics of bottled babies, and the 'Bokanovsky technique' ensures absolute uniformity within social classes by producing countless identical 'twins'. The babies are conditioned by neo-Pavlovian techniques while older children learn the appropriate credo and 'interests' of their class through sleep-teaching.[5] The liberal use of the happiness drug, *soma*, completes this catalogue of insidious, yet non-aversive, control techniques.

A comparison of the end-product of total conditioning with that of total coercion would show superficial similarities, such as total obedience; both societies require a commanding or manipulating élite. In some ways, then, the continuum is circular. But with regard to the economy of resources and the elimination of inconsistencies, uncertainties and painful decisions, conditioning is more conducive to happiness, whereas, evaluated with regard to freedom or dignity, coercion is preferable since the subjects of coercion are aware of their subjection and can aspire to freedom. Conditioning leads to the acceptance of a situation which would not otherwise be tolerable, and the enforced abdication of man as a rational and moral agent. Liberal opinion holds that the enslavement of the mind is more debilitating than the enslavement of the body, although in practice the two may be interconnected or inseparable. Certainly, both indoctrination and conditioning tend to destroy those values which the nineteenth-century utopians most esteemed — morality, rationality and truth.

The cluster of values which utopia cannot eschew without changing its own definition are incompatible with the methods of control at the extreme right of the continuum. Indeed, few methods of control avoid being debilitating, degrading or aversive. Those which remain — education, morality and inducements — reinforce and enhance the humane values to which the utopian subscribes. They have an important role in the utopias scrutinised here, but even they sometimes partake of the characteristics of indoctrination and conditioning and so cannot guarantee man's status as an autonomous and rational being. However, it is in the nature of controls to be ideology-laden, in the sense that they are tailored to support one system rather than another, and this should not blind us to the fact that controls are more or less humane and dignifying, and that their relative merits can be assessed on this basis.

THE CASE AGAINST LAW

Whips, axes and gibbets, dungeons, chains and racks are the most approved and established methods of persuading men to obedience, and impressing upon their minds the lesson of reason.[6]

Although such abuses of intelligence and humanity alone could be cited in support of his opposition to punishment, Godwin appreciated the need to destroy its theoretical basis as a prelude to installing humane systems of control and he stigmatised punishment as an institution contrary to human nature, reason and truth. His arguments were influenced by Beccaria, and typified the humanitarian attitude to crime prevalent during the Enlightenment. Godwin was seized by an emotional repugnance for law, and the hideous abuses of justice and the victimisation of offenders were bitterly portrayed in his most successful and impassioned novel, *Caleb Williams* (1794).

Godwin's wide-ranging attack on punishment calls into question the institutions of government, private property and law itself. He disputes received opinions that law has a denunciatory effect and helps men to recognise and eschew crime, and that it has an action-guiding function; 'all real crimes . . . are capable of being discerned without the teaching of law'.[7] This implies that there are categories of absolute justice and 'real' crime which are spontaneously recognised — a view deriving from his notion of a natural morality. It seems contradictory to argue as Godwin does that law serves no informative purpose, because only the law informs people of what is against the law. He concedes that 'law was originally devised, that ordinary men might know what they had to expect',[8] but the fact that it is often amended, and the labyrinthine complexity of the legal machine make it instead a daily source of uncertainty and misinformation. Godwin condemns too the procrustean spirit of the law which forcibly assimilates particular crimes to general categories.

Godwin formulates a definition of retributive punishment as a butt for refutation: 'there is apprehended to to be a certain fitness and propriety in the nature of things that render suffering, abstractedly from the benefit to result, the suitable concomitant of vice'.[9] 'The abstract congruity of crime and punishment' has no basis in logic or nature, and rests on ideas of freewill and responsibility, which the determinist rejects. 'The assassin cannot help the murder he commits any more than the dagger': this constitutes Godwin's chief condemnation of the legal system, that actions are determined by circumstance and are *not* manifestations of 'moral character'. The law falsely assumes that crime is the criminal's free choice, symptomatic of a permanently malicious disposition, which must be bludgeoned into submission.[10]

But assassins, unlike daggers, are creatures of habit, Godwin concedes, and their actions must be condemned for the wellbeing of the community. But the expression of disapprobation does not entail the infliction of suffering, which can only be justified when it will 'produce an overbalance of good'. (Then it should be inflicted, argues Godwin the Utilitarian, parenthetically and perhaps unwisely, irrespective of guilt or innocence, but it cannot be termed 'punishment'.) The justifying aim of punishment must be deterrence. 'The only sense of the word punishment . . . compatible with the principles of the present work, is that of pain inflicted on a person convicted of past injurious action, for the purpose of preventing further mischief: to punish . . . upon any hypothesis, for what is past and irrevocable . . . must be ranked among the most pernicious exhibitions of an untutored barbarism.'[11] Inconsistently, Godwin later attacks deterrence as well, stigmatising it as 'punishment upon suspicion', inflicted upon individuals whose violence is finished. Reformative punishment is unlikely to succeed, he says, for coercion, unjust in itself, cannot propagate just behaviour, but will produce alienation from the ideas which it is intended to inculcate, or slavish, unthinking conversion under duress. Exemplary punishment he rejects because 'when I am made to suffer as an example to others, I am myself treated with supercilious neglect',[12] a point evidently incompatible with his previous utilitarian contentions. But he also argues that 'to do a thing for the sake of example, is . . . to do a thing to-day, in order to prove that I will do a similar thing tomorrow'.[13]

Here is the most telling stricture against punishment: it has no improving effects and can never lead to a society in which punishment can itself be outlawed, because it does not penetrate to the springs of criminality (i.e. irrationality), and misconstrues the causally determined nature of human action. At most, it can make life safer and more tolerable, but it is impossible to find a humane method of punishment because Godwin identifies punishment with the unmitigated evil of physical coercion. Punitive coercion is the brutish, imperfect substitute of a lower civilisation for the forces of truth and reason: 'if he who employs coercion against me could mould me to his purposes by argument, no doubt he would. He pretends to punish me because his argument is strong; but he really punishes me because his argument is weak'.[14] The expedient of punishment is tantamount to an admission of failure. Embedded in these seemingly philosophical points there is a potential revolutionary critique of law as ideology: what arguments *could* the landowner ever produce to convince the poacher? Indeed, Godwin argues that 'the community is always competent to change its institutions, and thus to extirpate offence in a way infinitely more rational and just than that of punishment'.[15] Herein lies Godwin's hope for utopia: the flexible component, society, must adapt to accommodate man.

There is confusion and conflict in Godwin's diatribe against punishment, between his humanitarianism, which decrees an end to suffering, and his utilitarianism, which sanctions necessary suffering; also between his pragmatism, which acknowledges the social need to eradicate anti-social actions (and hence to identify and brand criminals), his determinism, which demands no victimisation of so-called criminals, and his concern for individual morality, which allows that individuals *have* a continuing moral character, and that they in fact differ with respect to worth and desert. These contradictions would perhaps be suppressed but not resolved in his system of moral control, where correction would never involve suffering or blame.

The philosophical scrutiny to which Godwin subjects punishment is not equalled by Owen, although he too bases his attack on the determinist argument. He shows punishment to be absurd and paradoxical. Firstly, the law supposes that men can feel and act as directed by law, instead of as they are naturally inclined; so law is based on the assumption that men can be what they are not, and punishment is patently absurd.[16] Fourier's assertion that Civilisation 'represses and mutilates' the passions supports Owen's point.[17] But this weak conclusion rests on two doubtful propositions; that laws invariably frustrate human desires, and that they have no formative effect on those desires, both of which could be refuted. This argument is also a complaint about the contemporary content of law, and not tantamount to an indictment of the institution itself.

The paradox lies in the fact that men's characters are formed by social circumstance; so society punishes men for crimes for which it is responsible. Society plays cat-and-mouse with the wretched criminal. The working classes are '*trained* to *commit* crimes, for the commission of which they are afterwards punished'.[18] (The meaning of 'society' changes during this overstated argument, for society *qua* policeman may have no connection with society *qua* educator.) Owen's environmentalism leads him to conclude that adults have permanent, irremediably determined characters, and therefore punishment is always unjust; by contrast Godwin, starting from similar premises, argues that men's characters can change so radically that punishment is never just. Owen always maintained that no fixed standard of goodness existed, and that one age tolerated what another would have punished — hence his ironic references to 'actions designated crimes'.[19] Contingency sets the standards and, furthermore, each man's role in society is fortuitous: the judge passing sentence should humbly consider 'There, but for the grace of circumstance, go I'. The subject of Owen's compassion is a special type of criminal whose crime is born of poverty, squalor and deprivation. Retributive punishment is misdirected, since social reform is the only answer. But Owen, being (sometimes) consistent, extends this exonerating principle too far, so that no invidious action can be condemned.[20] The determinist argument is powerful but too comprehensive: one is loath to extend its mercy to the professional criminal. Owen and Godwin unrealistically treat crime as a homogeneous phenomenon, but deliberately anti-social acts must be distinguished from those born of necessity. The determinist holds that need and greed are both involuntary, but society arguably has a responsibility to satisfy only the former impulse.

Owen's treatment of crime at New Lanark exemplifies a non-punitive control system. When he purchased the cotton-spinning community, he was confronted by theft, drunkenness and immorality. 'To remedy this evil (theft), not one legal punishment was inflicted'; instead, leaders of the community were lectured on how to increase their earnings honestly. Workers with hangovers were given a homily by the factory manager. To eliminate sexual promiscuity, 'fines were levied on both parties' but no social disgrace was inflicted. The managers arbitrated in quarrels between workers. Instruments of mutual surveillance were introduced: to encourage domestic hygiene, the 'Committee of Bughunters' was formed (women who inspected each others' houses), and in order to discourage laziness Owen fixed 'silent monitors' by each machine, coloured symbols which registered whether the day's work had been satisfactory. He relied heavily on reasoned persuasion, moral precepts, and on shaming men into better behaviour. He idealised self-control, taught in childhood, and in his utopia '*justice* will take the place of law . . . The only code of laws in this system will be nature's laws, made plain to all'.[21]

The crucial and vulnerable element in any theory of punishment is the notion of responsibility, which assumes that each individual feels a conscious connection with, and power over, his present and past actions: this notion is the conceptual foundation of social and legal relationships.[22] How then can Godwin and Owen dismiss it? Should not Godwin, an advocate of moral behaviour, want those who commit immoral acts to feel remorse? But Godwin argues that the immoral man knows that he is acting contrary to the public good, and is dismayed by this, and his departure from truth and sincerity; he feels not guilt but unease, not repentance but selfless distress at the harm done to society. According to his utilitarian philosophy, self-centred feelings such as guilt should not attach to wrongdoing. 'We shall therefore no more be disposed to repent of our own faults, than of the faults of others. It will be proper to view them both, as actions injurious to the public good, and the repetition of which is to be deprecated.'[23] Is it really credible that the wrongdoer could view his crime in this impersonal light?

In reality, determinists such as Godwin must implicitly accept a modified doctrine of responsibility, if only for the convenience of identifying those responsible for actions. Two paths are open to the determinist who wants to destroy the moral constructions put upon responsibility without crudely asserting that all actions are determined and the language of responsibility is meaningless. He might argue that 'responsibility' is generally used selectively and partially: to say 'I was responsible for the crime' is partly true, but 'so were my parents, teachers, society, etc., *ad. inf.*'. This longwinded qualification highlights the absurdity and arbitrariness of punishing an individual victim for a collective crime. Alternatively, the determinist can say that the use of 'responsible' simply establishes a direct connection between an individual and a certain event; used like this, causally, the term merely constitutes an empirical description, and is conceptually separable from any moral construction imposed on it. Owen would probably find the first definition of responsibility most suitable for his arguments and Godwin, the second. Both definitions would enable them to retain the normal, causal description of social behaviour without inconsistency.

The determinist's treatment of deviance requires the identification of the miscreant for the purposes of correction, and the imputation of responsibility without the attachment of moral blame or guilt, or imposition of punishment. 'Responsible' is not equivalent to 'culpable' for the determinist. Yet the notion of responsibility is inextricable from our ideas of personal identity, causation and individual morality; also, mechanisms of praise and blame seem to be ineradicable from the process of childrearing. So the idea of moral responsibility might persist at the individual, subjective level and in human relations, even if it were ousted from the social structure of utopia. The optimism of these determinist utopians can be challenged on these practical grounds.

Together, Godwin and Owen present a catalogue of all the possible (but not always compatible) arguments against punishment and the legal system. Fourier would support them, but his critique is immanent rather than explicit. Both Godwin and Owen reflected the general concern over the injustices of the English legal system of their time, and this polemical involvement tends to weaken the theoretical case, since it is not always clear whether they are objecting to the law *per se*, a particular bad law, or the bad enforcement of law. Often, the focus of their attacks is unequivocally law itself, which protects private property; the two must, they assert, be simultaneously abolished. The philosophical case against punishment is designed to eliminate the harmful retributive mentality from utopia. The implements with which Godwin and Owen demolish the legal system are variously philosophical, logical, humanist and practical. The problems which remain in the wake of this destruction will be raised in Chapter 5.

To categorise crime as deviance limits its significance and disguises the social conflict which law, by its very existence, acknowledges. Both law and its iron handmaiden, punishment, would be incongruous in a harmonious society. But the rejection of law and coercive punishment as instruments of control demands as a corollary the invention of new methods of control or conflict reduction, and the utopians' suggested alternatives to law will now be reviewed, within the framework which the first section provided.

ALTERNATIVE CONTROLS

Saint-Simon's theory of social organisation and control rests squarely on his analysis of economic classes; herein lies his strongest claim to be a socialist forerunner. He holds that all workers have a common interest, wherein lies the solution to social conflict between individuals, and between public and private interests. Once the 'drones' were eliminated, only the producers' interest would remain, and so there would be no further need for control, law and compromise. This economic version of the identity of interests doctrine must be challenged. Firstly, it assumes that each man's interests *qua* producer comprise the whole of his possible interests, i.e. that non-economic interests are a negligible part of his life. This assumption is patently false for a social theory, even if it is satisfactory for an economic analysis of capitalism.

Secondly, the equation of interests is empirically unlikely to hold. True, when Saint-Simon was writing it would have been in the interests of *all* producers to liquidate the parasitic class and seize the government machinery in order to make industry prosper. But the interests of different sub-groups of producers would surely have begun to diverge when this was achieved. Saint-Simon assumes for all purposes the necessary and permanent identity of interests of managers, workers and shareholders, displaying here a lack of understanding of the workings of industry. Clearly, Saint-Simon's notion of class interest in no way resembles that of Marx, who criticised his merely nominalist approach to the subject.

Saint-Simon attributes to an inegalitarian society the natural identity of interests only possible in an egalitarian industrial society,[24] by inventing an artificial equality among the producer class — all men are equal *qua* producers, just as they are *qua* citizens. Such a postulate could only hold for circumscribed situations. Certainly, an 'industrial régime' would favour all producers for prosperous industry benefits everyone involved, but it would do so unequally without redistribution. However, industrial morality might counteract the divisive effects of unequal distribution.

Evidently, Saint-Simon's ideas on social control cannot be examined in isolation from his theory of history. He explains the dialectical transformation of modes of control, arguing that each historical epoch produces men with certain capacities and a corresponding means of control. In master-slave society it was 'impossible to establish any reciprocity in the moral relation between the two races',[25] and coercion was the only viable mode of control. Industrial organisation rests on the newly-developed industrial and moral capacities of individuals and the new structure of relations between independent producers; it also takes inherited characteristics into account, he suggests. But an organisation based on physiological traits would differ from one based on capacities; the former implies a rigid and predetermined division of power, and probably an élite government, whereas Saint-Simon's idea of socially determined universal capacities leads to a co-operative society with an egalitarian basis. Saint-Simon does not confront this anomaly, but incorporates both hierarchical and co-operative principles into his system.

Since the qualities of the new industrial man are conducive

to the exercise of morality and self-control, Saint-Simon expected an extension of morality to occur spontaneously. Morality is that which organises the human race in society; politics is simply the application of morality to public administration. The industrial regime is by nature 'moral' because of its pacific tendencies, and the industrial morality features tangible, definite interests by contrast with the non-materialist, other-worldly morality of Christianity. Saint-Simon found the do-as-you-would-be-done-by principle of terrestrial morality too negative, failing to clarify man's duty to himself, and replaced it by the more positive command 'Man must work'. Such a morality is indeed de-moralised, lacking a categorical imperative and reference points of virtue and goodness, and relying on the self-evident truth that man's economic interests, and hence their happiness, are interdependent. *Pace* Durkheim, Saint-Simon is as emphatic as any later sociologist about the centrality of morality to society, but he gives morality a different structure. His later espousal of an altruistic Christian ethic represented a considerable departure from the secular industrial state and the terrestrial morality, probably because Saint-Simon feared that this would not be sufficiently progressive and redistributive; he was also counteracting charges of atheism. *New Christianity* did not propose a theocracy exactly, but suggested that religion should act as a curb to the temporal powers, and as the ethical system within which the sciences could progress. This contrasts with his earlier criticisms of Christianity as the outdated metaphysical system which hampered progress towards positivism. In all probability the earlier and later writings cannot be entirely reconciled, but both exhibit his pre-occupation with setting morality on a sound basis, preferably that of a single principle.

In Saint-Simon's earlier utopia the only task of government is to execute laws useful to industry, which individuals will follow *out of inclination*, in the expectation of personal benefits. Although man's new moral capacities fit him to live in and support the industrial régime, it is still his innate impulse to follow his self-interest which serves as the basic control mechanism. Of prohibitive control, or the problem of crime and laziness, Saint-Simon says little, expecting that material incentives will eradicate these. Indeed, the incentive elements of Saint-Simon's scheme are conceptually separable from the industrial morality and identity of interests doctrine, and might operate alone. But the industrial morality itself promotes co-operative production through which abundant and tangible rewards may be obtained, so there is mutual reinforcement. In this respect, the system is fully determined.

The alluring industrial morality appears as a vindication of materialism, which utilises greed as much as the new capacities. The pivotal assumption is the doctrine of the identity of interests (which Saint-Simon bases on a questionable economic analysis). This in turn supports a system of minimum control. The industrial regime is utopian, because of the harmony achieved between human satisfaction and socially desirable activities.

In Harmony, control is transcended and transformed into social integration, so that men can follow their liberated passions without hindrance. Fourier's perfectly co-ordinated society of free men could function entirely without prohibitive or persuasive forms of control. In addition, he invokes every available method of promoting social cohesion by voluntary means. His premiss is that the liberation of the instincts, through the dissolution of civilisation, would transform socially disruptive passions, such as envy, into their harmonious equivalents. Thus, there is no fear that socially harmful instincts or passions would require permanent, repressive social control.

The basis of social reorganisation is passionate attraction and attractive work, which makes it possible to organise the productive function of the community painlessly. All work in itself satisfies the passions and guarantees the enjoyment which makes backsliding and laziness unthinkable: it is the primary integrative element in the phalanstery.

But the organisation of the harmonious society round work is precarious, because it relies on enough people being attracted to unpleasant but socially necessary jobs. Fourier provides three safeguards: the passion for consuming a commodity is annexed to the passion for producing it,[27] which may be contingently true, but is not necessarily so. Distasteful tasks must be surrounded by special honours which make them indirectly attractive. Finally, Harmony sacrifices the consumption of goods whose production *cannot* be made pleasant: Fourier settles the residual problem of unattractive but necessary work by decreeing that goods with an exorbitant social cost must be foregone. Can we believe him?

Harmony is characterised by the passion for unity, which rests on a spontaneous identification of interests, unknown to previous societies. In Civilisation, conflicts of interest necessitated control: 'the general wellbeing was in opposition to individuals' passions, so that the government, in legislating for the public good, was obliged to use constraints'.[28] But in Harmony free passionate attraction connects individuals with ties of friendship, cabalism, etc., so facilitating the identification of personal interests with the general interest. This constitutes an empirical identity of interests, not mere conversion to a moral doctrine such as Owen advocates. Individuals' interests will coincide spontaneously: 'each individual, while simply following his own interests, constantly serves the interest of the whole'.[29] The destruction of the specialised division of labour system and the new interchangeability of roles make this unpremeditated empathy possible. Thus, Fourier is an *engineer* of the identity of interests rather than an advocate of the doctrine.

The links of attraction between individuals and the community are also formed by 'gourmandism', the major passion, and love, which has a minor role. Gourmandism, the refined development of taste, promotes universal social coherence because the young and the very old, who are incapable of sexual love, are still delighted by good food, a universal passion. Throughout history, small communities have emphasized the important unifying effect of communal eating, and the phalanstery too relies heavily on this device.

If unsatisfied the amorous passion is a dangerous and disruptive force. But the liberated love relationships of Harmony will fully exhaust individuals' energies, and establish a large network of connections, physical, spiritual, and even financial. The loves of Harmony will be 'convergent', uniting pairs of lovers with others, producing social friendships, unlike the monogamous love of the 'tender' republican and his spouse, which is exclusive, egoistic and, hence, divergent. As its central recreation, the phalanstery will organise delights such as the Court of Love, polygamous dances, the 'museum orgy', foot-tickling sessions, pleasures corresponding to the most capricious taste. Consequently, sexual pleasure will be strongly associated with the community's corporate being. Familism will also be transformed from being a fragmenting force into a unifying power. A woman may choose three different men as husband, lover and father of her children, and men have similar rights. This will ensure that within three generations all community members will have familial connections.

Two points of major importance for social control emerge from the preceding account of Phalanstery. Firstly, the arrangement of the community is such that every major pleasure is inextricably associated with communal life, and the community must inevitably be regarded as the provider of happiness. This, more than anything, will cause men to devote themselves to the common interest. Also of great theoretical interest is Fourier's idea of multiple group loyalties. The conflicting allegiances of individuals prevent them from rivalry, and reduce conflict and the likelihood of permanent divisions. Multiple allegiances enable each individual to identify with individuals unlike himself who nevertheless have some group membership in common with him. The broadness of his own interests make him unable to take a narrowly sectional approach to the general interest. Ultimately, the social mechanism of Harmony lies not in feelings of solidarity, or identification at the level of awareness, but in the organisation of a society so perfectly meshed that no individual action can ever be out of joint. 'The institutions and conventions of (Fourier's) society come about through the equilibration of calculable motives.'[30] Fourier himself made the necessary calculations, but the system remains flexible: no real governing mechanism is described by Fourier.

But can any elements of formal control be detected in the Phalanstery? The strictness in the Harmonian régime is in the embracing nature of the organisation, and not concerned with deviance as such. People are most likely to break the rules of procedure or act unkindly in the area of love, so obligations are made explicit, and penalties imposed for misbehaviour. This is the only mention of organised control. There is no supreme controlling mechanism, and no overall authority with the power of direction of enforcement:

> *Since no coercive measures are tolerated in Harmony*, the work to be done is indicated *but not ordered* by the Areopagus, which is the supreme industrial council . . . Thus the Areopagus cannot order that the mowing or harvesting be done; it can only declare that a certain time is propitious . . . thereupon each series acts according to its wishes. But its wishes can scarcely differ from those of the Areopagus whose opinion is held in high esteem.[31]

Fourier uses no conventional method of control and vehemently rejects morality and education which would induce self-control. 'To his mind self-imposed constraints were no better than constraints imposed from without. There was nothing virtuous or dignified about continence and rational self-discipline'.[32] The phalansterian will follow his every passion, wayward though it may be. Only by the constant adaptation of society to the calculable desires of men can the Harmonious state be attained.

Despite his explicit intention to adapt society to men, it might be argued, as by Marcuse, that Fourier's utopia embodies restrictions more insidious than the overt controls of existing societies. But Harmony dispenses with all explicit controls and also operates with the weakest possible administrative apparatus, because all aspects of phalansterian life lead to integration and cohesion. Fourier's utopia forms an organic whole in which the role of each member is fixed and secure, and carries its own rewards and duties. It nevertheless takes account of the differences between individuals in a way impossible in traditional organic societies. Fourier's use of musical analogies reflects the composition of Harmony as an integrative, organic whole, a representation of the most perfect and hedonistic society imaginable.

The Gradgrind philosophy of Education has a more than accidental resemblance to that of Owen.

> "Now what I want is Facts. Teach these boys and girls nothing but Facts. Facts alone are wanted in life. Plant nothing else and root out everything else. You can only form the minds of reasoning animals upon Facts . . . Stick to Facts, sir!"
>
> . . . The speaker . . . swept with (his) eyes the inclined plane of little vessels than and there arranged into order, ready to have imperial gallons of facts poured into them until they were full to the brim.[33]

But Dickens's parody of the rational education omits Owen's indisputably benign intentions. Owen's measures at New Lanark were strictly short-term; the long-term solution for crime, and the foundation for the good society, was to be a system of rational education, directed at young children, which would exercise preventive control by teaching 'positive' precepts to direct their energy into socially beneficial paths.

This education will exploit man's malleability, his capacity to acquire 'any language, sentiments, belief, or any bodily habits and manners, not contrary to human nature'.[34] Owen differed from some radicals who proposed education as a social and political force, in that his environmentalism committed him to education as the foremost instrument of reform, whereas for later socialists it was a second best, espoused in their disappointment at the lack of spontaneous working-class consciousness. In Owen's hands, education became in effect an instrument of embourgeoisement, creating well-socialised workers.

The influence of Helvétius ('Education can achieve everything') and Rousseau's *Émile* are visible in Owen's proposals; he, like Rousseau, argues that education must be equated with enjoyment, and must stimulate and interest the children. 'All their instruction is rendered a pleasure and delight to them.' The ideal education should infuse an inquisitive and instrumental attitude towards objects. The central lesson of Owenite education is the use of reason, and the teacher must never usurp the role of the children's reason by presenting him with unexplained beliefs of rationality. The three positive aims of Owen's education are to teach rational principles, relevant facts, and understanding.

The similarity of Owen's outlook to that of Mr Gradgrind is unpromising, and *Hard Times* brilliantly exposes the practical shortcomings and spiritual disastrousness of such an education. Numerous other criticisms can be made of his plans. Rousseau, speaking for the anti-rationalist reaction of the late Enlightenment, anticipated the basic fallacy of Owen's scheme: 'of all men's faculties, reason, which is, so to speak, compounded of all the rest, is the last and choicest growth, and it is this you would use for the child's early training'.[35] The project of developing rational morality is doomed because these faculties develop on different time-scales. In fact, Owen concedes that the very young will be taught morality through an authoritative statement of precepts, rather than through reason. Again, theoretical analysis and the orderly accumulation of knowledge requires frameworks of enquiry which cannot be deduced from facts, as Owen's crudely empirical approach would suggest. All these objections are commonplaces of modern educational theory.

The teaching of 'rational principles' usually denotes the teaching of an ideology and Owen's system was devoted to teaching his own humane ideology, which he referred to as pure, value-free rationality. Is Owen's system therefore one of indoctrination? The distinction between instruction and indoctrination typically hangs upon the method and content of the teaching, and the intention of the teacher.[36] Only with regard to content can Owen be interpreted as advocating indoctrination. The implantation of humanist principles was, he thought, acceptable since these were 'moral facts', not matters of opinion.[37] Nevertheless, this approach resembles indoctrination: or is it tantamount to conditioning?

It is necessary to distinguish between the mechanisms of conditioning which cause involuntary responses (i.e. purely physical or subliminally psychological) and those of education which elicit 'voluntary' behaviour (i.e. intellectually/rule-guided actions). The Mowrer-Eysenck distinction suggests that the two categories are entirely separate with respect to the human nerve system. Learning is a process of the central nervous system while conditioning involves the autonomic nervous system.[38] The effects of education are more easily subjected to rational correction than those of conditioning, which may be ineradicable. Hence, conditioning and education give rise to qualitatively different kinds of behaviour, with regard to the kinds of human responses involved. It can be hypothesised that voluntariness and consciousness, which characterise learnt activities, are desirable qualities. Owen's praise of rationality and explanation evidences that he wished to create a society in which voluntary, self-aware action was the norm, not conditioned, 'automatic' virtue.

Owen was certainly critical of the role which education can play in the maintenance of destruction of established social values: his own school repudiated the use of praise, blame, reward and punishment, and discouraged individualism and the competitive spirit. School accustoms children to notions of hierarchy, deference, achievement and merit: if these premisses and values can be eradicated, society's perverse ethical foundations can be undermined. So reasons Owen, expecting education to oust irrational ideologies and hypocrisy. Owen's education theory leads to the quandary: can we trust educators' benevolence? He, like Plato, places his educators above suspicion by furnishing them with independent, absolute values — truth, knowledge and reason — but these reveal themselves as potentially ideological too.

Owen was an instinctive moralist, as is plain from his description of the ideal society. 'This new life must be one of temperance and of well-combined and well-directed industry.'[39] His choice of methods of control indicate that he was as enthusiastic as Godwin about reciprocal moral correction. He was also willing to curtail the freedom to commit anti-social acts and personal excesses, hence the closure of the New Lanark public houses. But education is the pivot of Owen's theory: when only one generation has been educated under the home colony scheme, he predicts, all other methods of control will be superseded. The colonies will have codes of rules, seldom invoked, for the members will have so thoroughly imbibed the principles of social harmony. Owen claims that rational education would ensure spiritual development, creating 'feelings too high and pure to be expressed in forms or words'. But evidently the claims which he made for his system outreached its potentialities. Granted, the educability of man suggests exciting prospects of human development, crime prevention and non-aversive control, but any such scheme for education must also take account of the inbuilt biases in the method of teaching, the opinions of the teacher, and the context in which the education occurs. Owen scarcely takes cognizance of these problems. Although his premises are credible, his reasoning and conclusions embody inconsistencies which make the theory vulnerable.

In Godwin's view, the means of control lies within man's own moral nature and his ability to exercise private judgement; properly trained, these would automatically lead to socially virtuous action. Since there is one set of universal moral truths, judgements concerning morality are shared, or public. Yet Godwin utterly rejects external agencies as a means of inculcating these truths and attacks institutions that destroy that essentially human characteristic, autonomy. Objections to Godwin's solution may rest — in principle — on a disbelief that such universal truths exist, and — in practice — on the fact that agreement on ends does not entail agreement on means, over which conflict frequently arises.

In Godwin's parish communities there is to be no punishment, while law is reduced to a common sense code of justice. The retributive spirit and moral reprobation will also disappear, although recidivists will be encouraged to reform, or emigrate. Men will offer each other advice for the improvement of their conduct, as well as correction. In short 'the wise and the honest man . . . carries about with him a diploma, constituting him inquisitor general of the moral conduct of his neighbours'.[40] When each member of the community becomes a moral policeman, the mutual surveil-

lance will virtually eradicate crime; but for any residual mis-
demeanours there will be trial by a sympathetic neighbour-
hood jury.

Godwin summarises his system as follows:

> The principal object of punishment, is restraint upon a dangerous
> member of the community; and the end of this restraint would be
> answered, by the general inspection, that is exercised by the
> members of a limited circle, over the conduct of each other, and by
> the gravity and good sense that would characterise the censures of
> men, from whom all mystery and empiricism were banished.[41]

Evidently, all Godwin's proposals must be seen in the
context of improved, sweeter human nature. Men will
become increasingly moral, so that eventually no reciprocal
supervision will be necessary, and the system will operate
through self-control. But, in eliminating the merciless
impartiality of the legal system, may not Godwin in reality
be consigning offenders to a jury whose partiality could take
the form of hostility and vindictiveness rather than
sympathy? Also, the smaller the community, the greater the
pressure to conform, and so the enfranchisement of public
opinion in the parishes could virtually disenfranchise private
judgement. Proposals for mutual moral supervision
normally inspire emotional abhorrence due to a lack of
confidence in the goodwill or perfectibility of others. There
are risks inherent in being informally at the mercy of one's
fellows in situations which have previously been formalised
and depersonalised. The only safeguard is Godwin's prediction that men would become increasingly reasonable and
fair.[42]

But there are other weighty objections to Godwin's
system. The abolition of law is to be followed by the
extension of province of morality. Although the catholic
nature of moral responsiveness already noted suggests that
situations at present regarded as morally neutral could be
infused with moral content, morality cannot dictate solutions to the complicated non-moral situations which abound
in society. Secondly, the substitution of morality for law may
in practice mean the exertion of far stronger control on
members of society. Godwin implies that it would, arguing

that intemperance and 'the caprices of personal intercourse' which escape rebuke in a legal system would be condemned 'by the sincerity of neighbours'.[43]

But internalised precepts of morality dominate consciousness in a way that law cannot, and moral responses are basic and inescapable, associated with unease or mental pain. The moralisation of new areas of social life might generate tension and misery for everybody. Moral guilt may be harder to purge than legal guilt, and the censure of neighbours may be more far-reaching and distressing than punishment. Godwin's system lacks a guarantee that punishment will not be reintroduced disguised as moral disapproval and inflicted without legal restraint.

Godwin presumes a homogeneity of moral opinion; eccentric moral judgements are to be eschewed. Given scepticism about universal and absolute moral truth, it is nevertheless conceivable that this essential condition could be fulfilled in small parishes where ideals are shared and interests identical. But in larger, heterogeneous stratified societies there are bound to be differences of moral opinion according to class, situation and upbringing.[44] Godwin's theory would not hold. Thus, an examination of applied morality shows that in practice it may not be as universal, or as conducive to freedom, autonomy and happiness as its favoured position on the control continuum implies, and as Godwin hoped.

The semi-anarchistic philosophy of the utopians decreed that government should be minimised. Accordingly, they endowed other institutions with the former prerogatives and functions of government. The utopian himself usurps the task of formulating constructive social policies and embodies them in his blueprint. The other vital task, the reconciliation of interests, is no longer to be performed by agencies of government; instead, the utopians choose methods of control which can be operated by the people themselves. And, crucially, they make various catalytic assumptions: that individual interests are naturally co-operative, that crime is caused by imperfect social environments, and that social deviance is eradicable under ideal social conditions.

These devices and arguments render the apparatus of government and the state redundant.

The schema of possible control methods of Section 1 showed that few methods of control are compatible with the ideality of utopia, notably those which employ human reason and intelligence (Diagram 2: 4, 5, 6). These methods maximise a number of goods, as Diagram 3 indicates. Morality, education and reason are, predictably, the means of control favoured by the utopians, except for Fourier who favours the liberation of the passions in an integrated environment: his organic ideal is removed from the realm of control altogether.

Morality constitutes something different for each utopian. For Godwin it is a rational reflective process of judgement; for Saint-Simon it is the regulation of impulses of self-interest through the promise of material benefits; for Owen it is the automatic operation of rational precepts taught in school. The common feature of these moralities is their instrumentality in achieving happiness, and their demoralised nature. But there are objections in principle to the extensive use of morality; it is also true that inhumane ideologies have infused their doctrines with moral language and exploited the moral capacity for anti-social purposes. In view of these objections, it will be useful to consider the possible alternatives to morality which utopia might employ. The liberal view of man as rational agent suggests that a comprehensive set of rules which directed man's actions into socially beneficial channels, and was enforced through mutual reminder (rather than conscience), might be an effective substitute for morality: the justification for obedience would be the acceptance of the aims of society. But such a code could never contain a sufficient multiplicity of rules to cover all concrete situations. Eventually, rules of thumb would be devised for situations not in the catalogue, and these might again resort to moral justification.

The search for substitutes for morality reveals various impediments: an immense administrative apparatus would probably be required for enforcement and there is also the difficulty of categorising forbidden and permitted actions in terms both general and precise. Morality is in fact a uniquely economical, efficient and informal way of enforcing desirable behaviour. Where general principles and rules of thumb fail, there is to be a *presumption of goodwill* between men, an unwillingness to harm others. Thus, morality is a persuasive elaboration of the notion of natural sympathy or compassion. The infinite variety of human relations, and the total vulnerability of men to each other, both physical and psychological, make the presumption of mutual goodwill the essential ingredient of any life worth living.[45] Fourier's elimination of all moral premises leaves vast areas of human contact uncharted. Even if morality is, like other belief systems, ideological and subject to abuse, there are weighty reasons for maintaining it as an instrument of social control.

Finally, two qualifications to the use of 'control' in this chapter must be emphasized. Control, as it appears in the schema and in the works of the utopians, is not merely an instrument for the minimisation or elimination of social conflict and deviance, whose *modus operandi* is prohibition: in any society (even a laissez-faire society) social control has the second important function of inducing or forcing people to act constructively within society — to participate, to work, to co-operate. Secondly, it is evident that agencies of social control are often agencies of social cohesion as well: that which prevents conflicts also promotes consensus. The utopian methods of control described in this chapter perform a triple function, analysed further in the next chapter.

References
1. B. Barry, *Political Argument* (Routledge & Kegan Paul, 1965). Ch. 10 gives a thorough analysis. But he is analysing how policies, etc., may be 'in one's interests', whereas I am concerned with the activity of 'pursuing one's interests', which requires a slightly different approach.
2. *International Encyclopaedia of the Social Science*, ed. D. Sills (Macmillan Free Press, 1968), Vol. 14, p. 561.
3. For various definitions see *Concepts of Indoctrination*, ed. I. A. Snook (Routledge & Kegan Paul, 1972), pp. 1-8. The introduction summarises approaches to indoctrination through aim, method and content.
4. G. Orwell, *Nineteen Eighty-four* (Penguin, 1954), p. 169. See also Y. Zamyatin, *We* (Penguin, 1972).

5. The classes have antagonistic interests, but the indoctrination makes the individual identify completely with those of his class, and consider it superior to the rest, so that no other class could ever constitute a reference group for him. Utopian means, dystopian ends.

6. PJ I, p. 12. Godwin's attack must be seen in the light of the ruthless manipulation of the legal machine by the ruling elite of his time, and undoubtedly his views were also coloured by the government's misuse of legal processes for political oppression during the French Revolutionary wars. *Caleb Williams* vividly portrays the maladministration, abuses and cruelty of the judicial system of the time.

7. PJ II, p. 399 and pp. 303-4.

8. PJ II, p. 402.

9. PJ II, p. 323.

10. See PJ II, p. 324. The secondary theme of *Caleb Williams* is that Falkland, an ex-murderer is now a man of kindness and gentility, yet the judicial system cannot account or allow for any such inconsistency of character. Later in the book a philosopher brigand complains 'It signifies not what is the character of the individual at the hour of trial. How changed, how spotless, and how useful, avails him nothing'.

11. PJ II, p. 327.

12. PJ II, p. 346.

13. PJ II, p. 360, also p. 375.

14. PJ II, p. 337. Also I, pp. 179-80.

15. PJ II, p. 363.

16. *Six Lectures*, p. 14.

17. Fourier also wrote 'Your Civilisation persecutes us when we obey Nature; it obliges us to assume an artificial personality, to behave in ways that are contrary to our desires'. Beecher & Bienvenu, p. 174.

18. NVS, p. 99.

19. BNMW, pp. 74-5. These pages summarise Owen's arguments memorably. See also NVS, p. 99.

20. Even kings and rulers are 'blameless for all the folly, wickedness, absurdity or mad actions which they may commit'. *Six Lectures*, p. 36.

21. HC, p. 78. This echoes Godwin.

22. See P. F. Strawson, 'Freedom and Resentment', in *Studies in the Philosophy of Thought and Action* (Oxford U.P., 1968), who points out that differences in our nexus of responses occur when we are led to believe that those with whom we are dealing are irresponsible.

23. PJ I, p. 394.

24. W. Stark argues this point in 'The Realism of Saint-Simon's spiritual program', *Journal of Economic History*, Vol. 5 (1945), pp. 24-43, especially p. 28.

25. Markham, p. 109.

26. See Markham, pp. 83-5.

27. E.g., the girl who loves garlic but hates the idea of work can be persuaded to work in the garlic-growers series, etc. OC VI, p. 257 ff.

28. OC I, p. 63.

29. OC VI, p. 49. Note that Fourier believed the complete spiritual unit or 'communal soul' to be composed of 810 individuals. OC VII, pp. 461-2. Also see OC X, p. 59.

30. E. Mason, 'Fourier and Anarchism', *Quarterly Journal of Economics*, Vol. 2 (1927-8), p. 228-62, especially p. 249.

31. Beecher & Bienvenu, p. 252. My italics.

32. *Ibid.*, p. 206. (Editors' comment).

33. C. Dickens, *Hard Times* London, 1901), pp. 7-8.

34. NVS, p. 102. See also pp. 144-7.

35. *Émile*, (Everyman, 1911), p. 53.

36. See A. Flew's commentary on the views of J. Wilson and R. M. Hare in 'Indoctrination and Doctrines' in Snook (ed.), *op. cit.*

37. See, e.g., N. Postman and C. Weingartner, *Teaching as a Subversive Activity* (Penguin, 1971), esp. Ch. 6.

38. H. J. Eysenck, *Crime and Personality* (Paladin, 1970), pp. 114-5. It must be emphasized that the distinction is *not* that education is a verbal process: conditioning may also be verbal.

39. *Six Lectures*, p. 97.

40. PJ (1st ed'n) I, p. 106-7.

41. PJ II, p. 198-9. 'Mystery and empiricism' probably refers to the esoteric workings of the law. Bk. V, ch. xxii, gives an account of parish government.

42. Some of Godwin's remarks about the obligation to behave well (PJ I, p. 162-3, 165) may be intended to allay these fears.

43. PJ (1st ed'n) I, p. 109.

44. See, e.g., C. Davies, 'Four Hundred Burglary Suspects' in *Howard Journal of Penology,* Vol. XIII (1970). 'The men were detached and objective in their discussion of the offences as if talking about some act of quite neutral morality.' (p.45).

45. See K. Lorenz, *On Aggression*, trans. M. Latzke (Methuen, 1966), p. 209.

CHAPTER 5

COHESION IN UTOPIA

IN an ideal world, the individual is reconciled with society not merely at the level of action, but at the level of impulse, through judicious socialisation; only then can the utopian guarantee social solidarity and cohesion. Notwithstanding the utopians' professed faith in reason, they employed — perhaps unwittingly — a wide range of supplementary methods to guarantee a high degree of cohesion, especially in the social structure. Fourier's society is organised so that disruptive tendencies do not arise: the liberated passions are never anti-social, and all potential conflict is defused by multiple allegiances. Control and cohesion are indistinguishable in his social structure. Saint-Simon's physiologically-based class system operates similarly, for to allocate a class-based role to each member of society is to avert conflicting claims, uncertainty, and disruptive behaviour. With such examples in mind, this chapter will scrutinise the sociological and structural features of the utopias which were to promote integration and cohesion. The analysis is necessarily interpretative since the utopians neither thought nor wrote in terms of control or cohesion, although they were, as social scientists, instinctively aware of the need for such devices. Three conceptually and operationally different kinds of device can be detected: (a) organisational, (b) ethical or ideological, and (c) structural.

ORGANISATIONAL DEVICES: CO-OPERATIVE WORK AND THE NEW FAMILY

The utopians' presentation of the nature and role of work is distinctively socialist in its emphasis on the creative and co-operative nature of the process. The idealisation of work as a regular, creative and satisfying activity contradicted the facts of the contemporary work situation, marked by irregular and seasonal employment.[1] One necessary question, therefore, is whether the utopians' designation of work as the central social activity represents a capitulation to the incipient capitalist work ethic.

Work is an agent of social cohesion in two respects: *substitution* and *socialisation*. Saint-Simon and Owen saw work as a substitute for idleness and crime, and organised their societies round the productive process, so as to substitute rival behaviour patterns for these anti-social patterns. Saint-Simon condemned idleness and parasitism, and Owen, *qua* social reformer, suggested the provision of public works as a crime prevention policy. Fourier too uses labour to fill every moment of the phalansterian's day, which would inevitably minimise the chances for deviant behaviour. By contrast, Godwin looks forward to the minimisation of labour; the philosopher never doubts man's capacity to profit from leisure.

But the negative, prophylactic function of work as a substitute for anti-social activity is overshadowed by its positive role as a socialising influence. Saint-Simon believes that specialisation and interdependence in work, based on biological differences, make workers into collaborators and associates. 'The introduction of division of labour has bound men together completely. Things have come to the point where each depends on his neighbours.' Order and co-operation result. For Owen too, the provision of work turns men into industrious, co-operative, valuable citizens. The socialising role of work in Fourier's society operates not only through the norms which it engenders but through the loves and friendships which it fosters, the opportunities for the harmless release of passionate energy, and the provision of pleasure. Cabalism and ambition, two dangerous passions, will also find constructive outlets in work.

These accounts suggest that peer-group socialisation will continue into adult life, for where men work they exercise considerable control interdependently, because of division of labour, over each other's behaviour, and collective values and judgements assume importance for each individual. This tendency is reinforced by the co-operative ethic. Saint-Simon additionally gave work a moral value which would further extend its socialising influence. 'Work is the source of all the virtues', he asserts.[2]

Work evidently promotes social control and cohesion, but it may also erode human liberty by consuming time and energy, and subtend an oppressive social structure. It absorbs the energy of the workers so that they cannot function in the political and private spheres. For such reasons, Marcuse condemns the present dominance of work, which he equates with surplus repression and the achievement ethic.[3] Aside from the economic analysis of capitalist exploitation, it can be argued that any work-oriented and specialised system will have *socially* oppressive aspects: (1) the division of men into classes (according to wealth and productive role) with ultimately irreconcilable interests; (2) the disproportionate consumption of workers' time and energy, which severely curtails their freedom of action; (3) the alienating nature of production under the division of labour, and especially man's alienation from his own product, and (4) the work ethic, an ideological superstructure which justifies and reinforces oppression.

Could these work-based utopias, avoid the oppressive features while successfully exploiting the integrative aspects of work? Godwin was sceptical: in his devotion to intellectual life he repudiated the idea of a work-centred society, arguing that 'mechanical and daily labour is the deadliest foe to all that is great and admirable in the human mind',[4] and preferred to abolish work itself. The other utopians denied that class interests could exist in an ideal society. Although Saint-Simon supported a role-based class system, he argued that men would have a common interest in the general prosperity. Owen envisaged the ultimate abolition of class distinction in his colonies, and collective ownership of the means of production; work would be paid according to the labour standard of value and no profits would be extracted. Only Fourier tolerated the continuance of profits and wealth, but social distinctions and privileges would disappear, and the otherwise egalitarian arrangement of society would prevent a division of interests. The utopians hoped to abolish class oppression by making society more egalitarian, more mobile, by proclaiming the identity of interests doctrine or even by abolishing private property outright. Marxist critics argue that they misunderstood the nature of class conflict and its economic basis. But the utopians defined oppression as a situation where the poor produced luxuries for the rich, and were underpaid; this contradiction they successfully eradicated.

Their response to the physically oppressive aspects of work (2) must be taken in conjunction with their solutions to work-alienation (3). In their appreciation of the paradox that the worker's product is financially beyond his reach lies the germ of the idea of alienation. All were keenly aware of the horror of industrial production and monotonous labour, and protested against the division of labour in industrial processes, which produces humiliating dependency (Godwin) and boredom and lack of initiative (Owen, Fourier).[5] In utopia, the division of labour becomes specialisation according to talent and inclination which guarantees work satisfaction. The importance of variety in work was emphasized by Owen, and more so by Fourier.

With work a pleasurable activity, and with the products of labour freely available to the worker, there would be an end to alienation. But what of the time-and-energy-consuming aspect of labour, which prevents men from pursuing other activities? For Fourier, the question does not arise, since work is unmediated pleasure, and can scarcely be prolonged sufficiently. But Owen and Saint-Simon regard work less as pleasure than as a socially necessary activity, the *sine qua non* for consumption.[6] Fourier, by contrast, takes a wider view of work as a socially necessary institution, which is an instrument of unmediated pleasure apart from its productive aspect, and an integrating force within the social structure.[7]

It is in the utopian socialists' understanding of *the meaning of work in human life* that the cure for work-oppression is to be found. They postulate that human nature is creative and active, and pleasure essentially lies in activity, and the exercise of talent. Saint-Simon argued, influentially, that classes create themselves through work while Fourier's view of attractive work forms the basis of many socialist accounts of work.

The characterisation of man as *homo faciens* enables these utopians to abolish the four aspects of oppression which threaten a work-centred society. The creative view of man implies that a work ethic will not be oppressive, since it differs from the capitalist work ethic, which advocates satisfaction through 'achievement' within a work structure intrinsically devoid of unmediated satisfaction. The notion of satisfaction through creation prevents the utopians from viewing work as something performed only out of physical necessity. Although mechanisation and high productivity might dissever work from need-satisfaction, when men's physical needs are fulfilled, they will work for the pleasure of creation. The dangers attendant upon satiation are thus avoided by the new concept of creative work.

In summary, important links are established between work as the central activity of utopia and control, social cohesion and creative satisfaction, through the notion of *homo faciens*. Work has an essential macro-function in social organisation, and an important subjective function in the development of the individual. Both societies and individuals are self-integrated through work. Furthermore, the new co-operative organisation of labour will reinforce the integrating bonds, and redouble the pleasure of work.

Their independent discoveries of the virtues of co-operation caused Owen, Fourier and Saint-Simon to be grouped together as early socialists.[8] Co-operative theory rests on a presumption of men's natural sociability and mutual dependence, and their individual inadequacy when faced with natural forces. Only through combining, Saint-Simon argues, will men be able to master nature. These are the practical benefits of co-operation, while at the theoretical level it is seen as the antidote to competition and individualistic enterprise. Apart from its literal connotation, 'working together', co-operation can signify joint activity in a particular project or common rational agreement to obey certain activity-governing rules for mutual benefit. Again, there can be total co-operation in a way of life which includes agreement and understanding on aims and values, the shared mores which Saint-Simon suggests, as well as joint activity. Owen and Fourier also refer particularly to the co-operative 'spirit' in which people conduct their activities.

Saint-Simon characterises a co-operative society by contrast with one in which men have few skills, which rests on force; everyone has something to contribute and something to gain, and so society coheres voluntarily. The necessary precondition for such a society was the mass development of capacities, parallel with the extension of the division of labour, which makes men less individually dependent and more dependent on the whole.[9] Saint-Simon's utopia, built on the willing and spontaneous co-operation of the three classes, would reflect the involuntary co-ordination of the parts of the body. This harmony of classes rested on the producers' unity of interests in the industrial project. Saint-Simon's proposals for co-operation were in the sphere of constructive enterprise, and he probably envisaged co-operation as operating at the level of the *chefs d'industrie*, and being the pooling of resources in order to achieve more ambitious results; some moral and spiritual virtues of co-operation may have eluded him. Saint-Simon's programme is therefore a paradigm of the rational *ad hoc* kind of co-operation.

By contrast, Owen's statement that men's happiness rests on promoting that of others acts as the *philosophical* basis of a more comprehensive kind of co-operation, namely, men's voluntary co-operation in living and working together. He attacked the current fallacious idea that egoism is more beneficial to man than that of union and co-operation. Noting the proven success of destructive co-operation in wartime, he asks 'Would not a similar increased effect be produced by union, combination, and extensive arrangement, to *create and conserve*?'[10] Sometimes, admittedly, Owen's vision also seems to be of entrepreneurial economic co-operation, as when he mentions bridges and canals, and says that large firms will show men the possibility of further beneficial combinations.[11] But his own community experiments were explicitly for the benefit of the working classes: for Owen, co-operation utilised the still unharnessed powers of the many. In fact, the moral element of co-operation is always the strongest element in Owen's programme. Co-operation was a principle infinitely extendable, but useful in particular to the working classes as a means of promoting their own prosperity in the face of the entrenched wealth of other classes: it created some solidarity among workers in the 1830s.[12]

Fourier made friendly overtures to Owen on the grounds that Owen had 'foreseen' what Fourier called 'the principle of association'. But later, he attacked Owen's desire to form and modify the human character, arguing that it had to be left *au naturel*, whereupon the principles of attraction would ensure co-operation.[13] Fourier himself argued that the economy of God's system rests on the unity of the largest possible number, and therefore on co-operation, and denied that the individual or family is a viable unit, economically or socially. His own associationism rested on the primacy of the social group and he, like Saint-Simon, advocated 'organic' co-operation; the members of society co-operate spontaneously within the organic social unit.[14]

The notion of co-operativism was born of the need for people to act together, proposed in the face of an extreme, fragmenting division of labour, and doctrines of individualistic *laissez-faire* and cut-throat competition. Co-operative ideas originated in the gathering together of men in factories and *ateliers*, where their work necessitated co-operation and their proximity facilitated communication. The idea of economic co-operation emerged almost simultaneously among the utopians, signifying their understanding of the need for accumulated capital and investment as the condition for large-scale industry. Even Fourier, who hated industrialism, recommended the economies of scale in community life, and the need for mass production of necessities.[15]

Fourier's account of co-operation is largely sociological, with important implications for the arrangement of the whole of society. It is also redolent of the metaphysical naturalism to which all the utopians are in some way committed. Owen and Saint-Simon, however, saw co-operation as something essentially concerned with production and material welfare, an imposed principle of organisation; the utopian's task was to teach the principles of union and organise a scheme for participation in co-operative ventures. Co-operation, properly constituted, as participation in beneficial common economic ventures, can prevent work alienation and discontent, and extend production beyond the aggregate of individual contributions, through a humane division of labour.

The contrast of such views with Godwin's attack on co-operation is instructive. He deplores the fact that co-operation compels individuals to modify ideas and to accommodate others. 'We cannot be reduced to a clockwork uniformity. Hence it follows that all supererogatory co-operation is carefully to be avoided, common labour and common meals.'[16] Joint activities which detract from individuality, even playing in orchestras and acting in plays, should cease. As to the need for co-operation in heavy construction tasks, Godwin hopes prophetically that machinery will supersede co-operation. This veto on co-operative efforts is, of course, inconsistent with his advocacy of co-operation and interdependence in the moral sphere, and his doctrine of universal benevolence can be read as an account of co-operation.[17] Both Godwin and the other utopians see the same universal problem, man's weakness confronted by his desire to master nature. But the individualist abandons the endeavour, while the co-operative utopians take the nature of the task as given and necessary, and hope to alter human behaviour to accomplish it. Godwin's individualistic arguments distort the meaning of co-operation, making it denote uniformity and subordination of the individual. Later anarchists certainly did not follow Godwin into this extremity, for they posited spontaneously co-operative human nature. The desire to co-operate is formed, for Fourier, at an instinctual level and, for the others, follows from a rational perception of the need for, and benefits of, mutual aid. Neither way is it exclusive of individual thought or enterprise.

The theory of co-operation rests on a perception of human weakness. Joined with the premiss that men are irremediably selfish or antagonistic, this dictates a Hobbesian solution of imposed co-operation which naturally yields less satisfaction to the individual than voluntarily-constituted co-operation, just as the enforced co-operation between unfree workers in capitalist production provides none of the benefits of co-operation in a socialist utopia. The utopians' assumption that man is sociable, rather than selfish, is essential to their doctrines of co-operation: if universal or widespread selfishness were the case, 'free-riders' would jeopardise the co-operative utopia.

The natural tendency of co-operation as a social form is to promote integration and cohesion, engendering shared values and mutual restraint. As well as facilitating complex, large-scale manufacture, it creates a necessarily egalitarian ethic. Co-operation thus appears as a form of continuous peer-group socialisation for adults.

Radical critiques of marriage and the nuclear family appear in these utopias. Godwin's inexorable logic destroys the supposedly overriding moral ties between family members and reveals the threat which marriage presents to individual autonomy.[18] Owen and Fourier deplore the selfishness, exclusiveness and unhappiness of monogamous marriage, and its harmful effects on children. Fourier blames 'the tender republican and his tender republican-wife, who love only themselves' for the fragmented, un-productive state of the economy.[19] Such attacks partly reflect the breakdown of the economic family unit, well advanced in English towns by 1800.[20]

Fourier and Owen replace 'natural', intra-family co-operation by economic and social co-operation within the community. Their advocacy of an extended sense of kinship relates to this endeavour. Fourier, by separating the roles of husband, lover and father, and encouraging multiple love affairs, ensures that each member of the phalanstery will feel kinship with every other member. The work series also

generates loyalty between group members, and these
networks of kinship and comradeship are highly favourable
to social harmony. Owen, hampered by his reputation for
atheism, was less overtly radical and proposed, in effect,
divorce on demand, without explicitly advocating free love.
The wider sense of family will come through the communal
upbringing of the community's children: children will feel
stronger attachment to their peers than their parents, and the
sense of solidarity and commitment will be redirected
towards all members of the community. Godwin delcares
that the abolition of marriage will enable men and women to
form multiple friendships based on individual merit; this
would presumably have an integrating effect in the
community, as must any proliferation of personal ties.

The new, community-wide families are held together by
'socialist' sentiments such as friendship and solidarity rather
than by duty, sexual desire and dependency. The utopians do
not merely extend the idea of family but revolutionise human
relations, setting them on a rational, voluntary and enduring
basis. Interestingly, they sought explicitly to extend 'family
sentiment' to the community, rather than to counteract
atomisation by expedients such as the membership of interest
groups, better described as self-interest groups.

The demise of the family entails innovations in the treatment of children and sexual relationships. In Harmony,
children are brought up together and socialisation occurs in
dormitories, schools and workshops. Fourier calls this the
'natural' and most effective form of education.[21] Owen
concurs on the socialisation of younger by older children:
parental affection prevents proper education at home.[22]
Peer-group influence must begin early, and continue into
adulthood. Fourier's presentation of sex as a cohesive factor
is a revolutionary innovation, for the sexual impulse was
seen (especially by the Church) as an anarchic force whose
manifestations had to be suppressed or sublimated. The
experience of mass orgies and the resulting multiplication of
pleasure would strengthen the individual's commitment to
the community as an integral whole (*l'âme intégrale*), rather
than to the partner of the moment. In advocating such

novelties, Owen and Fourier were deliberately experimental, and daring.

Curiously, these would-be social scientists finally capitulated to the messianic impulse and designed religions to fill the empty temples of utopia. The Rational Religion of Owen and the New Christianity of Saint-Simon perhaps answered the metaphysical yearnings of their old age. But there is a strong case for arguing that these were the consequence 'of mature doubts as to whether their societies could function successfully with only industrial morality or rational education as instruments of socialisation. Their spiritual father, Rousseau, had been converted to the social virtues of a civil religion, and other *philosophes* agreed.[23] Saint-Simon gives a historical account of Christianity as a social instrument, and his New Christianity, with its emphasis on improving life on earth for the poor, seems to have a primarily social purpose; it is to propagate the idea of brotherhood, a more integrating doctrine than the industrial morality. Similarly, Owen and Fourier create social religions apparently to reinforce their central instruments of socialisation. Fourier's Religion of Love lacks spiritual pretensions and is patently a device for promoting order in the community's sexual antics. The social functions of these new religions are important, but the details are immaterial here. Essentially, they do not constitute what Becker describes as an intellectual secularisation of earlier Christian concepts, but are invoked as social safety-nets, and resemble the rational religion of revolutionary France.

One other organisational feature of these utopias worth attention is the preference for the small community. The justification for limiting the size of social units is concisely expressed by a modern sociologist writing on the role of the police:

> The communities with the highest level of social control are small, homogeneous, and stable . . . In such communities social order is maintained to a very large extent by informal controls of public opinion . . . Village societies are usually tightly knit communities because everyone is so dependent upon everyone else.[24]

Whether protesting at urbanisation, regurgitating Rousseau, or following instinct, the utopians, except perhaps Saint-Simon, adopted the village as the basis of their societies. The absence of government would not detract from the cohesion of such societies, for utopian inhabitants are active and relate constantly to their fellows, participating in many areas of social life: the paraphernalia of government would be superfluous.

IDEOLOGICAL BONDS: THE IDENTITY OF INTERESTS

By promoting harmony of belief the utopian can guard against disharmony of action. Consensus is the basis for social cohesion. Crucially, individuals' belief systems in utopia must be changed to support socially desirable ends; re-education is essential. Men are impelled to act in accordance with their beliefs, to avoid 'cognitive dissonance'. Among the methods by which the utopians restructured belief were the 'demoralised social morality', a doctrine with personal and moral overtones removed, and the work ethic and co-operative morality, which integrate the individual's desires with the general productive aim of society, and with the interests of his fellows in the everyday work process.

The doctrine of the identity of interests merits analysis as the major device by which the utopians persuade their audience to suspend disbelief. It operates at two levels: firstly, as an ideology within utopia, which reduces the conflict of interest by assuring individuals that their interests are ultimately identical, and secondly as a methodological statement in the utopian's theory, whereby he convinces readers that his utopian model would function without conflict. The utopians claimed for the identity of interests doctrine a scientific basis in human nature. 'Collective and individual interests must be brought into accord with each other' Fourier argues, and the other utopians concur. In utopia individuals pursue their own interests through the common good, and achieve happiness in a orderly way. The minimal state merely maintains order, while its members provide the dynamic energy. But greed and selfishness would invalidate this social equation, so the utopians, following Smith and Bentham, offer a solution in the form of the doctrine of identity of interests, which is sometimes empirical, sometimes persuasive. The empirical formulation states that all actions will naturally harmonise in utopia where a form of social organisation attuned to human nature will eliminate all conflicts of interest. The persuasive version seeks to unite action and belief, and may appear as a moral or a prudential doctrine. It states men's real interests in opposition to their apparent, selfish and often erroneous desires. There is a logical separation between the two versions. The moral doctrine is not derived from the empirical doctrine, and each functions differently. But if it is empirically true that interests coincide, the invocation of the moral doctrine over-determines the case.

Fourier's prediction that each will serve the interests of the mass while 'blindly following his own passions' indicates that the willing contributions of individuals to their favourite work groups increases the general sum of happiness. Self-interest is in everyone's interest. Because no interest is entirely selfish, pleasures are multiplied; even the sexual fetishist will find a lover who enjoys the same fetish. This results from the carefully balanced composition of temperaments in Harmony and the close co-ordination of the small community. Fourier explicitly states that individuals have no conception of the parts they play in the whole: once society is ideally organised, the passions do the rest. The identity of interests doctrine is neither moral nor persuasive nor functional in Fourier's utopia; it is rather a theoretical explanation to his readers of the celestial mechanics of Harmony. His solution is reminiscent of the radical liberal's mechanistic explanation of social harmony, the 'conception of society as a network of activities carried on by actors who knew no principles of authority'.[25] But Fourier needs no invisible hand, for harmony is latent in nature, and human nature.

By contrast, Owen presents the doctrine persuasively as a moral principle, and his dictum that the happiness of self . . . can only be attained by conduct that must promote the

happiness of the community'[26] is part-moral, part-factual
and will be a self-fulfilling prediction, once it is widely
taught and believed. Another version substitutes 'his fellows'
for 'the community', a significant difference. Unlike
Fourier, Owen asserts the need for consensus, and for
rational comprehension and conscious effort in the
reciprocal promotion of interests. His magic wand formula
begs the question of how precisely individuals' happiness is
interconnected, and so seems moral rather than factual.
Experience suggests that happiness often demonstrably does
not lie in promoting that of others, quite the opposite. A
negative version of Owen's doctrine is weakly true: others'
blatant misery may mar our own happiness — but this is not
the substantial moral doctrine which he sought. Evidently
the individual's happiness depends on the prosperity and
security of his community, and he would be wise to contribute to these. Nevertheless, 'if all individuals *less one*
continue refraining from doing A, the community loss is very
slight, whereas the one individual doing A makes a personal
gain far greater than the loss he incurs as a member of the
community'.[27] Whatever interest-identifying moral rule pre-
vails, moral renegades and amoral free-riders will flourish,
so the identification of the interests of individual and community is fallacious. Even so, Owen's stipulative definition
of happiness as altruistic activity has an exhortatory value.
The definition which refers to the community is not easily
translated into action, for it becomes entangled with that
problematic concept, the common good, and the individual
cannot meaningfully set out to promote this, even if he can
be made to identify imaginatively with it.[28]

Saint-Simon, wrestling with the problem of socially
disruptive egoism, argues that 'the solution to the problem
consists in having a means which is common to particular
interests and to the general interest'. The adoption of
combination is evidently the solution: 'the whole human
race, having one end and common interests, each man must
consider himself, in social relations, as engaged in a
company of workers'.[29] Saint-Simon's version of the
doctrine rests on the economic axiom that the interests of all

producers is identical. 'The "solidarity" between the
interests of the industrialists, and the law of association, give
Saint-Simon and his followers the conviction that (class)
conflicts can be transcended.'[30] The economic axiom has
already been shown to be not *necessarily* true, and Saint-
Simon also overlocks the fact that individuals' interests may
be incompatible in other respects, even if coinciding
economically. But Saint-Simon's analysis of interdependence
in an industrial society (each depends on 'the mass')
reinforces the economic argument. He also says 'A man can
only be truly happy in seeking happiness in the happiness of
others'.[31] But the statement that prosperity, peace and order
are in everybody's interest is a less idealistic, more credible
version of the doctrine. Godwin's view that each individual is
to count as part of a common stock, and his exposition of
happiness through benevolence, is a straightforwardly moral
and persuasive identity of interests doctrine, making less
claim to a scientific basis than the other formulae.

Analysis of the doctrine must first clarify which interests
are identical. The utopians usually see individuals' interests
as identical and consider the general interest an aggregate of
these: the community has no separate interests. Evidently,
the equality of individuals in relevant respects is a prerequi-
site for their interests being considered *the same*, but *not* for
their interests being comprehended *within* the general
interest.

The chief criticism of these identity of interests doctrines is
that they do not analyse the notion of interest, or adequately
consider the conflicts that arise owing to differences between
individuals' wants and the needs of the system itself. They
assume that men resemble each other enough to make their
interests identical in all important respects (or to differ
predictably — Fourier): a premiss useful to the social
scientist. But they reinterpret 'interest' in order to formulate
the doctrine. The *ex post* hypothesis that the same things are
good for all men because of their common humanity is too
weak to support the doctrine: a strong version must be
located *ex ante*, and at the level of *wants*. Here, even in
utopia, identity of interests may have to be achieved by

teaching men what their 'real', not apparent, interests are; this was what Owen and Saint-Simon intended. Such education is feasible with a definition of 'interest' like Barry's (that which puts me in a better position to satisfy my wants, is in my interest)[32] which suggests that my interests are not merely what I consciously desire. But the concept of an identity of interests then becomes increasingly sophistical. The utopians do not prove that the identity of interests doctrine is objectively true, but cause it to become true by an authoritative re-definition of interest. Yet unlike Bentham, whose legislator would impose an artificial identity, the utopians insisted that identity would be natural.

The utopians advanced beyond the archetypally eighteenth-century ideal of a mechanical, unconscious equation of interests. Owen, Godwin and Saint-Simon offer moral reasons and material inducements for men to harmonise their interests actively which makes the process conscious and voluntaristic, not mechanical. But Saint-Simon argues that the pre-conditions for harmony are automatically generated in the productive process, and Fourier relies on totally mechanical equilibrium. *All* the utopians emphasize that self-interest will remain a driving force, albeit deflected from totally selfish goals. As Saint-Simon argues, 'egoism is essential to the security of organisms: every effort to combine the interests of individuals is a step in the right direction, but every argument of the moralists which tries to destroy egoism, is an error which is easily recognizable'.[33] This passage clarifies the difference, also implicit in Barry's formulation, between *interests*, which can be made identical, and self-interest, an individualistic force essential to society. The identity of interests doctrine appears most convincing when viewed in the light of the co-operative ethic, for, in specific projects, co-operation combines individual and general interests. But it is questionable whether it could apply throughout society, which is a complex structure. If the doctrine is to become true, it will have to be made so by utopia's social organisation.

These utopians attempt a fusion of the characteristics of what Weber called the 'aggregative relationships' of society constituted as a 'purely voluntary union based on self-interest', and the 'communal relationships' typical of a society based on subjectively felt solidarity and social cohesion.[34] The utopians accommodate and exploit self-interest, but their attempts to establish social cohesion and morality indicate that they consider communal relationships ideal. In Durkheim's terms, the utopias seek to realise both egoism and altruism simultaneously. The distinction between the two principles remains clear, and the vacillation between them signifies the incompatibility of their desire to explain the workings of society mechanically (i.e. scientifically) and their wish to run utopia according to idealistic principles. The utopians presented the identity of interests as a factual and scientific truth about men in utopia, whereas they were actually attempting a conceptual reconciliation of real social conflicts to convince readers that social harmony is possible, and control unnecessary. The doctrine was thus a powerful item in each utopian's ideological arsenal.

BONDS IN THE STRUCTURE OF UTOPIA

Certain structural features of the utopias which also promote social cohesion can be regarded as the parameters determining the forms which utopian organisation may take; they are determined by the conceptual structures favoured by the utopians.

Three interlinked concepts are those of *social rationality*, *consistency* and *homogeneity*. Owen attempted a critique of contemporary society in terms of its rationality, and found it wanting.[35] 'Irrational', applied to society, refers to aberrations such as inefficiency (the inappropriate matching of means and ends), injustice, hypocrisy (the use of double standards), inconsistency in the treatment of individuals, and the pursuit of short-term aims at the expense of long-term goals. Owen is not explicit about the connection between irrational beliefs and human misery. Nothing in his analysis of the intellect proves that merely exposing men to forms of irrationality can cause suffering, and the misery that he hated had primarily material causes. Undoubtedly, certain

kinds of inconsistency might be 'contrary to human nature'
as Owen believed: if men had to worship God and Mammon
on alternate Sundays, unendurable tension could result, so
that the irrationality of the system directly caused misery.[36]
But subtler inconsistencies may not distress people.

Must utopia therefore be rational, consensual and consistent? Certainly, its structure must be logically coherent in
terms of its own purposes, and it must be consistent so far as
that is necessary to promote justice. But is utopia bound to
foster consistency of values and behaviour? A pluralist
society necessarily fosters multiple, potentially inconsistent
value systems through its different institutions, which in
practice are mutually accommodating; such inconsistencies
can even be shown to be functional.[37] The utopians may be
wrong in thinking that inconsistencies produce a divergence
between individual and social interests. Living in a pluralistic
society entails playing different roles, perhaps displaying inconsistent behaviour, but this may in fact be more pleasurable than distressing. Godwin feared that the identity and
honesty of the individual would be threatened by such inconsistencies, and in making homogeneous society
axiomatic, he and Owen fail to see that cross-cutting loyalties
and values can lead to overall harmony. By contrast, Fourier
demonstrates that a plurality of dovetailing differences and
inconsistencies can generate cohesion as efficiently as uniformity. Homogeneity thus appears not to be a *sine qua non*
of utopia, although utopias are definitionally homogeneous
through their elimination of deviance by successful control.

The utopians assert the desirability of shared beliefs,
especially moral ones. Owen's utopia, by giving all children a
common education, would deliberately produce considerable
homogeneity of belief, knowledge and manners. Utopians
can hardly afford to promote diversity among their citizens
which might disrupt the social equilibrium; and diversity also
presents difficulties at the theoretical level. Homogeneity
sanctions universal behaviour assumptions, although controlled heterogeneity, such as Saint-Simon and Fourier
hypothesize, can also operate as a theoretical basis. *Prima
facie*, homogeneity is likely to engender consensus and social

cohesion most successfully, as Rousseau argued; the onus is therefore on the pluralist utopians to prove the feasibility of their own systems; as Fourier does.

Another premiss built into the structure of utopian societies is that men are interdependent. Rousseau was no doubt an intellectual influence here, for he emphasized the degradation which the dependency of man on man entails.[38] The solution of the *Social Contract*, the dependence of each on all, is echoed in Saint-Simon's writings, and is implicit in the other utopias. One form of fruitful and non-exploitative inter-dependence which the utopians advocate is economic co-operation. Of course, a conceptualisation of the structure of interpersonal relations, entailing some solution of the 'dependence vs. autonomy' debate, is a necessity for the social scientist. The utopians opted for a de-personalised, non-exploitative dependence which is mediated through society as a whole, and so contributes to harmonious integration.

Typical of the structure of utopias is the judicious *circumscription* of possibilities. A planned environment excludes the variety and unpredictability of unplanned life, and curtails some opportunities. In utopia, disharmonious and disruptive possibilities may be by definition excluded at the planning stage. Owen, for example, recommended the repeal of a number of enabling laws, especially the lottery and alcohol laws. Evidently, he judges that the permanent limitation of opportunities by diminishing the range of possibilities in utopia is a legitimate method of control. Undoubtedly, homogeneity, consistency and cohesion will be furthered by judicious circumscription.

Many utopians are seduced by the ideal of an *organic society*, in which the individual's roles and tasks are fully defined and integrated. For Fourier and Saint-Simon, this takes the form of a non-oppressive hierarchy. The concept of an organic state has been popular since Aristotle but the distinctive attribute of the utopians' organic ideal is that it was to rest on rational human characteristics and a logical hierarchy, not on the traditional stratification of power typifying the organic feudal epoch that many conservatives took as a prototype. Rational, co-operative organisation would produce a quasi-organic society within which individuals have pre-determined functional roles and tasks, proof against anomie.

Saint-Simon's class system, which he repeatedly likens to the human anatomy, is an overt expression of this predilection for organicism, as is Fourier's description of the 'integral soul'. Organicism can only ever be said to exist at a theoretical level since it rests on the analogy between society and a genuinely organic structure, and analogising is a mental activity. The theory of the organic utopia remains merely an analogy. Evidently, the nearer that utopia approaches perfect integration and coherence, the more properly can it be said to have an organic structure, but this predicate adds nothing to the reality of the social structure. Organicism is as much a persuasive as an analytical device.

Clearly, many of the structural characteristics of utopia (rationality, consistency, homogeneity, interdependence, organicity) which promote cohesion are themselves overlapping and mutually reinforcing: predictably so, since they are themselves derived from the underlying conceptual structure on which each utopia is based. This structural cohesion is as important for harmony as the control and socialisation processes.

The utopians' devices for eliminating conflict can be summarised as follows, in logical progression:

1. *Circumscription* of available possibilities for aberrant action. For example, the abolition of divisive institutions such as marriage and property; the prohibition of strong drink.
2. *Substitution* of rival patterns for anti-social behaviour. For example, substituting work for crime, free love for adultery.
3. *Organisation* — the appropriate structuring of society so as to eliminate divisions and conflict between members. For example, Saint-Simon's physiologically-based class society, which removes possibilities of comparison and envy.

4. *Extensive socialisation* E.g. peer-group socialisation, then education, then mutual dependence and surveillance in the co-operative work process, and so on.

In addition to these mechanisms, Saint-Simon and Fourier make an open bid for the hearts of their utopian citizens by planning public festivals and events that are obviously intended to increase the sense of communal solidarity and cohesion, so persuasion at the ideological level is also countenanced.[39]

CONTROL OR COHESION?

The utopians manifestly made ample provision for the control of conflict and the integration of society by means congruent with their various conceptions of human nature. Their proposals were influential: educationists developed Owen's ideas, Durkheim criticised but built on Saint-Simon's secular morality and notion of organic solidarity. The methods favoured were those suggested by man's rationality, educability, sociability and natural moral sense. The prevalence of morality or altruism in some of the utopias does not detract from their appeal to rationality, for morality was to become a positive science based on observation and calculation. Rejecting Christian morals, they de-emphasized piety and virtue, but dwelt on morality as a social instrument. Fourier's alluring account of self-abandonment to instinct is in fact a substitution of total organisation for partial control, an innovation which abolishes all the old categories.

It might be argued against the utopians that the legal system which they rejected has intrinsic advantages which would make it a useful utopian device. According to Hart, law 'is a method of social control which maximises individual freedom' since 'members of society are left to discover the rules and conform their behaviour to them'.[40] Another view, with conflicting consequences, is that law articulates the shared moral principles of a society and induces moral conformity and social cohesion. However, the theoretical freedom which the law allows is of no interest to

these utopians, whose societies necessarily limit and determine the possibilities of action. Nor is the law as the embodiment of social mores attractive, for they have devised other
means of achieving solidarity. Since institutions can be
changed so as to eradicate crime, legal methods can be
avoided altogether, although some substitutes, such as moral
surveillance, might prove even more rigorous and intrusive.

Control and cohesion might be separately categorised on
the grounds that control is externally imposed and cohesion
is the product of voluntary adherence. But this distinction is
overturned in the utopias, where many controls rest on
voluntary self-control and the mechanisms of cohesion are
impositions of the utopian designer. Control and cohesion
together constitute a seamless web in which utopian inhabitants are contentedly enmeshed. In this respect the utopias
are fully-determined models of social harmony.

The analysis demonstrates a basic divergence between the
theoretical structures of Saint-Simon and Fourier and those
of Owen and Godwin. The latter presume similarity among
men and construct, by deduction, simple, homogeneous,
egalitarian, consensual utopias where social cohesion results
from near-uniformity, as in Rousseau's ideal society. By
contrast, Fourier and Saint-Simon suppose human diversity,
which points to a complex and stratified social structure,
which is inevitably harder to systematise in social science
because of the multiplicity of variables. Both resort to the
organic analogy to fuse the strata into a cohesive whole. In
theory, then, there are two roads to social cohesion.

Empirical and theoretical work on communes and utopian
communities has an important bearing on the problem of
ideal control, especially Kanter's *Commitment and
Community*, which contains an exhaustive account of the
means whereby nineteenth-century and modern utopian
communities achieve cohesion. The 'commitment
mechanisms' of the early communities embraced all the
devices of utopian theory, including institutionalised mutual
criticism: this is no surprise, since many such communities
deliberately modelled themselves on these theories. Kanter
categorises the ideals of communal life as perfectibility,

harmony with nature, order, brotherhood (including communal property and work), unity of body and soul, deliberate experimentalism and subjective coherence as a group. These ideals too are in the theories, as is the pivotal assumption that 'in utopia what people want to do is the same as what they have to do'.[41]

Kanter measures the practice of utopian communities against their expressed idealities. The fact that these are voluntarily constituted groups, often formed in opposition to contemporary society, and having a siege mentality, leads them to emphasize *commitment*, the central theme of her analysis. As Abrams and McCulloch argue in *Communes, Sociology and Society*, communes and 'intentional communities' share this need, being 'essentially oppositional'. Today's communes often have a comfortable cushion of resources and tend to 'exclude the damaged, the disabled and the demanding'.[42] So voluntary communities, although requiring more positive commitment than utopia, can also avoid the problem of deviants and misfits, with which utopia must cope. Only Owen's transitional colonies would require the element of intentionality and commitment: the difference here between utopian theory and communitarian practice is that the communities are trying to achieve change, while utopian theories assume it. The former process needs active commitment, but automatic adhesion would suffice to maintain the achieved utopia, although subjective allegiance would be encouraged.

Many of today's (and yesterday's) utopian communities aim at extensive 'ego-abolition', and operate de-individuating mechanisms, but the commune movement seeks to establish individuality — hence 'personal growth' communes — and not to submerge the individual in the group. Taking a middle way between subordination and possessive individualism, they 'attempt to master the issue of identity through the practice of mutuality', but many collapse because of disruptive individualism. Although the utopians were individualistically inclined, notions of identity and individuality were less well-defined than they are today, perhaps because there had not yet been dehumanising régimes which make the assertion of individuality an imperative. The utopians saw the individual in terms of material needs to be satisfied by rectifying inequalities; 'mutuality' was to be attained by making interests identical, and personal growth and individual subordination were equally irrelevant to this process.

Kanter and others analyse communitarianism by applying their own sociological structures, and supplementing these with the expressed philosophies of the communities. Their studies impose frameworks of analysis on existing practices: the utopians, by contrast, were inventing practices simultaneously with developing theoretical analyses. The categories of their analyses are perhaps as old as community itself, but the manipulation of non-coercive varieties of control to produce spontaneously harmonising societies was an innovation which experimental communities have tried ever since to emulate, as Kanter's analysis suggests. In this respect, social harmony is more than an idealist invention: it is a goal attainable by specific devices.

What has been referred to throughout this analysis as 'social cohesion' would be termed 'consensus' by many modern theorists.[44] The literal meaning of consensus suggests a sharing of beliefs, and solidarity at the level of consciousness, which is not, however, a *necessary* condition for cohesion. Owen and Godwin intended to achieve consensus through the propagation of the identity of interests doctrine and other socialising propaganda, whereas Fourier expected to create an unconscious cohesion through the perfect dovetailing of desires and temperaments. For Saint-Simon, cohesion is largely non-consensual, being based on a coincidence of economic interests. On the narrow interpretation of consensus the two latter are somewhat deficient, but by solidarising *interests,* they have created the important material conditions for cohesion which must underlie a consensus of ideas.

References
1. E. P. Thompson, *op. cit.*, p. 277. See also E. Hobsbawm, *The Age of Revolution, 1798-1848.* (Weidenfeld & Nicholson, 1962), pp. 49-50. In the late 18th century a steady job was still exceptional, and skilled workers

would work until their income needs were satisfied. French itinerant factory hands would drift back to their shareholdings for the summer.

2. *Catéchisme*, p. 43.

3. H. Marcuse, *Eros and Civilisation*, (Sphere, 1969), ch. 4, and *One Dimensional Man* (Sphere, 1968), pp. 25-6.

4. *The Enquirer* (London, 1797), p. 171.

5. See Beecher and Bienvenu, pp. 122-50, for a compilation of Fourier's acute observations on unattractive labour.

6. See *L'Industrie*, t.i., pp. 128-30. Possibly these utopians have not entirely shaken off the biblical idea that work is man's curse.

7. Dautry makes a similar point: Saint-Simon's interest went *beyond* work, to the organisation of production, while Fourier's interest was at the psychological level. See 'La notion de travail chez Saint-Simon et Fourier', in *Journal de Psychologie*, LII (1955), pp. 59-76.

8. See, e.g., P. Lambert, *Studies in the Social Philosophy of Co-operation*, trans. J. Létargez (Publishers' Co-operative Union, Manchester, 1963).

9. *L'Organisateur*, p. 151, and *Suite à la Brochure*, p. 514.

10. RCL, pp. 231-2, 264.

11. HC, pp. 27ff, and *Six Lectures*, pp. 56-8. All the utopians were obsessed with canals and bridges, even Godwin, for obvious historical reasons.

12. See E. Yeo, 'Robert Owen and Radical Culture' in Pollard and Salt, *op. cit.*

13. See H. Desroches, 'Images and Echoes of Owenism in 19th century France' in Pollard and Salt, *op. cit.*, pp. 242, 246, and see also OC VI, p. 4. In England, Fourier's doctrine was known as Associationism.

14. OC VI, pp. 2-3, OC XI, pp. 320-1, and OC VII, pp. 461-4.

15. OC VI, pp. 6-8; and Beecher and Bienvenu, p. 202 and editor's note.

16. PJ II, pp. 501-506, especially p. 502.

17. As it is by M. Taylor: *Anarchy and Co-operation* (John Wiley, 1976), pp. 138-9.

18. PJ II, p. 499ff.

19. See OC VII, pp. 237, 276, 284, 461-4, for typically venomous attacks.

20. E. P. Thompson, *op. cit.,* p. 332ff.

21. Full details are given in OC X, p. 111ff. See also Beecher and Bienvenu, p. 262.

22. *Revolution*, p. 78. See also *Six Lectures*, p. 77.

23. *Social Contract*, pp. 113-4.

24. M. Banton, *The Policeman and the Community* (1964). Quoted in *The Sociology of Law*, ed. V. Aubert (Penguin, 1969), p. 301.

25. S. Wolin, *Politics and Vision* (Allen & Unwin, 1961), p. 301.

26. NVS, p. 103.

27. V. Pareto, in *The Mind and Society*. Quoted in B. Barry, *op. cit.,* p. 198.

28. These terms may be philosophically meaningless, as J. P. Plamenatz argues in *Consent, Freedom and Political Obligation* (Oxford U.P., 1938),

Ch. 3. Or they may simply be useless for guiding individuals in any course of action, though perhaps with some exhortative value. See also the concluding paragraph of J. R. Pennock, 'The One and the many' in *The Public Interest*, ed. J. R. Pennock (Lieber-Atherton, 1962).
29. *Lettre*, pp. 43-44, and *L'Industrie*, t.i., p. 188.
30. F. Perroux, *L'Industrie et Creation Collective* (Paris, 1964), Vol. I, p. 55.
31. *L'Industrie*, t.i., p. 238.
32. B. Barry, *op. cit.*, p. 183.
33. Markham, p. 9.
34. *Basic Concepts in Sociology*, M. Weber, trans. H. P. Secher (Peter Owen, 1962), p. 91.
35. Marcuse and Ivan Illich criticise contemporary society in similar terms. See Marcuse, *One Dimensional Man*, Ch. 6, and I. Illich, *Deschooling Society*, (Penguin, 1973), Ch. 5.
36. Orwell's dystopian parody of Soviet communism, *1984*, delineates a society in which the law of non-contradiction is suspended in this way by self-asserting re-definitions of crucial terms, such as the often quoted WAR IS PEACE, FREEDOM IS SLAVERY. Marcuse argues that similar distortions are taking place in capitalist society, *ibid.*, Ch. 4.
37. Studies in political science of cross-cutting cleavages may held such a refutation. See, e.g., H. Eckstein, *Division and Cohesion in Democracy* (Princeton U.P., 1966). For positive advocacy of multiple role-playing, see R. Dahrendorf, *Essays in the Theory of Society* (Routledge & Kegan Paul, 1968).
38. *Discourse*, p. 220. 'Social man lives constantly outside himself, and only knows how to live in the opinion of others.' There are extensive references to the ills of dependency in *Émile* also.
39. *L'Organisateur*, pp. 53-54. This is clearly influenced by the secular festivals of the French revolutionaries.
40. H. A. L. Hart, *Punishment and Responsibility* (Oxford U.P., 1968), p. 23, and *Concept of Law* (Oxford U.P., 1961), p. 38.
41. R. M. Kanter, *Commitment and Community* (Harvard U.P., 1972), p. 1.
42. P. Abrams and A. McCulloch, *Communes, Sociology and Society* (Cambridge U.P., 1976), Ch. 7 especially.
43. *Ibid.*, p. 202.
44. See P. H. Partridge, *Consent and Consensus* (Macmillan, 1971), especially Ch. 4 and the bibliography.

CHAPTER 6

UTOPIAN VALUES

VALUES have a multiple function in society, for they must encapsulate human aspirations while ministering to human weaknesses and limitations. They function crucially as ideological controls, endowed with quasi-moral content, directing activity to socially-desired ends. Evidently, the utopians' values are tailored to fit their views of the human predicament, as well as their aspirations to social perfection.

The primary utopian values are those operating in the utopian's own methodology, which structure his reasoning, or are explicitly acknowledged as dominant values. Other ideals may be openly displayed or dealt with at the level of polemical or ideological debate, as the utopians deal with liberty. The utopian's favoured values may either operate as part of the ideology with which utopian citizens are imbued or be built into the organisation of society from the start. However trustworthy men's natural morality and rationality, values are needed to galvanise them.

Harmony and happiness are the supreme values of these utopias, and their final goals. Supporting them are other instrumental values which are not derivable from harmony or happiness but which, according to the utopian's calculations, will promote their realisation within the given framework. The utopians frequently present their values and ideals as directly and scientifically derived from human nature, and so validated. Such values could not be disputed, they imagine.

The first section discusses the utopian's treatment of received political values and, in particular, of the nexus of liberal-democratic ideas to which they were so opposed. Then, the innovatory values of harmony and happiness are analysed in relation to the structure of utopia.

NO CHEERS FOR DEMOCRACY

Indisputably, the content of ideals is historically determined, and the utopians, philosophising about freedom, equality and democracy after the French Revolution, were compelled to reinterpret them in the light of its failure. Likewise, they set out to re-define these ideas in opposition to the increasingly prevalent values propagated by liberal democracy, which clothed its economic hard-headedness in romantic notions of the individual, freedom and equality.

The discussion of control in utopia raises questions about the nature of utopian freedom. Dare the close-knit utopian collectivity idealise freedom? Is freedom essential to happiness, and therefore to utopia? To answer these, a definition of freedom is necessary, to serve as a standard of comparison.

Three conditions can be formulated for the maximisation of freedom:

1. The opportunities for free action must be maximised by (a) the removal of restrictions and impediments (i.e. negative liberty) and (b) the creation of opportunities and choice (positive liberty).[1]
2. A social minimum of civil human rights must be established by law or convention.
3. External control and coercion must be minimised. External controls are excessively restrictive of freedom, detract from human dignity and autonomy, and entail the existence of a class of superior beings, the controllers.

These conditions chart an open-ended concept of freedom. It is impossible to determine a limiting point at which maximum freedom is reached and so the conditions can be interpreted as recommending ever-increasing liberation, and aspiration.

Godwin, despite his opposition to free will, approves of liberty as an ideal which glorifies mankind. (Liberty, for the determinist, is the placing of limitations on *which* causal factors are allowed to operate in society, e.g. the whims of the autocrat are prohibited, but rational self-control is permitted.) Liberty as self-control and the absence of restraint is inextricably connected with the exercise of private judgement.

Godwin emphasises freedom primarily as a liberation of mind which may resolve the seeming paradox between his individualism and his utilitarianism, for such freedoms as freedom from unjustifiable beliefs and prejudices might indeed co-exist with conformist utilitarian social behaviour. Godwin also makes freedom necessary to happiness and refuses to endorse the happiness of the contented slave as valid, maintaining that we must strive to disabuse and illuminate him.[2] This argument is a necessary corollary of his views on truth and sincerity.

Owen's approach to liberty is brisk, assertive but equivocal: he advocates 'the utmost individual freedom of action compatible with the permanent good of society'.[3] The voluntary nature of his colonies means that the formal elements of restriction are slight, but the organisation of the colonies themselves circumscribes individual development, and the Institution for the Formation of Character undermines the freedom *not* to be formed.

Saint-Simon, like a *laissez-faire* liberal, insists on the economic basis for freedom: 'what is liberty? It is the free development, both physical and spiritual, of industry, it is production'.[4] He remarks that liberalism only represents sentiments, not interests, and must be superseded by interest-based industrialism.[5] He condemns the liberal espousal of formal political and economic liberties which ignores the material conditions necessary for the exercise of those liberties: 'the basis of liberty is industry'. He attacked the individualistic ideal of liberty as being divisive and destructive of co-operation and harmony. But a new interpretation of freedom makes its debut: it is an active ideal, the freedom for self-development and fulfilment, and he infuses into the term the typically socialist meaning of the self-realisation of *homo faciens*. For the *industriels* liberty 'is not to be hindered in their productive work, and not to be bothered in the enjoyment of what they have produced.'[6]

Fourier is vehement about the need to remove the real obstacles to freedom, hence his advocacy of the social minimum. More acidly than Saint-Simon, he disposes of bourgeois liberal values. 'By these words, "natural rights", I do not mean the chimeras known by the names of liberty, equality. The poor man does not aspire so high'.[7] The chimeras were to be replaced by a new conception of total freedom, located in the psychological plane. 'Each man gives himself over to the frank instincts of nature pure and simple'[8] which offers defiance to the psychological repression of Civilisation. This passionate liberation will engender maximum scope for individual action (Condition 1.) although it connotes no formal freedoms (2.) and is opposed to self-control (3.), which Fourier denigrated.

No method of keeping order is necessary in the phalanstery, but the minute-by-minute organisation of the phalansterians' time may be restricting. Marcuse asserts that Fourier 'hands (society) over to a giant organisation and administration and thus retains the repressive elements'.[9] But activity will be based on voluntary inclination, and group organisation and co-operative work are natural and automatic. Contrary to appearances, Fourier maintains, man is not naturally lazy, and passionate attraction provides the necessary stimulus to work.

How do the utopians' accounts of liberty measure up to the three criteria? They expressly minimise the extent of political authority, and espouse quasi-anarchistic social forms which enhance negative liberty. There is also total agreement on the need to maximise opportunities for individual development, *according to chosen criteria*. The formal political rights valued by the *philosophes* and French revolutionaries were disdained by the utopians, and rendered superfluous by the abolition of the political sphere as such. As to Condition 3, the methods of control replacing law emphasize self-control: private judgement, rationality and morality minimise external control.

How do the utopians' social blueprints, as opposed to their theoretical statements, measure up to the three conditions? The formidable list of utopian controlling agencies includes some which would short-circuit the rational process, and stunt the individual's capacity for choice: also the structure of a planned society limits the objective conditions for choice. All chosen options exclude rival plans, as the essence of decision taking *is* such exclusion. But at least with societies modelled on human nature the exclusion of opportunities is not random, but optimal.

Saint-Simon's class system might be thought particularly inimical to freedom since it limits the scope of action of members of each class, by predetermining their occupations. But freedom is not restricted by laws which men do not desire to break: similarly, if men's desires *are* rooted in their physical characteristics as Saint-Simon believes, the limitation of the possibilities would not curb the freedom of individuals to enact their preferred class roles.

The diminution of external control and increase of self-control should augment freedom, unless involuntary self-control is induced by methods such as Skinnerian conditioning, or the fear created by a hell-fire religion, for then external control and internal irrationality prevail. The self-control on which the utopians (except Fourier) rely is not an imposed inhibition, but a rational policy which each man formulates for himself. But self-generated self-control, completely free from external influence, is a contradiction and the persuasive content of the utopians' rationality and morality is clear.

Freedom has been variously represented as the *sine qua non* and as the antithesis of happiness by adherents of different ideologies. Liberals built freedom into the definition of happiness, and did not explore the possible dichotomy between the concepts. Others did: conservatives, theologians and advocates of totalitarianism have all argued that man is unable to support or endure total freedom. Freedom has often been correlated with uncertainty, disorder and unhappiness by some psychologists, although others idealise the psychological effects of freedom. Fromm deplores the 'fear of freedom', the human desire for security and authority, and advocates freedom because of the moral virtue attached to the act of choice. 'Free man is by necessity insecure; thinking man by necessity uncertain.'[10]

The juxtaposition of such conflicting and tangential arguments is inconclusive, but some relevant points can be made. Firstly, there is the compelling argument stated by the utopians, that freedom is useless to those without the means to benefit from it. Their concern with the material conditions to make freedom meaningful explains their lack of interest in civil rights. A point at which freedom and happiness diverge was illustrated in Diagram 2.2b: happiness is achieved despite a diminution of choice if men are deprived of the *conception* of possibilities outside their grasp, or alienated from these, as might happen in a utopian society. This fails to maximise freedom in two ways, but may successfully promote happiness. Thirdly, even free men may 'misuse' their liberty and become miserable. Utopia must strike a balance between freedom and guidance.

The connection of happiness and freedom partly consists in the pleasure of knowing oneself to be free, which in turn seems to be a culture-specific pleasure, for it is possible to envisage a free and happy society with no theory of individual freedom. Predictably, utopia would gradually supersede the idealisation of personal and 'felt' freedom as redundant ideology while maintaining the conditions for freedom.

The utopians, sceptical of liberal values, sought a new approach to freedom. Their first innovation was the devaluation of *choice*, a market value beloved of liberals, which they distinguish from freedom. Harmonious organisation necessarily restricts choice. The devaluation of choice is also entailed by the determinist position common to the utopians. The extent to which environment precludes courses of action for each individual makes it absurd to idealise the remaining areas of choice and call them 'free'. Such a definition of freedom is riddled with inconsistencies. For Godwin freedom of choice would anyway be an arbitrary, capricious ideal.

The utopians' new approach to negative freedom consists of a fierce radical attack on political authority and repression. For Godwin and Owen, the eradication of ignorance, superstition and irrationality are essential, while Saint-

Simon, Fourier and Owen destroy the economic base of un-freedom through the creation of abundance. Instinctual freedom is Fourier's ideal.

The new definition of positive liberty is self-realisation, usually through work: for Saint-Simon, the development of the creative capacity, for Fourier, the free play of the passions, and for Owen, the 'fullest exercise of all the faculties'. Godwin viewed freedom more cerebrally, as individual autonomy and leisure for intellectual self-development. Freedom seen in these ways furthered human perfection. The utopian socialists thus confronted the liberal definition of freedom as non-interference with a new definition: creative activity.

With the new definition of freedom, social harmony is compatible with individual freedom whereas if freedom is made synonymous with choice, it is incompatible. If freedom is defined as the absence of coercion, the harmonious state is ideally free since it outlaws coercive methods. And if freedom is equated with self-realisation as in these utopias, harmony can be so constituted as to promote this ideal.

> Equality is poison in harmony (Fourier)
> It is impossible not to see the beauty of
> equality. (Godwin)[11]

The utopians inherited several superficially conflicting attitudes to equality. The view that men should have sufficient means to make them independent, since dependency leads to inequality and servitude, is expounded in Rousseau's *Discourse* and echoed by Godwin. Egalitarians such as Morelly and Restif de la Bretonne established equality of property but preserved social hierarchies. A more revolutionary interpretation was Babeuf's advocacy of absolute equality, which gave rise to Fourier's fears of enforced, inappropriate uniformity.

On the other side were those who held that inequality was vital to the structure and quality of society, as indeed were vices and dishonesty, and Godwin criticised Mandeville and Hume for such arguments.[12] Saint-Simon and Fourier, who followed the inegalitarian school, thought inequality of talent and reward was productive, and compatible with social justice.

The considerable variations in the utopians' attitudes to equality can be directly traced to their analyses of human nature. Godwin postulates a Babouvian premiss, 'that man and man are beings of the same nature, and are susceptible, under certain limitations, of the same advantages'[13]. This leads him to advocate the abolition of property, though by consent rather than by decree. The economic independence resulting from equality will bring greater independence of mind and greater intellectual equality. But his theory of equality seems to be inconsistent with his arguments on the moral deserts of individuals. Again, Godwin the moralist and Godwin the radical political theorist are at odds, and the difference is never resolved.

Owen's attack on private property is as vehement as Godwin's: 'private property is one of the great demoralising and repulsive powers, arising from the laws of men, and is the cause of innumerable crimes and gross injustices; as well as of selfishness and callousness'.[14] Owen advocates 'a just and pure equality' which extends to wealth, status and political power. Human malleability alone does not directly entail equality, but diversity among individuals in aggregate 'produces a perfect equality of rights, privileges and happiness among all of the human race'.[15] In Owen's communities, workers will be paid in kind, and class divisions and hierarchies will disappear.

The utopian protagonists of inegalitarianism are Fourier and Saint-Simon, who see inequality as inherent in the varieties of human temperaments and physiologies. Inequalities of talent divorced from wealth and privilege will not be socially divisive, but productive. Fourier states 'if this scale of inequalities did not exist, it would have to be created', and that 'man has an instinctual aversion to equality and a penchant for hierarchical patterns' (sic).[16] Ordered inequalities abound in harmony but they promote wellbeing. There would be a gradual, but not total, redistribution of wealth. Admitting divergent needs and capacities, Fourier's society nevertheless rests on equality of treatment and satisfaction, and hence — despite Fourier's intentions and protestations — cannot be called thoroughly inegalitarian. Each man works until he is tired and feeds until he is satisfied.

Saint-Simon establishes equality of treatment and satisfaction within a stratified society and considers the industrial society to be truly egalitarian, as co-operation is an egalitarian venture. 'The industrial system is founded on the principle of perfect equality; it is opposed to the establishment of any rights of birth, and even any kind of privilege'.[17] This is not the absolute, levelling egalitarianism of the revolutionaries, for his society will be governed by a hierarchy of talent. The principle of equality of treatment will be distributive: 'each man obtains a degree of importance, and benefits, proportional to his capacities and resources; this constitutes the highest degree of equality which is possible and desirable'.

The intimate connection of equality with justice makes it desirable that utopia should be egalitarian, although if everyone can be given a feeling of the incomparability of his own role, relative deprivation can be prevented. Fourier's society achieves this by promoting change and mobility, and Saint-Simon's physiological class structure might also achieve this: where comparisons are impossible, envy cannot exist. Upon the premiss of human diversity can be constructed a society which promises equal contentment for all, so that equality is achieved in that most important area of utopian policy, human happiness. Eventually the question becomes empirical: is inequality really rooted in human nature to the extent that Fourier and Saint-Simon suggest?

'Equality' generally relates to the quantitative distribution of resources and cannot be a *part* of human nature because it cannot characterise an individual, just as equivalence can be the property of one isolated number. The idea of equality is essentially an intellectual pattern against which social phenomena can be measured. Several objections can be made against simple distributive equality as an ideal: men have different tastes and different abilities to benefit from opportunities, and may indeed enjoy 'distinction', i.e. be averse to equality, as Fourier suggests. Furthermore, the structured organisation of complex societies leads to inequalities of power, and the division of labour allocates some individuals less pleasant and remunerative work.

Against these anti-egalitarian predispositions of men and organisations, the egalitarian must resort to measures which follow an indirectly egalitarian principle, as do the seemingly inegalitarian utopians. Men's different consumptive and productive capacities must be equally satisfied, by differential measures if necessary. Even the love of distinction can be diverted from acquisitiveness into public-spirited actions, if society honours such actions, as Godwin proposes.[18] As remedies for the inequalities rooted in the social structure, society can be re-organised so as to eradicate inegalitarian hierarchies and the work patterns can be changed so as to eliminate unpleasant labour, or offer compensating rewards.

Taking 'equality of treatment' as an operational principle leads to unpredictable results, an indefinable outcome, whereas 'equal shares' means that the outcome is predictable, a perfect procedural justice and pure procedural justice.[19] Evidently, the greater the diversity which the utopians admit in human nature, the more purely procedural and the less specifiable must their egalitarian solutions become. Fourier and Saint-Simon are not espousing injustice but acknowledging these realities in adopting procedurally egalitarian policies although they do not lead to uniformity of results, whereas Godwin and Owen are attempting to achieve uniform equality through perfect procedural egalitarian policies. For the utopians, all individuals are equally deserving of happiness, and equally capable of pleasure. Their policies take need as a basis for distribution which entails considerable redistribution of property (if not equalisation) and the rendering of residual differences of wealth socially unimportant: their abolition of private property is thus consequent upon their perception of human needs and human equality, rather than upon any analysis of exploitation.

Individualism for the social theorist is partly an epistemo-

logical assumption, partly a value, partly a policy orientation. The function of individualistic doctrines varies
accordingly, and depending on which human qualities the
individualism rests. Three varieties of individualism, current
in the utopians' time, can be distinguished.

1. *Political and legal individualism* defined the individual
   as the bearer of political and legal rights. Being concerned to delineate the position of the individual versus
   the state, it erased the differences between individuals
   and conceived of them abstractly.
2. *Capacity-regarding individualism* credited men with
   active capacities which are valued for their contribution
   to society. In *Representative Government*, J. S. Mill
   portrays men as universally rational, active and
   educable. Society is seen in terms of the functioning of
   individuals, and such individualism supports theories of
   participatory democracy.
3. *The concern for individuality*, exemplified by Mill in
   On Liberty, rests on the differentiating qualities of
   individuals. The emphasis on individuality may have
   adverse effects on social organisation, as it reduces conformist behaviour.[20]

Clearly, different forms of individualism derive from
different analyses of human nature and morality. The
utopians vociferously attacked the selfishness which
masqueraded as individualism under *laissez-faire*, and
political individualism was of as little interest to them as
politics itself. As for individuality, as was argued with
reference to communes, the utopians lacked the conception
of unique personal value on which this rests; in any case,
individuality cannot easily be accommodated to a scientific
model of society. However, capacity-regarding individualism is an orientation which they readily adopted,
although capacities were to be turned to social, not political,
uses.

In addition, the utopians all shared the concern with the
individual in respect of his needs and wants, given that their
ultimate aim was human happiness, and they adhere to what

is best termed *want-regarding individualism*, which emphasises man's need for material and spiritual satisfaction, born of his rational and sensual faculties, and prescribes for the satisfaction of the resulting wants. The distinction between human wants and capacities may vanish under close scrutiny, but their social functions undoubtedly differ, and the two kinds of individualism influence different aspects of social theory. The utopians therefore treat individuals variously as active bearers of capacities, and as passive candidates for satisfaction. The latter emphasis produces the want-regarding individualism intrinsic to most utopianism. This orientation is not tantamount to absolute surrender to the whims of self-interest, because implicit in the utopian's theories is the notion of *reasonable* wants and needs: no wants would be regarded which encroached on the integrity of other individuals or harmed them.

Owen's premiss of human malleability has an ambiguous connection with individualism, for it does not single out attributes on which an individualistic doctrine can be posited. On the contrary, the notion of adaptability may support a state-centred theory and the subordination of the individual to the organisation. Owen might thus be accused of undermining man's 'individuality' by his emphasis on malleability, but he maintains a policy of want-regarding individualism not logically deduced from the premiss, by elevating perceived wants in contemporary society to the status of universal wants. In fact, the utopian determinist *must* logically espouse want-regarding individualism temporarily: if individuals cannot change their wants, what else can utopia do but satisfy them?

The idea of equality seems to govern all versions of individualism, even the concern for individuality, for it dictates that we should not value one man's individuality in excess of another's; equal treatment or consideration seems to be the basis of consistent individualism, of whatever kind. The concepts are logically separable, but equality is a limiting value. Individualism is instrumental in the creation of a hedonistic utopia whose perfection turns on personal happiness. The utopians do not explicitly glorify the individual as J.S. Mill does or as communitarians glorify personal growth: they are concerned simply with the qualities which make men capable of happiness and useful to society. Yet in effect they create opportunities for the development of the individual as well as the satisfaction of his immediate, felt needs.

Why, when revolutionaries and liberals were clamouring for democratic self-government and popular sovereignty, did democratic institutions and values play only a minor role in these utopias? It can partly be explained by the utopians' hostility to government as such, partly to their disillusionment with the attempts at popular rule in the years after the Revolution. But, crucially, there is innate antipathy between the basic principles of democracy and the conditions necessary to utopia which makes the two incompatible. Hostility to government caused the utopians to search for other ways of ordering their societies and consequently makes them uninterested in democratic methods. The utopians comprehended the reinforcing connections between, for example, government, the law and the Church, and intended to abolish these mutually supportive institutions simultaneously.

The entry under 'Government' in Godwin's index runs '. . . its negative character . . . the evils of political society . . . founded on ignorance . . . the enemy of change . . . no scheme of government perfect or final . . . abstractedly considered, an evil . . . all government a tyranny . . . no more than individuals, infallible'. His main objections rest on the wrongness of coercion and the encroachment on individual independence which governments attempt, although their only legitimate tasks are to prevent injustice and invasion.[21] Saint-Simon argued that government was outdated, and entailed the power of men over men, with corresponding possibilities of abuse and humiliating dependency. The 'administration of *things*' will be impersonal, incorruptible and minimal.

Of the utopians, only Godwin enthuses about democracy, praising it by contrast with other conventional forms of government, as a lesser evil. He admires the spirit of *ideal* democracy, which 'restores to man a consciousness of his value, teaches him, by the removal of authority and oppression, to listen only to the suggestions of reason, gives him confidence to treat all other men with frankness and simplicity',[22] but condemns the practical aspects, and the vices of parliament.

Public deliberation is valuable in itself, but private judgement must prevail: 'when the deliberation is over, (the individual) finds himself as much disengaged as ever. If he conform to the mandate of authority, it is either because he individually approves it, or from a principle of prudence'.[23] So Godwin disposes of political obligation and solves the paradox of democracy! The self-government which *he* idealises lies in the sovereignty of the individual over himself, to which democracy is but a poor approximation, despite Rousseau.

Saint-Simon's views typify the post-Revolutionary distrust of Rousseau. Direct democracy failed because of the mob's ignorance and inability to perform the duties of citizenship. In consequence, he pleads for elite government by those well-versed in positive knowledge. Or, as Talmon interprets, 'it having been proved that popular sovereignty has no better claim to legitimacy than divine right of Kings or the Apostolic succession, and being more costly, more wasteful and more erratic than they, we have to recognise that legitimacy is acquired from competence'.[24]

Saint-Simon echoes Rousseau, finding the necessary basis of an ideal, world-wide community in 'conformity of institutions, unity of interests, agreement of maxims, community of morals and of public education'.[25]

Fourier's attitude to self-government is similar to his attitude to self-control: when the passions are liberated, neither will be necessary. He has often been classified as a wayward imitator of Rousseau, but Lichtheim indicates the point of divergence. 'Fourier had seen too much of early capitalism to regard popular sovereignty in the Rousseauist sense as a panacea . . . In a sense he may be said to have become a socialist because he had no faith in democracy.'[26] Fourier denied the possibility of a homogeneous egalitarian society, Rousseau's pre-condition for direct democracy, and insisted on the permanence of a plurality of desires. Yet it has been argued by Talmon that the phalanstery is 'calculated to create and realise the conditions of genuine direct democracy' since members know each other, have a free and equal vote, and usually agree unanimously.[27] But in fact, 'democracy' in the phalanstery is instinctive and involuntary, not intellectual and deliberative: the daily business of the Exchange (which Talmon might liken to a democratic assembly) is conducted through intrigue, cabalism and factions, not democratic processes. Furthermore, the language of democracy is entirely absent from Fourier's theory and government is reduced to a co-ordinating mechanism. Owen's communities, based on 'a complete reciprocity of interests, should be governed by themselves, upon principles that will prevent divisions, oppositions of interests, jealousies'. The education system will raise each individual to a high level of competence and so guarantee the essential condition for 'a pure democratic government, of a just and practical equality, that will not require any election to offices'. Official posts are to be filled *by rota* it seems — a feasible procedure if all are well-educated — and the governing body will be composed of senior members. Rotation embodies safeguards absent from an elective system, for the rulers soon become subject to the consequences of their own administration.[28] Alas, contemporaries of Owen such as Lovett suggested that his own overbearing behaviour betrayed his professed ultra-democratic ideals.

Liberal democracy, with which these utopias contrast so sharply,[29] can be descriptively defined as follows: a method of deciding the aims and policies of a society in which every capable member of the community has an equal chance to voice his opinion, usually through a representative. Clearly, both the mechanism and a set of social and political values contribute to the complete, evaluative theory of liberal democracy. Liberal democracy holds that each man is best equipped to look after his own interests; political equality is the precondition for this, and associated conditions are freedom of thought and action, an individualistic ethos and justice, which also become democratic values. Political life is considered important, even valuable, *per se*. Democratic theory boasts that its system is flexible, that change and adaptation can occur when public opinion dictates it.

Even when the utopians seem to espouse democratic ideals and methods they invariably change the nature of the concept. Where lie the general differences between a democratic and a utopian community? Comparison suggests that the differences are fundamental and structural. Essentially, utopia is committed to a final solution, democracy is not, and many of the other distinctions relate to this quasi-metaphysical divergence. Differences also spring from differing views of human nature, and hence, of what constitutes human good. Democracy presupposes that men are by nature enquiring and rational, and claims to develop these attributes, which constitutes one kind of human good. But Owen, Fourier and Saint-Simon consider that human nature is fulfilled through creative activity, not through nugatory political participation. Although those human qualities pivotal for democracy, such as rationality and educability, are also utilised by the utopians, they are made to function in non-political contexts, and the emphasis on perfectibility and malleability imparts to human nature a dynamic dimension which might jeopardise democracy. The concept of the general good in a democracy is a complex notion in which values like liberty and justice are included, but of which a substantial element is left open and uncertain, to be determined at particular times by the will of the people. Essentially, democracy offers men the opportunity to debate and deliberate upon the nature of good and happiness: the question is left open, and the answer may change, as may the means of achieving the good. But the utopians derive definitions of human good from their analyses of human nature, and design societies specific to the achievement of these goods, in the certainty of the rightness of their vision.

Typically, utopian societies do not need democratic assemblies for policies are determined by the utopian designer, who creates a perfect system. The motif of a prophet or a revelation, which occurs in many utopias, makes dispute over the forms of organisation into heresy. In any case, no debate should be necessary, because utopians claim that their schemes embody the truth, and will therefore gain instant acclaim from all rational men. So, the organisation of utopia, resting on the true principles of human happiness, can suffer no correction or improvement.

The absence of debate about social policy correlates with the atrophy of government, and with its conversion to administration, a goal of all the nineteenth-century utopias. Administration appears a desirable method because it excludes the strife and dishonesty of politics and simply implements agreed policies. Saint-Simon argues that the industrial system under *laissez-faire* is peaceful and self-regulating. Durkheim elaborates, 'where economic relations form the basis of communal life, social unity is above all the rest of a solidarity of interests . . . governmental forms are reduced to a minimum.[30] After the replacement of institutional controls by mutual and self-control, the residual administration retains few of the characteristics of government, and little of the idealism of democracy. But an important consequence of minimising government and policy is that a state of petrified perfection will obtain in the ideal society, without possibility of change. This is the antithesis of democracy in the Rousseauesque and Madisonian tradition, which was potentially revolutionary, and always open-ended, offering opportunities for change within wide but idealistic parameters. In democracy, consensus needs extend only to the political machinery and the parameters,[31] but from the inception of utopia consensus must extend to the whole of social organisation.

One undemocratic method of government with a long utopian history is government by nonpolitical experts or meritocratic government. Its proponents justify it on the grounds of expediency and efficiency: since the 'general good' is a sophisticated concept, beyond the ordinary citizen's understanding, there is a strong case for dispossessing him of his political powers and vesting them in experts. Democracy intentionally endures the inefficiency that its methods breed in order to preserve its ideals, but many utopians are committed neither to these ideals, nor to the liberal-democratic perspective which engenders them, and so are free to opt for expertise and efficiency, as did Saint-Simon in his scientific-industrial government.

Characteristics intrinsic to utopian theory render utopia and democracy antithetical: for example, utopia is necessarily changeless and circumscribed, often a-historical and almost invariably a- or anti-political. The nature of utopia prevents a special value being placed on freedom of choice, since the ideal solution to all dilemmas has been found, whereas democracy institutionalises freedom of choice in the area of policy-making. These differences can ultimately be located at the level of epistemology. Most utopians since Plato, and certainly those considered here, adhered to absolutist epistemologies, which lent their utopian theories an absolute validity in their terms; as a result, utopia has the appearance of being a closed system, and the utopian — often unjustly — is branded as totalitarian. (A successful escape may be made via a theory of historical development, *vide* Saint-Simon and Marx, but not Fourier). By contrast, the starting point of the democratic theorist is an empirical and experimental (i.e. relativist) epistemology, and the structure of democracy is correspondingly open-ended. Democracy is, in the final analysis, an idealised process of conflict resolution of which the harmonious utopia has no need since conflict is to be eliminated at source.

If these utopias are antipathetic to classical democracy, they might be thought to have more in common with modern democratic theory, which relies on the existence of a wide consensus in favour of the system and its ideals (as does utopia) and confines policy debates within these agreed limitations, and encourages the acquiescent population to withdraw from the political arena.[32] But the new democratic theories are still essentially political, while utopian theory is fundamentally *social*, and dwells on aims such as the development of a close-knit community, goodwill between men and personal satisfaction, which are beyond the scope of modern democratic theory.

The language of liberal democracy and *laissez-faire* was the medium which surrounded the utopians and against which they reacted strongly and unequivocally. As a consequence of their rejection of democracy, they preferred socialist versions of the political ideals which liberal democracy had interpreted in such a formalistic and individualistic spirit: liberty as self-realisation, not self-advancement, and equality of treatment, not a crude numerical equality blind to human differences. They reconciled the collective ideal with individualism by developing want-regarding individualism and postulating abundance. Democracy as an ideal was discarded (being merely a second-best method which resolves, but cannot eliminate, social differences) or transformed — e.g. Owen's rota system — but often government by a 'natural elite' was preferred.

Since political values are under discussion, it may finally be asked how the utopians proposed to deal with the age-old problem of political obligation. Although the etiolated and primarily political notion of obligation was of little interest to them, the utopians in fact devised numerous methods of procuring obedience, and their most powerful instrument was the Good Life itself. They had no need of traditional contractual or consensual devices, which make indirect appeal to the reason and intellect through the concept of rights and duties, for *pleasure* makes a direct appeal to the senses and self-interest, to the intellect, and a happy society exacts obedience without the mediation of quasi-moral devices.

HAPPINESS AND HARMONY RULE

Berlin has argued that 'the belief in the possibility (or probability) of happiness as the product of rational organisation . . . is the heart of all the utopias'.[33] If so, utopian theory flatly contradicts Freud's assertion that 'happiness is not a cultural value' and so cannot be the goal of social organisation. Happiness in fact features in these utopian theories as a primary ideal which directs the analysis. Admittedly, the 'general good' is also the professed goal of most political theory, but the concept is too often used as an anodyne general justification, and individual happiness may yield to macro-values such as efficiency, nationalism, solidarity — values utopia would consider secondary or instrumental. But the utopians try to analyse the nature of this *summum bonum*, a process intimately bound up with their perceptions of human nature and destiny.

The utopians' view of what constitutes happiness have been referred to throughout this analysis, and need not be reiterated here, particularly as they are fairly pedestrian, with the exception of Fourier's novel theory. Saint-Simon and Godwin have a basically individualist approach to happiness, while the other two have a collectivist approach, as Owen's much-quoted dictum about interdependence suggests. Over and above the maximisation of individual happiness, the phalanstery offers the hyper-perfection of the 'integral soul'. There are both consumption-based and activity-based elements in each utopian's definition of happiness, and personal development and social participation appear to various extents in each theory. Clearly, this fundamental value eludes precise definition, although we might agree with Owen that 'man is born with a desire to obtain happiness, which desire is the primary cause for all his actions'.[34] Happiness has to comprehend pleasures of reason and of sense, and the wellbeing of society as well as individual contentment, although the concept of general happiness is parasitic on that of individuals, since happiness is subjectively-felt wellbeing.

One innovatory theme is the utopians' insistence on the connection between knowledge, truth and happiness. This, and their emphasis on the mastery of nature, may be dismissed as a product of nineteenth-century scientific pride, but it also suggests that understanding and control of the environment are necessary conditions for human wellbeing. Saint-Simon acknowledges this explicitly, and Fourier and Owen also wish to control animate and inanimate nature.[35] Understanding counters alienation from the phenomenal world, and the exploitation of natural resources also provides active and consumptive satisfaction. In terms of this analysis, these also signify the endeavour to achieve flawless harmony by assimilating a menacing portion of the phenomenal world, Nature, into the part which is man-made and under-control, Society.

Some utopias treat individuals as candidates for satisfaction while society, as the mere agent of satisfaction, is reduced to a subordinate role. In these utopias, a contrasting emphasis on creative and productive activity indicates the individual's duty to society as a whole, and counter-balances the passive definition of happiness as consumption. They progress beyond the 'gastronomic utopias' by reconciling a high standard of living with a high quality of life. The medieval celebration of the act of satisfaction was no doubt appropriate in situations of relative scarcity where religion raised deprivation to the status of a virtue. Likewise, the legitimation of needs was correlated with the beginnings of industrial capitalism which offers plenty (at a price) and relies on consumer demand for the impetus of its own development.

The consumer man of these utopians is unlike the market man of liberal economic theory, however. His rationality is a quasi-moral quality, not one which directs his every action towards profit, and he is far from being the abstraction or cipher to which market man is reducible. Saint-Simon and Fourier acknowledge individuality in consumption patterns and are adept at solving the problem of the tension of the particular and the general which plagues a satisfaction-orientated utopia.

Activity is at a premium in these utopias, and since achievement and reward stand in a non-exploitative relation to each other the secondary enjoyments of consumption will not be tainted with injustice. The characterisation of *homo faciens* allows the utopians to assert that socially necessary work will be performed willingly, and that abundance is attainable. But their greatest innovation was to remove happiness from the philosophical limbo of 'the general good' and place it in the realm of concrete detail. Happiness thus became a meaningful socio-political ideal and could be located in the social minimum, the development of knowledge, the exercise of capacities and the satisfaction of passions. These suggest policies for the promotion of happiness and internal standards for measuring the success of these policies.

Fourier alone has a revolutionary vision of happiness, and a total commitment to its realisation. 'That which gives pleasure to several people without harming anybody is always a good.'[36] He accords to the immediate satisfaction of the passions a value far greater than that with which he credits the accumulated achievements of Civilisation. The triumph of the pleasure principle, so maligned by Freud, in Fourier's utopia constitutes a revolution which entails the rejection of the whole structure of Civilisation, which he asserts is built on sacrifices and deprivations justified by the perverse achievement ethic, and hypocritical morality. Achievement-directed activities are absent from the phalanstery for each activity constitutes its own goal because of the passionate satisfaction intrinsic to it. The aggregation of short-term individual satisfactions produces long-term collective wellbeing.

The *summum bonum* for Fourier is the liberation of the instincts. He chooses the pleasure principle and rejects the reality principle, along with its benefits. 'Repellent work' in Civilisation shows the reality principle at its worst, while in the phalanstery work is reclassified as *play* under the pleasure principle. Reading Fourier's account of Harmony is like reading *Civilisation and its Discontents* backwards. The shift from reality to the pleasure principle means the end of sublimation and the reclaiming of the instinctual gratification which had to be renounced as a condition for civilisation. The end of sublimation and delayed gratification may however entail the atrophy of intellectual and scientific enterprises which require a prolonged time-scale. Presumably another consequence would be the loss of our conceptions of time, continuity, progress and achievement, which give society its subjective, historical identity, since such conceptions rest on experiences of delay and achievement which instant gratification will preclude. But the reign of the pleasure principle generates unprecedented forms of happiness, and for his revelations of delight Fourier can be acclaimed as the utopian who offered the profoundest and most revolutionary analysis of pleasure, and whose utopia came nearest to ideality.

Among the instrumental utopian values promoting happiness is expertise. The role of the expert in Saint-Simon's utopia is the Enlightenment's deification of knowledge. If knowledge is man's most precious possession, the *savants* must be the leaders of men: so the argument flows easily from the approbation of expertise to the advocacy of meritocracy. The connection has long been typical of utopian thought, for Plato's Republic and Magnesia were meritocracies. The confidence in expertise does not constitute the humiliating dependency which Saint-Simon deplored in other contexts. Although his scheme constitutes a rejection of democratic politics, it represents an avowedly idealistic approach to problems of power. Fourier's Harmony makes appropriate use of the inherent superior skills, experience and wisdom of individuals by giving them special advisory roles. 'By natural right and common consent, the more sophisticated personality types take charge of the administration of three or four phalanxes.'[37]

However, the elevation of expertise and a meritocratic arrangement of society may lead to evils unsuspected by the utopians. The utopians approved of expertise because they did not envisage the now lamented divorce between knowledge and application which diminishes the control of the experts over the use to which their discoveries are put. Also, they mistakenly held that *by definition* the application of knowledge by rational experts would benefit mankind. But science may be put to anti-social uses, and the ruling experts may develop different interests from those of the people, a favourite theme of dystopian novels. The utopians' only safeguard is the necessary goodness of wise men, another version of the fallacy, dating from Plato, which links knowledge with benevolence.

Aesthetic values are not absent from the theories of these writers, despite the assertive functionalism of some of their schemes. Owen's plans originated as a solution for desperate unemployment, and so predictably lacked grace and embellishment. But Saint-Simon wanted men to transform the environment and beautify the countryside with pleasure gardens and convenient hostelries, and Fourier wished the phalansterians to adorn the countryside by landscaping.[38] He also provided cultural entertainment — ballet, opera and concerts — and described in detail the 'aesthetic perfection' of each passion. Godwin's notion of individual development also certainly includes cultural and aesthetic pleasures. The utopians were by no means artistic or cultural pioneers, and their major constructive proposals are in the field of town-planning rather than in the fine arts, but they made the innovatory assertion that society must provide cultivated pleasures, rather than leaving these to the mercy of chance and free enterprise.

The utopians' ideas of justice have not been discussed as such; the reason for the omission is that justice is regarded chiefly as a term of approbation which each utopian strove to attach to his system. Even Godwin, despite the title of his *magnum opus*, hedges on social justice and again invokes a universal and absolute standard: justice consists of 'those laws of reason that are equally obligatory wherever man is to be found'.[39] Because of the superordinate position which justice normally holds in our ordering of values, justice must be a definitional property of utopia as well as an ideal within utopian society, for the perfect society can hardly be less than perfectly just. Some common elements of justice emerge in the utopians' analyses. They agree on the necessity of abolishing the exploitative basis of society, the polarity between extremes of wealth and poverty and the consequent social contradictions, before a just society can be constructed. The nature of distributive justice in these utopias is determined by equality of treatment and want-regarding individualism which dictates distribution according to need and want, as far as possible, But in these theories justice is always reducible to some combination of the instrumental social values. Although it remains a primary value, it is attributable *ex post* rather than being an operational force within the utopias.

According to Kateb, utopianism is 'that system of values which places harmony at the centre', and, as Borges remarks, 'a system is nothing more than the subordination of all aspects of the universe to any one such aspect'.[40] The present analysis has shown that the supreme and culminating value of these utopian theories is harmony. Any conflict or disintegration would make society definitionally sub-utopian. Harmony is intimately connected with peace and orderliness but qualitatively different, being a second-order property, like perfection. The idea of harmony, prevalent in the natural sciences since Newton's analysis of the ordered and harmonious universe, was raised to the philosophical status of a metaphysic during the eighteenth century, and then extended to the social sciences as an explanatory principle.

Harmony pervades the method and structure of these theories as well as being a property of the utopias. The utopians sought to make a theoretical structure out of their metaphysical conviction of the possibility and necessity of harmony, and then to create ideal types of society to embody and exemplify this theory. Because all possible contradictions are eliminated *a priori* at the mental level, the resulting utopia is entirely harmonious. These theories resemble a self-contained logic: the deductive method, the circularity of some arguments, the anticipatory removal of deviant variables, all reinforce the simile. A closed system inevitably has a 'harmonious' character.

Fourier gives harmony a specific meaning within his schema. The universe is structured on a musical model with harmony as its final resolution, and God himself embodies the principle of unity and 'integrality of movement'. But man is out of harmony with God, and in discord with the 'four movements', through his self-indulgence, enfeeblement and incapacity to deal with natural phenomena.[41] Fourier's theory of harmony may contain some worthwhile insight: his idea of the passion for unity, 'harmonism', has been linked with Freud's 'oceanic feeling'[42] and certainly, the idea that man is a creature that unwittingly follows the laws of the natural universe from which civilised man has become disastrously severed, is a persisting theme.

In social science models, harmony connotes the absence of social conflict, disruption and incongruous social institutions. A prescription for the achievement of harmony must therefore eliminate social conflict structurally, primarily through the reconciliation of diverse interests. Political theorists seek political mechanisms: for example, the utilitarians portrayed the state as an arbiter between antagonistic interests. The utopians solved the problem by creating a correspondence between men's capacities and the organisation and structure of society, an enterprise which was indicative of the contemporary predilection for an all-inclusive social science. Many attributes of the utopias such as cohesion and integration are necessary and contributory to harmony, which also rests on the identity of interests.

The choice of a small community as the ideal unit fosters homogeneity among the inhabitants and maximises social awareness, incidentally minimising control. Typically, the organisation of these utopias combines a high degree of socialisation with a small amount of overt, non-aversive control which is not destructive of human dignity. The eminently 'socialist' ideas of co-operation, solidarity between workers, mutual dependence and natural sociability and creativity contribute to social cohesion, and to all the utopias is superadded a strong quantum of ideological persuasion to reinforce solidarity and integration. It follows that harmony is as much a state of mind as a structural or material reality.

The attendant properties of musical harmony such as perfection and fixity are also attributes of utopian society. All these utopias have a quality of timelessness, changelessness, closed-ness and perpetuation. Change within specified limits is envisaged, but there is no allowance for revolutionary change of whatever kind. The prevalent view at the time was that scientific progress was almost at an end, and the only remaining task was the correct application of scientific principles to solve social problems. The static nature of utopian society may also derive from the attempt to build theories on the Newtonian model, which assumes a static universe: not until after Darwin, a half-century later, did dynamic theories come into vogue. The historical theories of Saint-Simon and Fourier attempt to counteract this fixity, but utopia is still seen as the final stage. Another reason for the changelessness of utopia is the vision of human nature as unchanging; the attained utopias depend on a finally perfected human nature, and so have a static quality. A dynamic view of human nature interacting progressively with society would inevitably imply unstable situations and historical progress, which utopia outlaws.

The disconcerting a-historical character of the utopias is closely related to harmony. They are a-historical, because the utopians do not envisage further social progress within utopia and because their utopias are cut off from all previous states by the break with continuity. The utopians envisage progress *to* but not *beyond* their chosen goal. The folly of trying to halt the progress of history is revealed in the appearance of petrification common to most utopias.

Utopian theory, in order to maintain social harmony in practice, must reconcile the particular with the general, and cope with the problems of universality and diversity which permeate society. One successful device for effecting the reconciliation at the theoretical level, popular since Plato, is the organic analogy. There is no question of the human organs' being *subordinated* to the social whole, yet there is no likelihood (except in a pathological state) of their rebelling and behaving dysfunctionally. This approach to the parts and the whole is more satisfactory than that of Godwin and Owen who reconcile conflicting elements through an imposed uniformity. But the idea of harmony and the organic ideal are both conceptual analogies, and are therefore unattainable *as such* in society; these notions remain ultimately metaphorical, and metaphysical.

The special role with the utopians claim for truth, and the closed view of knowledge on which this relies, reflects the closed nature of harmony. Truth and harmony, as they function in these theories, are two facets of the same aspiration. The subordination of the system to the requirements of harmony is not characteristic of all utopias, although almost

every utopia has certain properties conducive to the achievement of harmony. But the desire to establish an equilibrium
in the ideal society, and to dispose of all potentially
dangerous social elements in advance, is typically utopian.

Various other criticisms may be made of the harmonious
ideal, which has often been presented as a totalitarian ruse.
Adherents to the democratic ideal consider the 'closed'
nature of harmony an obstacle to freedom and progress. The
utopian can defend his ideal by pointing out the compensating delights of harmony, and the vulnerability of the notions
of freedom and progress; also by sceptically questioning the
boasted open-ness of democratic systems. Next comes the
related criticism that utopia is a 'monolithic' structure,
lacking variety, choice and interest because of its fusion of
the economic and political and private spheres of life in an
integrated whole. The term 'monolithic' is as much an
analogy as 'harmony' in this context. When does society
become a monolith? Or totalitarian? The listing of empirical
conditions may produce an answer, but this will be equally
controversial. Fourier demonstrates that a closely integrated
and 'closed' society need not be monolithic if the premises
on which it is built do not assert or impose universal uniformity, and the building blocks of the construction are
varied and dissimilar. He offers proof that a pluralistic
society could be conflict-free and happy, and that harmony
is, ideally, a polyphonous composition.

All such points made by critics of utopia for its would-be
totalitarian nature can be turned against the critic firstly by
challenging his definitions and the artificial polarities which
he sets up between open and closed, totalitarian and
democratic, and so on, and secondly by questioning whether
open and pluralistic societies in fact genuinely offer a more
extensive range of choices and opportunities, since they
certainly do not guarantee continuous happiness or freedom
from conflict. The protagonist of utopia may well argue that
the trade-off between these commodities leaves utopia with a
surplus. The objector who favours pluralistic social
structures will finally expatiate on the virtues of a conflict-
based society: antagonisms are refreshing, conflict is

bracing, the release of aggression is healthy,[43] courage and the endurance of uncertainty are desirable and (as a last resort) conflict is inevitable anyway, being 'human nature'. Again, the utopian must retort that his product generously compensates for these astringent and dubious delights, offering intenser forms of happiness, and the additional pleasures of cooperation and integration unknowable in strife-filled societies.

Although harmony is hedged about by these complications and objections, it is, as Fourier suggests, essentially a 'composite', uniting and aggregating ideal, the property of the *whole*, not of its components: thus it constitutes the crowning virtue of utopia. Returning to the axiom of Borges, it has been shown that for these thinkers utopia is a system subordinated to two parallel values, happiness and harmony. Happiness is necessity of any utopia, embedded in its definition which refers to the Good Life. By contrast, harmony is a value which the nineteenth-century utopians, influenced by the scientific and metaphysical concepts of the eighteenth century, extol. They make harmony a necessary condition for happiness and hence a necessary property of their utopias: disharmony is synonymous with unhappiness for those who suffer in social conflict. These two goals must really be treated as equal and parallel ideals: happiness is the individual-oriented ideal of utopia, while harmony is the ideal attribute of the social whole.

References
1. K. Deutsch in 'The Widening of Choices and the Chance of Goals', *Liberty* ed. C. Friedrich (Lieber-Atherton, 1962), defines freedom as the range of choices open to actors and makes allowance for self- transformation and the change of goals over time. See also I. Berlin, 'Two Concepts of Liberty', in *Four Essays on Liberty* (Oxford U.P., 1969), p. 129.
2. PJ I, pp. 443-4. Without such value, a utopian might be tempted to create the illusion of freedom. See Appendix, Note 2, for a discussion of illusory freedom, and its connection with happiness.
3. HC, Appendix 4, p. 25.
4. *Système*, p. 16n. and *Oeuvres* (Paris, 1865-78), XXXIX p. 224. 'L'industrie' connotes 'the industrial society' as well as 'industry'.
5. *Catéchisme*, p. 180.

6. *L'industrie*, t.i., p. 128. See also *Système,* pp. 16-17.
7. OC XII, p. 624. Also see OC III, pp. 136-137, 171ff.
8. OC VII, p. 211.
9. *Eros and Civilisation*, p. 174.
10. *The Sane Society* (Routledge & Kegan Paul, 1956), p. 196. See also *The Fear of Freedom* (London, 1942) for the main arguments.
11. Fourier, OC IV, p. 55 and Godwin, PJ II, p. 476.
12. For Godwin's attack, see PJ II, p. 490.
13. PJ II, pp. 487, 423.
14. *Revolution*, p. III ff. See also *Sex Lectures*, p. 29.
15. BNMW, p. 30. 'Privileges' here means advantages or benefits.
16. OC VI, p. 6, and Beecher & Bienvenu, p. 227. Equality is of course not synonymous with uniformity.
17. *Catéchisme,* p. 61.
18. PJ II, p. 428.
19. J. Rawls, *A Theory of Justice* (Harvard U.P., 1971), p. 85.
20. There are many resemblances between this approach of Mill and Godwin's individualism. See, e.g., PJ II, p. 500. An extensive analysis and categorisation appears in *Individualism*, S. Lukes (Blackwell, 1973).
21. PJ I, pp. xxxvii-xxxviii, and PJ II, p. 197.
22. PJ II, pp. 117-9.
23. PJ I, p. 219.
24. J. L. Talmon, *Political Messianism, The Romantic Phase* (Secker & Warburg, 1960), p. 42.
25. *Réorganisation*, p. 205.
26. G. Lichtheim, *The Origins of Socialism* (Weidenfeld & Nicholson, 1969), p. 33.
27. *Op. cit.*, pp. 152-3 There is in fact little mention of voting in the phalanstery's proceedings.
28. See RCL, pp. 255-6 and *Revolution*, p. 127.
29. See B. Holden, *The Nature of Democracy* (Nelson, 1974) for an account and comparison of liberal and Rousseauesque democracy, Ch. 2 esp. Rousseau's account of direct democracy contrasts with the utopians' views as well as the liberal doctrine.
30. É. Durkheim, *Socialism and Saint-Simon* (Antioch Press, 1958), pp. 148-9.
31. See Schiller 'On the Logic of being a Democrat' in *Philosophy*, vol. 44 (1969), pp. 46-56, for a development of this view.
32. E.g. modern democratic apathy as presented by W. Morris Jones in 'In Defence of Apathy', *Political Studies,* II (1954), pp. 25-37.
33. I. Berlin, *Four Essays on Liberty*, p. 60.
34. NVS, p. 152.
35. Owen as well as Fourier places great importance on the control of animals and inanimate nature — BNMW, Bk. I, p. 75. C.f. Spiro's arguments about the need for a 'universal world view', in Spiro, *art. cit.*, pp. 26-9.
36. OC VII, p. 335.

37. Beecher & Bienvenu, p. 221.
38. *L'Organisateur*, p. 52n, and OC VI, p. 119.
39. PJ II, pp. 382 and 326n.
40. G. Kateb, *Utopia and its Enemies* (Collier-Macmillan, 1963) p. 7, and J. L. Borges, 'Tlön, Uqbar, Orbis Tertius' in *Labyrinths* (Penguin, 1971), p. 34.
41. OC X, p. 43. See also OC VII, p. 410.
42. The Freudian connection is suggested by K. White in his introduction to Breton's *Ode*.
43. This argument occurs in K. Widmer, 'Libertarian Reflections on Human Aggression', *The Personalist* LIII (1972).

CHAPTER 7

UTOPIAN SOCIAL SCIENCE

THESE thinkers did not claim to be utopians, although it has been a convenient abbreviation to refer to them as such: they *did* claim to be social scientists. In this chapter their significance within social science will be evaluated, some problems in their methodologies highlighted, and the relation of utopianism to social science will be discussed.

The dangers of generalising about four such different thinkers are apparent; inevitably, many differences between them have become evident during this analysis. But the justification of the comparative approach lies in their common claims to have produced social theory with practical implications which pointed the way to a better society. Not all of them achieved the same acclaim for their endeavours, and only Saint-Simon is now habitually mentioned in histories of social science, although in the nineteenth-century Fourier and Owen were also cited.[1] Saint-Simon's influence on Comte and his affinities with Durkheim are well-charted, for he had a catalytic effect on both these thinkers.[2]

The common basic element of these theories is their positivist emphasis on the establishment of human and social truths on which to base social policy. Their methods are simple, not easily assimilated to today's complex social science terminology. Furthermore, because social science methods were fluid in their time, they cross and re-cross the now defined boundaries between positivism, realism, ideology and metaphysics without scruple. Social science writings of that period have a methodological innocence no longer possible.

The inclusion of Godwin in this grouping may occasionally have seemed incongruous, apart from his direct influence on Owen. But Godwin illustrates *par excellence* the transitional process by which philosophy became social science. The presumptions and structure of social science are visible in his arguments, but they are not yet made empirical or given a deliberately scientific methodology, although he states the need for observational data, and systematises his argument. Saint-Simon too aspires to a philosophy which will order all other forms of knowledge. Such conceptions suggest that the work of these thinkers must be viewed in part as philosophy, and treated accordingly. Ultimately, their theories are unclassifiable in terms of the modern disciplines, for they are not yet sociology as such, and are explicitly intended to unify social science in the face of increasing specialisation. Hence the admixture of precepts from political economy, psychology, moral philosophy and political theory of which they are constituted. Each discipline is now thought to require a special methodology but, however inconsistent, they were then unified in an overall framework by logical deduction, dialectic or analogy. The theories are both diverse and at times lacking in dimensions or perspective because some elements have been simplified or minimised in order to control the system as a whole and reduce disparities between the diverse elements.

INTELLECTUAL GENEALOGY

The intellectual background of the Enlightenment affected both the content and structure of the theories, for the ideas of the *philosophes* were still common currency when the utopians were writing, and permeated even the work of such autodidacts as Fourier and Owen. Although the genesis and genealogy of their ideas are not closely germane to this study, it will be useful to enumerate the strands of Enlightenment thought prevalent in their theories. There was, as Engels asserted, a necessary connection between the thought of the utopian socialists and that of the Enlightenment — necessary because inescapable, but also because these thinkers had to locate themselves intellectually in order to depart from tradition.

In its theoretical form, modern socialism originally appears osten-
sibly as a more logical expansion of the principles laid down by the
great French philosophers of the eighteenth century . . . modern
socialism had, at first, to connect itself with the intellectual stock-in-
trade ready to its hand, however deeply its roots lay in material
economic facts.[3]

A multitude of tangents and parallels exists between the
thought of the *philosophes* and the utopians.[4] Their
utopianism can be seen as a reaction against the negative-
critical approach, an attempt to create positive, constructive
theory. The acknowledgement of reason as an active,
energising force, Diderot's notion of the physiological basis
of morality, Helvétius's account of egoism as the basis of
social solidarity, and the French utilitarians' reinterpretation
of virtue as a socially useful quality are all echoed by the
utopians. Rousseau's optimism about human nature no
doubt prompted Fourier's dictum 'There are no vicious
passions, only vicious developments'.[5] Turgot's conception
of the Four Stages of material progress, and Condorcet's
account of intellectual progress and indefinite perfectibility
are clearly reflected in these utopians' theories, although
transformed to suit their own ends. The importance of the
identity of interests doctrines of Smith and Bentham has
already been emphasized. The humanism and humanitarianism of the utopians also mirrored the Enlightenment
tradition.

The utopians' versions of the doctrine variously known as
materialism, determinism and (more recently) environmentalism, derive directly from seventeenth-century and
Enlightenment views. The *tabula rasa* theory of human
nature and the materialist view that all thought is derived
from sensation, owe their origins to Locke, Hartley and
Condillac. Determinism, the social, moral and philosophical
application of materialism, was developed particularly by
Hume, Holbach and Helvétius, who also stated its corollary,
the importance of education. This doctrine constituted a
final refutation of the notion of Original Sin, with the consequence that social evil was in future to be located firmly in
the environment. Concurrently, progress in the natural

sciences heralded the possibility of the mastery of nature and self-improvement for man.

The deification of nature was maintained by the utopians: the *philosophes* had used the concept 'to embody the standard by which they could judge existing institutions, morals and forms of government'.[6] Used in this way, the umbrella term 'natural' is synonymous with 'good', and 'Nature' is often interchangeable with 'God', although the *philosophes* would have vehemently denied that. Naturalism as a doctrine goes further than this, however: it dictates that men should be treated like other natural objects, and made the subjects of scientific investigation, and that human action should be causally or even mechanistically explained. Thus, the naturalist metaphysic promotes the development of social science. Environmentalism represents such a development, showing men's characters and behaviour to be formed by the interactions between themselves and their surroundings, natural and social. Naturalism has a second function in Enlightenment thought, serving as a unifying and metaphysical doctrine in a disorderly social universe. This aspect of naturalism is directly associated with the intellectual rejection of Christianity.

In fact, the conceptual residue of religion was a further determinant of the utopians' social theorising, covert but important. Christianity as the dominent form of social knowledge and sole source of social prescriptions had been much undermined by the seventeenth and eighteenth centuries and was fated to be replaced by the social sciences; as a form of knowledge about the natural world it had long been defunct.[7] So pervasive, however, was the intellectual apparatus and world-view which Christianity had supplied, that the nascent social scientists employed many of its devices, transformed but did not altogether negate its concepts, and even resorted to a similar rhetoric: Owen's surpasses that of a hell-fire preacher. For the new generation of thinkers there was a need to create a secular history to locate humanity in the world, since the Christian interpretation was discredited. Saint-Simon, following Condorcet, developed a theory of ever-increasing enlightenment, as did Godwin, which contrasted with the Christian account of increasing decadence. Fourier too mimicked Christianity in his eschatological predictions. Again, these thinkers, even as social scientists, were unable to abolish completely the teleological elements which had given the Christian world its impetus, and so provided doctrines of human perfectibility to achieve utopia. These parallels could be extended to the notions of causality and will, important in the Christian intellectual vocabulary and not easily eradicable from secular thought.

The secularisation of intellectual Christianity occurred not only at the level of ideas but at the level of logic and the framework of thought itself. Christianity had evolved certain thought structures and explanatory forms such as notions of a *fons et origo* and purposiveness, which affected the way in which language was used and directed analysis towards causes, agents and intentions. These the usurping social sciences chose at first to assimilate rather than reject: to do otherwise would have meant radically reconstructing the logic of human and social explanation, perhaps beyond recognition. In time, social scientists eschewed the individualistic conception of society, dispensed with the notion of free and rational will as the cause of action, and ridiculed teleological explanation. But these devices had for so long constituted the stuff of social explanation that early social theorists were obliged to utilise them, if only for the convenience of being understood, and so that their theories should leave no gaps which religious doctrines had customarily filled. The rise of secular social science was in itself the culmination of a long endeavour to oust suprahuman explanations of human phenomena.[8]

The metaphysical and materialist elements of naturalism both relate to the *idée fixe* of the *philosophes*, the social science which would integrate the ever-increasing volume of knowledge about man and society, and serve as a basis for further observation. The problem was to find an appropriate methodology and a universal governing principle. During the first half of the century, the opinion prevailed that this should be modelled on the physical sciences, of which Newton's theory constituted an ideal model. He first established a mathematical regularity in the universe and successfully combined analytic and synthetic techniques. The principle of attraction sounded seductively comprehensible to laymen, and Fourier was certainly seduced by 'the Newtonian conception of the physical world as a mechanical equilibrium, a universe in which every atom attracts every other atom'.[9] Hence, 'celestial mechanics'.

Later, changing philosophical opinion decided that physiology, superseding Newtonism and philosophical psychology, should provide the model. Saint-Simon followed this fashion, calling his universal science 'la physiologie sociale', which treats of the whole organism, rather than the parts. The defection from Newton was also symptomatic of the move from calculation to experiment in the sciences.[10] The utopians were therefore writing in a period when slavish adherence to natural science methods had been abandoned, but little consideration had yet been given to social science's need for a unique method, and to the historical and cultural elements which distinguish the social from the natural sciences. The utopian theories continued to emulate the natural sciences in some respects, for they were seen as reflecting and conceptualising universal harmony.

EPISTEMOLOGY AND METHODS

As *soi-disant* social scientists, the utopians were eager to lay bare the innovatory principles which constituted their methods and the epistemological justification of their theories. All felt the allure of an absolutist epistemology. Truth was, they considered, the correct perception and account of relations between natural and social entities, relations which when correctly functioning were always harmonious. There are no contradictions in nature. A malfunctioning society, conversely, is the embodiment of men's incorrect perceptions, and untruth. There is some confusion in this attribution of logical properties to the phenomenal world: Fourier believed truth to be absolute, cosmic, eternal and incarnate in the very organisation of the physical universe. Social truth was accessible through analogies with musical and mathematical systems which he acclaimed as the paragons among ordering systems. There was for him nothing developmental about social or human truths, for the history of human life on earth was predictable from beginning to end. Fourier exemplifies the resurgence of a tradition as old as Aristotle, which merged absolutism with naturalism and found social certainties by inspecting the universe.

For Godwin, truth is a human invention, parasitic on language, imposed on the world from within, yet no less absolute since it reflects the universals of human nature. Certainty about human and social life can be achieved; moral truths are discoverable and universal and a state of absolute justice can be reached. With Saint-Simon, and Owen to some extent, the absolutist epistemology is much tempered by an understanding of the historical process. Each historical period has necessary truths, such as the appropriateness of the correspondence of the industrial economy, liberal regime and positive science. Owen too perceives that moral truths are relative to time and place, but he also locates absolute truth in the workings of rationality and, particularly, in the social relations prescribed by his own rational science. The truths which the utopians consider absolute are part of the nature of things physical, social and human, and thus rest on an essentialist perception of the phenomenal world. The teleological nature of the utopian theories, with their absolutes of human perfection and social harmony, is a further, logically consistent, manifestation of this absolutism. Their styles of theorising derive from these epistemological preconceptions and deductive arguments fit best with their notions of truth.

The chronologically short progression from Godwin to Owen and Fourier, and then Saint-Simon, represents a shift of emphasis from anthropocentric to socially-orientated social science. All retain the dual focuses of the individual and the social entity, but the perspective changes as the idea of a social science replaces the philosophy of man. Their views differ as to what constitutes social knowledge, how it is to be accumulated, and how employed. According to Godwin, social knowledge elaborated by introspective methods is profitable for the observer, as self-knowledge, and for society, as social science. For some, social knowledge ideally consists of scientific observation of men in groups or in the aggregate, for others, of generalisation about individual motivation on the basis of experience. The latter method, the method of philosophical psychology, is Godwin's; it is also, covertly, the basis of Fourier's systematisation of the passions. The former is exemplified by the social physiology of Saint-Simon. Owen has a foot in either camp. The embryos of the social scientific methods developed later appear in these perceptions of method. Differently structured utopias resulted from these methods: Godwin's individualism entails self-improvement for all, while Saint-Simon's macro approach entails improvement for all carried out by enlightened planners and scientists.

Advocating that all disciplines, even philosophy, must become positive, Saint-Simon states that his customary approach to politics is to base his principles on the observation of facts, and then to test them against events, i.e. he employs an analytic (inductive) method, then verifies the induced principles. But he also says that the industrial regime is based on general principles, and so could be constructed *a priori*, i.e. he seems to be deducing a model of society from historical conditions.[11] He also maintains that because his system rests on human nature it is not utopian. The two latter statements could be taken to signify a synthetic (deductive) method. He professed to favour a mixture of the two opposing methods, and in *Réorganisation* he advocated a parliamentary constitution with balancing and cross-checking synthetic and analytic elements. The doubtful notion that a method of theorising can be incorporated in social organisation is a recurring theme in these utopias.

Durkheim traces Saint-Simon's deduction of the need for a social physiology from his philosophical endeavour to order all the sciences encyclopaedically. Verifiable scientific principles had to extend to human, as well as social, phenomena.[12] Saint-Simon says of the social physiology that 'it soars above the level of individuals who are, from its viewpoint, no more than the organs of the body politic whose organic functions it must study, as specialised physiology studies that of human individuals'.[13] But the social physiology scarcely operates as an investigative method: it seems to stipulate how society *should be* organised, on the basis of the organic analogy. Of greater interest is Saint-Simon's historical method which analyses the social determination of human capacities and corresponding changes in economic organisation, social relations and the community of ideas. This represents a significant attempt to suit the method to the subject matter, with a consequent departure from the physical sciences. Ultimately, however, he expects a science of man, the conflation of all other sciences, to develop on the physiological model, and this could scarcely accommodate historical elements. Saint-Simon's methods vary and are hard to classify, but he himself did not always practise the positivism which he heralded as the science of the future.

Owen effused about the 'harmony, unity and efficiency' of his method, invoking nature as the ultimate standard. 'The proof of the truth of any science is in the harmony of each part with the whole, and its unity with all nature; for, of necessity, each truth upon any subject must be in strict accordance with every other truth; it being contrary to the laws of nature for one truth to be opposed to any other truth.'[14] He repeatedly sets out the principles of his deductively organised 'science of Man', which proceeds from human nature to society, then deals with problems of production, distribution, education and government. 'Each part has been devised with reference to a simple general principle . . . There is a *necessary* connexion between the several parts.'[15] The Rational System, then, is intentionally deductive and the only structural principle which Owen acknowledges is the law of non-contradiction; as a result, his disorderly ideas are surrounded by a shell of logical consistency. But his science of society rests on the fallacious or inadequate definition of science as a self-consistent entity. Innumerable fantastic systems might be devised that were self-consistent but in no way scientific: consistency is not a sufficient condition for scientificity. The 'deductions' which Owen makes are actually based on contingent facts about contemporary society and on an evaluative framework that determines which connections are made — but the absolutist epistemology causes Owen to present contingency as necessity.

Fourier rejects empirical social sciences as 'the uncertain sciences' because they deal with contingencies, and seeks to substitute absolute, necessary principles. Attraction, which rules the physical world, applies also to man and society. 'Where is the unity of the divine system if the mainspring of the general harmony, attraction, is not just as applicable to human societies as it is to the stars and the animals?'[16] So Fourier argues the case for a naturalistic approach to social science on the metaphysical assumption of universal unity. His chosen scientific method is mathematical: the social, animal, organic and material 'movements' are co-ordinated by the mathematical principle which constitutes attraction. In reality, it serves only as a basis for Fourier's idiosyncratic taxonomy, which is only pseudo-scientific. The analogy is his second innovation, which will replace deduction. Certain analogies exist (sic) in the natural world and can be applied to the social sphere to produce an ideal social entity which harmonises with the natural world and abolishes the tension and duality between them. But are there analogies in nature any more than contradictions? Fourier's theory is overtly teleological, with cosmic harmony as its declared aim, and so departs from experimental natural science. But its organic elements are incipiently social-scientific, and the conception of the functioning of different human psychologies in a diverse but harmonious whole is a model of great interest to social scientists.

Godwin's thought constituted a typically eighteenth-century synthesis of the philosophical and the scientific. *Political Justice* in highly deductive and its 'Summary of Principles' is axiomatic, yet there are also attempts to support the assumptions with empirical generalisations, and an acknowledgement that the analytic-synthetic method is the proper one to be pursued. 'If politics be a science, investigation must be the means of unfolding it . . . there must be one best mode of social existence deducible from the principles of (human) nature.'[17] The apparent contradiction here between investigation and deduction shows the predicament of the philosopher-cum-social-scientist. Godwin consistently employs a materialist and determinist approach in his discussion of human behaviour and social matters, and thought this rigorous approach appropriate for the new social theory.

Evidently these utopians shared a naturalistic approach to human life and behaviour, and a concomitant desire to investigate society and order the results scientifically. But while purporting to adhere to natural science methods, their theories are preponderantly deductive, with sorties into the factual world to find evidence for their *a priori* principles and inferences; some also rely on analogical and dialectical logic. The absolutist epistemologies and teleologies made deduction a tempting procedure, and the shortcomings of the approach for social scientists are manifest. But the utopians contributed to the development of two *sui generis* methods of social scientific theorising, environmentalism and historical determinism.

Environmentalism offers in principle a causal explanation of human and social phenomena, and the possibility of prediction, but may lack a historical dimension. Godwin's determinism is individualistic, while Owen's operates at an aggregative, communal level. Both present men as a natural object, motivated by the desire for self-preservation and aversion from pain, but moulded by external, social forces. Saint-Simon switches the focus of the theory from the immediate determinants of individual personality and behaviour to the social conditions which govern the development of classes, making environmentalism a determinant of his historical theory. Fourier's somewhat token environmentalism explains the changing manifestations of the passions in different societies. The old assumption that there is a constant human nature is undermined but not entirely destroyed by the environmentalist approach, since innate faculties are still conceded. Environmentalism and the *tabula rasa* clearly entail no prescriptions for social organisation such as the utopians proceeded to 'deduce', without a large injection of values. One major radicalising consequence of the doctrine *per se* was its refutation of Original Sin; another was that the manipulation of men as natural objects was seen to be possible (and not blasphemous), which suggested the possibility of human betterment.

Saint-Simon's historical determinism links class development to a historical process propelled by independent factors such as the progress of knowledge. New variables are thus introduced into determinism, making it a more powerful and wide-ranging form of explanation, capable of explaining the variations of social phenomena at different times, a capacity which social science needs. The historical factor also rebuts the stultifying dogma that human nature is constant. A-historical determinism generates unrealistic, universal propositions and predictions which are generally invalidated by circumstance, whereas the predictions of historical determinism are specifically related to the continuing progress of history and hold good only at particular times. Utopia for Saint-Simon is therefore something to be attained in the fullness of time, rather than created miraculously when the right formula is discovered. Fourier's theory of history does not rank with Saint-Simon's, for it is classificatory, not deterministic, and identifies no causal elements or agencies of change, except the metaphysical impulse to universal unity, although it makes the correlation between women's emancipation and social improvement.

Judgement on the utopians' standing as social scientists will be suspended until the final section, so that some problems specific to their methods can be considered.

HUMAN NATUROLOGY

Since assumptions about human nature are so fundamental to these thinkers, both as utopians and as would-be social scientists, this Achilles' Heel of their theories must be examined. The now controversial principle of basing social theory on ideas of human nature, with the resulting intrusion of subjectivism, will not itself be challenged, as that was their chosen method, and a common one at the time.

Certain principles govern the choice and form of the assumptions in any theory, such as consistency and universality, which suggest that operable assumptions about human nature must refer to predictable and universal attributes. Ideally, a minimum of assumptions should be made. Godwin and Owen satisfy these dictates, but their models are consequently vulnerable to deviations from the assumed normality. A sounder approach is perhaps to modify the universality requirement by making separate assumptions about groups of men differentiated by particular characteristics. In this way, Saint-Simon assimilates human diversity without admitting a dysfunctional, unpredictable variable. Fourier combines the premiss of an overall regularity of behaviour with a multitude of particular assumptions about individuals. Assumptions with different logical forms, universal or particular, support different analyses of the social structure: Fourier's particular assumptions necessitate an extensively pluralistic society, Saint-Simon's class assumptions dictate controlled pluralism,[18] while Godwin's and Owen's universal assumptions support unified, egalitarian societies.

The centrality of human nature in these theories detracts from their scientificity in that, because they are predictive and deductive models, the only elements which can be scrutinised, apart from the deductive logic, are the basic assumptions. But when such assumptions concern human nature they cannot easily be verified. Furthermore, as Chapter 3 argued, the utopian often amalgamates the descriptive, the prescriptive, and the teleological in his account of human nature, so that parts of the assumption are not even verifiable in principle.

All four thinkers could be classified as methodological individualists because of the attention which they devote to human nature, although this label is used in many ways. Certainly, they hold to what Watkins describes as 'the central assumption of the individualistic position . . . that no social tendency exists which could not be altered *if* the individuals concerned both wanted to alter it and possessed the appropriate information'. This expectation is crucial to their utopianism. Yet Saint-Simon and Fourier criticise contemporary society in ways which seem incompatible with the alternative formulation of the position, 'that no social tendency is somehow imposed on human beings "from above" . . . social tendencies are the product (usually undesigned) of human characteristics and activities and situations'.[19] There are elements of holistic explanation in these theories, less so in those of Godwin and Owen. All the utopians, however, are psychologistic in the sense which Popper deplores, i.e. in beginning their analysis with postulates about human nature, rather than tracing back events and so locating explanations ultimately in individuals, as the methodological individualist should. But none of these writers, *qua* utopian, exemplifies the aspect of utopian or holistic engineering which Popper condemns, the disregard of the 'human factor'.[20] Enough has been said to show that individually and collectively these thinkers present problems of classification because criteria of methodological consistency were only incompletely formulated when they were constructing their theories. Like mythological beasts, they are composed of oddly assorted parts.

One question which the psychologistic individualist must answer is whether his assumptions about individuals will hold without modification in a social context, since individual behaviour is often transformed in different social settings. Attempts to base theory on human nature conceived of *in vacuo* are perpetually dogged by this problem. Only Fourier anticipates it, and asserts that the true social unit is 810 individuals whose behaviour contributes to the functioning of the whole, which qualitatively differs from its aggregated parts because additional forces, such as harmonism, are generated. He thus reconciles the organic or holistic approach with individualistic premises. Godwin and Owen believe that the aggregate of their assumptions about individual behaviour will function unmodified as predictions about society as a whole, which indicates their confidence in the individualistic method.

The assumptions which the utopians, other than Fourier, make about human nature cover only a narrow range of characteristics and behaviour. Why such exclusiveness? They were influenced by the contemporary moral philosophy and psychology which focused on such attributes as rationality and self-interest, and may have considered their manifestations to be constant, and so more manageable as theoretical assumptions. But if other apparently universal human attributes, such as the desire to emulate, the capacity for play, and the creative imagination were postulated, might not the result be a more diversified and fulfilling utopia?[21] Fourier was uniquely radical in his argument that *all* passions can be socially functional, and embarked on a full-scale analysis of psychology instead of making the standard simplifying assumptions about motivation.

The narrowness of the other utopians' conceptions of human nature may endanger their systems, for it excludes consideration of some human instincts conventionally regarded as socially disruptive, notably human aggression. Freud's conservative conclusions concerning Eros and Thanatos and the need for perpetual repression have been contested by theories which suggest that sexuality can be integrative and that aggression is functional in society, and can hold itself in check.[22] However, the utopians omit to discuss the problem of aggression, which might threaten social harmony if it is indeed universal — except for Fourier, who puts it to good use in the slaughterhouse. Their noticeable neglect of the possibility that criminality is hereditary differs, since it is a consequence of their social determinism, which entails that criminals are made by society itself.[23] However, their concentration on 'virtuous' human attributes and neglect of the more intractable elements seem to be the result of policy decisions to operate in the optimistic mode.

The utopians' operations on human nature must also be scrutinised in the light of the current state of the 'nature or nurture' controversy, to which they postulated solutions. The possibility of their utopias rests on the hope that human nature can be changed by the elimination of culture-specific characteristics. But the assumption that when the harmful environment is destroyed human nature will become 'natural' begs many questions. Within the philosophical tradition, there have been four basic approaches to the nature-nurture problem: (i) the assumption of an 'original constitution' which does not, however, preclude modification by society, (ii) the assumption of a set of formal powers or faculties such as perception, judgement, memory, (iii) the *tabula rasa* assumption, and (iv) the assumption of a human nature that can only be conceived of historically and collectively, through its manifestations in culture.[24] The distinction between these categories breaks down as conditioned and hereditary elements interpenetrate, and even the *tabula rasa* must, as for Owen, include the idea of capacities able to deal with sense information.

In all branches of psychology the centrality of conditioned responses (nurture) is emphasized. Freud saw the libido as a quantum of energy, given shape through interaction with the external world.[25] But this pre-social mass of energy is an *ex post* deduction, for the theory pivots on the forms it takes in reality. Behaviourism concedes a 'natural' aversion to pain, but it is the stimulus of the external world which produces all behaviour patterns. Even the most ardent champions of heredity still attribute considerable influence to the environment. One social anthropologist deduces the existence of a universal human nature, detectable in behaviour motivated by needs, values, ego-processes (which include perception, learning, cognition) and defence mechanisms, and concludes that 'the structure and functioning of human personality constitutes man's universal human nature, psychologically viewed'.[26] Yet he refrains from deducing a human essence, for even basic behaviour patterns presuppose a social and cultural structure. Monod, the evolutionary biologist, confirms the impossibility of distinguishing the native from the acquired: although *everything* springs from experience, that experience is transmitted precariously through random mutations and may be incorporated into the genetic heritage. Biologically it is not feasible to distinguish between acquisition and inheritance.[27]

In summary, 'biologists, anthropologists and psychologists may now generally agree that human behaviour patterns are shaped by a complex interaction of genetic endowments ('nature') and environmental variables ('nurture'),[28] and 'taking a long enough time span, it is fruitless to try to distinguish between the nature and the acquired, the original and the derived'.[29] For the purposes of utopian or critical theory, and all social science which purports to go beyond the descriptive, it is necessary to distinguish nature from nurture in order to envisage social change. But since we only meet nurtured, culture-specific man, such a distinction is irremediably speculative. Assumptions such as perfectibility and educability offer unscientific escape routes from the impasse of a fixed present in which men perfectly match their social context. Saint-Simon offers the most sophisticated solution to the problem, bringing in the notion of changing ideology and capacities. Since the analysis of the proportions of human nature is ultimately guesswork, the utopians cannot be refuted, but their guesses, on which their whole structures rest, are ever open to challenge.

SCIENTIFICITY

To what extent, then, can these theorists be regarded as progenitors of social science and, in particular, sociology? Martindale has argued that eighteenth-century political theorists were too concerned with the endeavour to derive social forms from an original contract to study them as such, i.e. sociologically.[30] This contrasts with the position of these utopians. Firstly, since they wished to destroy, not legitimise, existing systems, the social contract was not a focus or first cause; Godwin took pains to elaborate Hume's refutation of the social contract myth, significantly. Furthermore, they regarded contemporary institutions as part of a historical progression, contingently caused by, but not justified by, earlier societies. The doctrine of historical improvement to which they subscribed quelled any nostalgia for an original state, however innocent. They were thus in a position to examine socially phenomena as temporally independent, though historically formed, entities.

Martindale posits two basic conditions for the development of a social science, naturalism and objectivity.[31] It has been shown that the utopians' methods were naturalistic and that, although they did not ignore essentially mental phenomena such as intention and will, they tried at least to treat these deterministically, as in Godwin's account of the necessary effect of motivation. Fourier provided the most nearly mechanistic account of instinctual human behaviour with the element of self-consciousness removed, but even he was far from being a behaviourist.

As to objectivity, the utopians willingly allowed a proliferation of evaluative elements in their thought, often disguised as absolutes. They needed ideologies for their utopias, and the aspirational ideals of equality of treatment, freedom of development, co-operativism, goodwill, replaced traditional notions such as honour, duty, charity, which had habitually lubricated social relations. The ideology of the theorist himself is reflected in the organisation of his society, while the persuasive ideology which he teaches utopian citizens appears as a device for control. But these elements seem ill-attuned to the scientific approach which the utopians' *alter egos* boasted. Are their claims to scientificity therefore discredited? How, for example, does the promotion of social harmony in these theories tally with the endeavour to be scientific? Its intrusion is explicable historically in part, for the utopians were emulating a natural science tradition which hankered after Newton's conception of harmony. But society itself was seen to be fraught with conflicts, so that the paradigm did not derive from the existent, and was undoubtedly an imposed value. The social theories of these eminently naturalistic utopians are informed by the conviction that there is harmony in the physical world, so they postulate it as an organisational, non-evaluative goal for the social world, which is also part of nature.

Harmony, as the supreme determinant of the framework of analysis, dictates certain perspectives and optimistic forms of reasoning: it structures thought so that the investigator expects to find, or by intervening to create, non-conflictual solutions to social dilemmas. Harmony sets what Taylor refers to as the 'crucial dimensions of variation' for the theory, and is part of the investigative framework which also secretes values.[32] The strong postulate of social harmony and its theoretical counter-part, logical consistency, determine the form of these theories, entailing critical analysis of existing, discordant society and the construction of an ideal model and, no doubt, rejection of contradictory evidence. Taylor also argues that such a structuring of theory is almost inevitable, and need not altogether impugn the attempt at scientific objectivity.

The attempt to develop a scientific method was impeded somewhat by the conceptual devices inherited from Christianity. Also, while striving to infuse the *esprit systématique* into their theories, the utopians sometimes fell prey to the metaphysical *esprit de système* which the *philosophes* had detested in earlier thinkers. Also, as has been shown, the utopians' absolutist epistemologies enabled them to view the evaluative parts of their systems as objective truths. But none of this seemed problematic to these thinkers because of the fluidity of their definitions of social science. They were of course aware of the need to avoid subjectivity, and knew that data collection and testing betokened an objective and positivist approach, but they were not positivist to the extent of outlawing values: instead, they 'objectivised' their dearest values, in the best social science tradition.

An objection to the consequences of this kind of social science is made by Hayek, who finds the rational-deductive method which the utopians mainly favoured, far from being objective, to be based on hubristic 'constructive rationalism' and to entail a manipulative and authoritarian model of society.[33] On examination, this objection revives the confrontation of rationalism with traditionalism and some forms of liberalism, and echoes the conservative reaction to Enlightenment philosophy. Any radical thinker must join the rationalist camp in this particular war, for therein lies all hope of social change. But the distinction has no greater relevance to the scientificity or otherwise of utopian thinkers, and can here be disregarded.

Debate on the utopias' merits as social sciences must take

into account Marx's and Engels's critiques of the early socialists, much of which also applies to Godwin. They wrote as scientific socialists and interventionist social scientists, and the burden of their criticism was that the utopians were insufficiently scientific and interventionist. Marx conceded that they were writing before the *economic* conditions for the emancipation of the proletariat had developed: they had therefore tried to expedite this by inventing *social* laws.[34] Although himself influenced by Saint-Simon's historical theory,[35] Marx deplored the lack of historical perspective, and located in this the utopian's neglect of the class struggle. 'Only from the point of view of being the most suffering class does the proletariat exist for them . . . (They) consider themselves superior to all class antagonism.'[36] Consequently, 'they do not claim to emancipate a particular class to begin with, but all humanity at once'.[37] The more developed the proletariat, the less relevant utopian socialism, which impeded the workers' movement by its denigration of political methods and class confrontation.

Engels argued that the utopian's methods, redolent of eighteenth-century rationalism, were the antithesis of scientificity. 'The solution of the social problems, which as yet lay hidden in undeveloped economic conditions, the utopians attempted to evolve out of the human brain. Society presented nothing but wrongs; to remove these was the task of reason.'[38] Problem-solving through abstract ratiocination is doomed to failure, and harms the revolutionary movement because the elevation of the intellect supplants praxis, even when turned towards propaganda. Reason thus becomes a surrogate for revolution. Engels also criticised the utopian socialists' absolutism and lack of historical vision. 'To all these, socialism is the expression of absolute truth, reason and justice and has only to be discovered to conquer . . . absolute truth is independent of time and space.'[39] He noted that absolute truth was in the mind of the beholder.

A common methodological preoccupation which the utopians shared with Marx was the conviction of the need for a comprehensive explanation, *the* social science. These generations were visibly haunted by the encyclopaedic spirit.

Measured by this criterion too, the utopian theories were found by Marx and Engels to be unable to comprehend social reality and change in their simplified, rationalist structures, so on this score they could again pronounce their socialism to be superior to that of the utopians.

With regard to the criticism of the utopians' lack of awareness of class conflict, the present analysis suggests that they were conscious of the obstacle which social conflict presented to the attainment of social perfection. But they conceptualised the problem differently from Marx, having a largely classificatory attitude to class which lacked an explanatory dimension and saw stratification as accidental. Their endeavours were intended to reconcile the individual with his fellows, and with society, not to eliminate class conflict. Lacking a structural analysis, although they perceived various levels of conflict, they saw the eradication of economic and social conflicts as parallel, co-equal enterprises, and made every symptom of discontent a suitable case for treatment. Inevitably the utopians failed to qualify as scientific according to the sophisticated criteria developed by Marx and Engels decades later, and indeed drawn up with some intention of excluding Owenites, Fourierists and Saint-Simonians from the mainstream of revolutionary socialism. But in-fighting apart, the marxist critique of their methods is instructive, although the canons which are being applied in this study are those of 'bourgeois', not marxist, science.

The utopians' own perceptions of the purpose and function of their theories suggest that they certainly shared the conception of a *sui generis* social science to which they adhered. The belief in intervention, a central part of the conception, justified them in concluding social analysis with utopian prescription. They would base the argument for intervention on the invariable connection between knowledge and human happiness and improvement; indeed, the utopians constantly boasted the usefulness of their own theories and recommended them as social manuals. For them, social science, like natural science, had its applications, and social technology in their hands became utopian planning. Prescribing and planning is as respectable a role as observing and analysing.

In addition, they postulated a correspondence between conceptual structures and social reality: Social organisation could be made to mirror their own deductive/synthetic/analogical methods of social analysis. Saint-Simon's proposal to model parliament on scientific methods was one such attempt. These meta-theoretical claims are both contentious and mysterious, for there can be no similarity between logical structures and physical or social reality. Of course, it has been argued that the world determines our thought structures, but the utopians wanted their thought structures to determine the world. They were fond of attributing logical processes and constructions to nature and society, and Engels praised Fourier's dialectical account of the universe, having similar aspirations himself, but these are impositions of human thought patterns on impervious and non-rational matter.

In assessing the scientificity of these utopian theories, their deductive procedures, on which so much depends, must be challenged. Evidently, no given human nature logically entails a particular form of society as the utopians hoped (once more finding logic in nature). Instead, humane social values must provide the criteria for compatibility between man and social forms, so evaluative elements are integral to the supposedly factual argument. This point has already been pressed to its conclusion, but a rehearsal of modern views on social science suggests that the utopians were not so much at fault for failing in the impossible aim of neutrality, but for being insufficiently secretive about their evaluations. There is at least an inner logic and unity to the theories, although they lack scientific rigour and empirical data, for the values derive from the assumptions about human nature, and in turn determine the ideal form of social organisation, and the dominant paradigms of happiness and harmony give the whole a unified and systematic quality which deceptively suggests scientificity.

The respect in which the utopians departed most from future social scientists was in the undisguisedly prescriptive nature of their social theories. All were manifestly enamoured of the idea of an interventionist social science. The Enlightenment had idealised philosopher-practitioners such as Turgot, and the utopians saw no possible objection to a theorist who, by way of conclusion, offered social prescriptions. His evaluations and prescriptions would, after all, be deduced from his investigations and so, necessarily, valid. Furthermore, since knowledge must be useful to mankind, a non-interventionist social science would be mere academic self-indulgence. So the utopians fused positive and normative elements in theories which deduced how society should be arranged from an analysis of the necessary attributes of all societies and all men, which was in turn derived from the observation of existing societies. This procedure is reminiscent of the so-called practical syllogism, the deduction which concludes with an imperative. Godwin's dictum that 'every perfection that human beings are competent to conceive . . . (they) are competent to attain' also intimates a relation between thought and action that would sanction intervention by the social scientist.

The polarity between social science and utopian theory also appears in procedures. The social scientist selectively simplifies social phenomena in order to analyse social organisation. By contrast, the utopian must recognise the diversity and abundance of such phenomena in order to satisfy desires and needs. The goal of happiness makes it mandatory to provide for both the particular and the general, a quandary which makes it difficult to be a good social scientist and a successful utopian. Once again, Fourier makes the best of both worlds, while others simplified, and so veered towards social science.

These utopias fail every major test of scientificity, and evaluation would be the only way to judge their speculative elements. They may in part be checked against social observation, but as integrated wholes, which they are claimed to be, they cannot be submitted to verification, even in principle, let alone falsification. Despite their would-be scientific structures and formulae, and their authors' intentions, these theories more often conform to conjecture than

to the positivism to which they aspired. It may be more fruitful to plunder the utopias for illuminating insights than to
insist on measuring them against criteria which they are incapable of satisfying. For example, by analysing the
utopians' work *qua* social scientists, we can understand the
concerns of early practitioners of social science. Measurement and evidence were less important than general explanatory laws, despite the desire for positivism, the infusion of
values was permitted and, most of all, intervention by the
investigator was sanctioned. The correspondence between
the form and the content of social investigation, between the
original framework and the conclusions, is manifest. The
preoccupation with logical consistency and deduction makes
the social scientist into a utopian preoccupied with social
cohesion and harmony. Even in natural science, input
determines output: just so with these theorists, whose frameworks, methods and selection of evidence conspired to give
them the desired results. In this, they are examplars of the
methodological problems of early (and later) social science.

But these theorists may perhaps be rescued from this
merely illustrative role. Their claims to be social scientists
can be defended in two respects against the charge that their
neglect of the need for objectivity and of the fact-value
distinction, leading to interventionism and utopianism,
devalues them as science. Analysis of the 'laws' of social
science shows them to differ from those of natural science in
being reflective. The self-defeating or self-fulfilling prophecy
illustrates this unique characteristic, and is reminiscent of the
performative aspect of promising which captivates philosophers. It is accepted that men can change social laws by
altering the conditions under which the laws operate, and
a social scientist might achieve this simply by making his
results public. The possibility of intervention in this way is
not considered out of bounds by many social scientists
today. Gewirth argues that 'man through his awareness of
the impact of the laws of social science on his values may
intervene, in a way which is impossible in the natural
sciences, to remove some of those laws from actual operation
and to create new laws of social science. In this sense man

can effect a factual change in the laws'.[40] This suggests that it would be perverse to ignore or deny the reflexive nature of social knowledge and the special character of social, as opposed to natural, science. From this can be derived a legitimisation of the theoretical and practical intervention attempted by the utopians who were, in effect, exploiting the performative aspect of social science.

The second argument which supports the utopianising of these social scientists rests on the interpretation, alluded to throughout this book, of the utopias as models of social functioning. Watkins's succinct account of individualistic ideal types applies to these utopias without modification:

> An individualistic ideal type places hypothetical actors in some simplified situation. Its premises are: the form (but not the specific content) of the actors' dispositions, the state of their information, and their relationships . . . The ideality of *this* kind of ideal type lies: (i) in the simplification of the initial situation and in its isolation from disturbing factors; (ii) in the abstract and formal, and yet explicit and precise character of the actors' schemes of preferences and states of information; and (iii) in the actors' rational behaviour in the light of (ii).[41]

The utopian models have, first of all, explanatory value as to what would happen in a world without 'disturbing factors' such as property and government and other causes of conflict, and *with* natural sociability and rationality. But then their ideality also suggests that such models should be realised, given the reflexive nature of social knowledge, rather than remaining academic solutions of real social problems. The interventionist impulse converts the ideal type into a virtual utopia, which appears variously as a scientific imperative, manifesto or mandatory revelation.

Interpretative as this account may seem, it supplies a justification for regarding these thinkers as serious social theorists, whose utopias constitute models showing the interaction of familiar human variables outside the familiar social contexts. As ideal types, they offer solutions to social problems which are, in reality, obscured by a multitude of incidental phenomena. They constitute models for the resolution of social conflict under idealised conditions; they also provide alternative structures for social relations (moral, non-contractual, etc.) and for the organisation of production (non-exploitatively, co-operatively, etc.). From our perspective the utopians can be seen to offer analyses of particular social problems of their time, but also ideal solutions to generalised versions of these problems. Furthermore, their theories can be historically viewed as instructive pioneering experiments in the social scientific method which stimulated and influenced the future course of social science.

References
1. See, e.g., J. Lechevalier, *Études sur la science sociale* (Paris, 1834) on Fourier, A. Paget, *Introduction à l'étude de la science sociale* (Paris, 1841) on the utopian socialists, and W. L. Sargent, *Robert Owen and his Social Philosophy* (London, 1860).
2. Indeed, Durkheim developed many of his own analytic devices through the criticism of Saint-Simon, as can be seen in *Socialism and Saint-Simon*.
3. F. Engels, 'Socialism: Utopian and Scientific', MESW, vol. III, p. 115.
4. See works by Becker, Cassirer, Gay, Crocker and Venturi cited, or listed in the select bibliography.
5. OC VII, p. 410.
6. P. Gay, *The Party of Humanity* (Weidenfeld & Nicolson, 1964), p. 199.
7. As J. W. Burrows states in his *Evolution and Society* (Cambridge U.P., 1966), the 19th-century intellectual typically wanted social science to provide the basis for political theory and ethics; the present analysis, however, shows that this could only happen after a considerable infusion of values *into* social science.
8. This is a development beyond Carl Becker's argument which rests chiefly on the secularisation of concepts.
9. E. Mason, *art. cit.*, p. 244.
10. See H. Guerlac, 'Newton's Changing Reputation in the Eighteenth Century' in R. O. Rockwood (ed.) *Carl Becker's Heavenly City Revisited* (Cornell U.P., 1958).
11. *L'Industrie*, p. 190 and *Catéchisme*, p. 61.
12. É. Durkheim, *op. cit.*, Ch. VI.
13. *La Physiologie Sociale*, p. 177.
14. BNMW, Part I, p. 72.
15. RCL, p. 267. My italics.
16. Beecher and Bienvenu, p. 212.
17. PJ I, p. 314.
18. Certainly, Saint-Simon had plans to introduce a unifying, anti-pluralist ideology through public education. See E. de Witt, *Saint-Simon et le Système Industriel* (Paris, 1902), pp. 141-2.

19. J. W. N. Watkins, 'Historical Explanation in the Social Sciences' in J. O'Neill (ed.) *Modes of Individualism and Collectivism* (Heinemann, 1973), pp. 168-9.

20. K. Popper, *The Poverty of Historicism* (Routledge & Kegan Paul, 1961), Ch. 3 especially.

21. Various works testify to the universal existence of such impulses and attributes. See, e.g. H. Schoeck, *Envy: A Theory of Social Behaviour* (Secker & Warburg, 1969) and J. Huizinga, *Homo Ludens* (Paladin, 1970). Renan criticised the 18th and 19th century tendency to identify perfection with moral perfection and suggested other valuable qualities such as wisdom, curiosity and passion. J. Passmore, *The Perfectibility of Man* (Duckworth, 1970), p. 250.

22. Theorists such as Marcuse, Reich and N. O. Brown have challenged Freud's interpretation and his pessimistic conclusions (*op. cit.*, pp. 62, 86-7) and a compendium of their arguments appears in R. King, *The Party of Eros* (N. Carolina U.P., 1972). The chief apologists of aggression are Lorenz (*op. cit.*, pp. 213, 257-8) and A. Storr, *Human Aggression* (Allen Lane, 1968), Ch. 6.

23. The argument that criminality is hereditary is expounded in H. J. Eysenck, *Crime and Personality* (Paladin, 1970). But see also A. W. Griffiths, 'The XYY Anomaly', *The Crimonologist*, 6 (1971), pp. 55-62, which contains many useful references on the controversy, and supports the opposed view.

24. *Encyclopaedia of the Social Sciences*, ed. E. Seligmann (Macmillan, 1932), vol. VII, p. 533. (The entry is by Dewey).

25. S. Freud, *The Ego and the Id*, trans J. Strachey (Hogarth, 1927).

26. M. E. Spiro, *art. cit.*, pp. 19-30.

27. J. Monod, *Chance and Necessity,* trans. A. Wainhouse (Collins, 1972).

28. F. P. Willhoite, 'Ethology and the Tradition of Political Thought', *Journal of Politics*, vol, 33 (1971), p. 620.

29. *Encyclopaedia of the Social Sciences*, p. 533.

30. D. Martindale, *The Nature and Types of Sociological Theory* (Routledge & Kegan Paul, 1961), p. 41.

31. *Ibid.*, p. 29.

32. C. Taylor, 'Neutrality in Political Science' in P. Laslett & W. G. Runciman (eds.) *Philosophy, Politics and Society*, 3rd series (Blackwell, 1967).

33. F. A. Hayek, 'Kinds of Rationalism', repr. in his *Studies in Philosophy, Politics and Economics* (Routledge & Kegan Paul, 1967), pp. 82-95.

34. *Communist Manifesto*, MESW, vol. 1, p. 134.

35. See the first part of R. Fâkkar, *Sociologie, Socialisme et Internationalisme prémarxistes* (Neuchâtel, 1968) for Marx's experience of Saint-Simon.

36. *Communist Manifesto,* p. 134.

37. *Socialism: Utopian and Scientific*, p. 117.

38. *Ibid.*, p. 119.
39. *Ibid.*, p. 126.
40. A. Gewirth, 'Can Men Change Laws of Social Science?' in J. O'Neill, *op. cit.*, p. 139.
41. J. W. N. Watkins, 'Ideal Types and Historical Explanation' in J. O'Neill, *op. cit.*, p. 145.

CHAPTER 8

APPRAISAL

ALTHOUGH they appeared as utopias, the theories of Godwin, Owen, Fourier and Saint-Simon were intended as scientific models, ideal types of conflict-free society, based on radically environmentalist accounts of human psychology. Social values and modes of social control and conflict reduction are deduced from the basic analysis of man, and the revolutionary impulse to realise these harmonious and perfect societies is the consummation of the new social scientist's enterprise which justifies both his utopianism and his interventionist intentions. He provides the constituents for the scientific reconstitution of society as a harmonious entity. To what greater heights could social science aspire?

These theories are instructive in many ways. The acceptance that social scientific reasoning may have a performative conclusion suggests one solution to the 'theory vs. practice' debate. The fusion of fact and value in these theories, and its constructive results, invites us to scrutinise that controversial 'fact or value' disjunction again, and to consider the benefits, such as social potency, of evaluative theories. The utopians' conviction of the need to intervene in a malfunctioning society is a useful corrective to the often exaggerated claim that the social scientist's place is on the side-lines.

The 'special theory' of early nineteenth-century utopianism suggests that utopia is necessarily harmonious, with secondary characteristics such as social cohesion and stability deriving from the dominant value, harmony. Such a society best fosters happiness, the permanent goal of utopia. These utopians also give an innovatory account of the nature of utopian theorising: it is the development of a set of social imperatives derived from scientific analysis. Other characteristics of these thinkers are their human perfectibilism and resulting optimism, and that special innocence engendered by the thoroughgoing environmentalist account of human nature. They are philosophically absolutist without being politically authoritarian, and are necessarily opponents of the democratic outlook — opponents from the left, who seek to realise the essence of democracy while dispensing with its accidental forms. The motivation for their theorising is not the Enlightenment's formalistic desire for a rationally organised society, but compassion, humaneness and benevolence towards mankind. Out of context, Marx's condemnation becomes a vindication: 'they claim to emancipate . . . all humanity at once'. Yet in a sense, the utopian endeavour is a doomed attempt to force mental constructs upon an intractable phenomenal world, which signifies unwarranted confidence on the utopian's part of the universality of his own conceptions; Marx appropriately criticised the utopian socialists for this hyper-rationalism.

Viewed as socio-political theory, and thus absolved from the strictest conditions of scientificity, these utopias deserve credit for their transcendence of the given reality. The utopian mechanism for transcending the existent can be characterised using the fashionable Kuhnian terminology of paradigms and scientific revolution. The nineteenth-century utopias are deliberate attempts to change the paradigms within which political and social theorising takes place. Familiar political ideas, and concepts of the state, are discarded. The old ideals are transformed: freedom without choice, democracy without government, control without coercion. Harmony, integration, cohesion and co-operation become the dominant paradigms with reference to which social theory is conceived, society operates, and to which all other principles are subordinated. If utopian theories are like revolutionary science, little wonder that there was a spate of them in the early nineteenth century, when a proliferation of anomalies discredited the established paradigms of normal, liberal-democratic theory. Even the idiosyncratic theory of a self-taught, isolated individual such as Fourier is an expression of the general disquiet. The creation of new paradigms is a major endeavour of these theories. Indeed, it has always been the critical function which makes Utopia socially important and palatable (since one man's fantasy is another's boredom). The influential, no-holds-barred criticism of the nineteenth-century utopians was as accurate and mordant as their utopias were constructive and critical.

But the articulation of social alternatives is the greatest service which the utopian can perform for those of his fellows who are prisoners of the prevailing ideology and lack the imagination to escape even in spirit. Owen's metaphor of 'withdrawing the mental bandage' describes exactly the function which he and the other utopians hoped to perform for their contemporaries. Their publicisation of alternative societies converted some intellectuals from liberalism to socialism or anarchism, and stimulated working class consciousness, if not in the way that Marx proposed. Working men's reading clubs raised subscriptions of three guineas to buy the seditious *Political Justice* — an indication of the unexpected influence that these thinkers achieved. The pioneering role of the utopians in applying the liberating philosophical ideas of the eighteenth century to the unliberated conditions of society at the turn of the century and after, cannot be overstated.

The social alternatives which they offered have been historically superseded, but the permanence of some human dilemmas, and the snail's pace at which ideologies and paradigms change, make the study of these utopians fruitful today.

APPENDIX

Long notes not included in references.

1. It is doubtful if Owen made such subtle distinctions about malleability. He appreciated the fact that children are especially vulnerable in early life, and even mentions ante-natal influences, without distinguishing the early process of character formation from the later process. But the distinction between conditioning and learning must be made before planning socialisation and education policies, since the resulting aptitudes differ qualitatively, and in efficiency.

Relevant here is the theory of B. F. Skinner, who favours the use of the conditioning process in socialisation. His utopia rests on his experimental psychological work on reinforcement. *Contingencies of Reinforcement* and his more technical works expound the theory. Reinforcement is any environmental response to human action which encourages or discourages the continuance of the action. Its effects carry over to future occasions, tending to establish a behaviour pattern. Skinner's argument is that this can effect complex behaviour, even social behaviour. He wishes to transfer previously voluntary social and moral behaviour into the involuntary sphere by effectively conditioning young children. Social progress is marked, he argues, by the movement from aversive methods of control to nonaversive and inconspicuous ones, which makes notions such as freedom, dignity and automomy redundant (*Beyond Freedom and Dignity*). His idea of 'automatic goodness' aroused a liberal outcry. The implication of Skinner's work is that *any* kind of behaviour can be reinforced, or conditioned out of existence — which strongly supports Owen's arguments.

2. Skinner also argues that freedom is a culture-specific ideal, called into existence as a form of countercontrol when

the methods of control in society are both conspicuous and aversive; the awareness of restriction and the desire for freedom rest on the natural aversion to pain. But 'the feeling of freedom becomes an unreliable guide to action as soon as would-be controllers turn to non-aversive measures'. (*Beyond Freedom and Dignity*, p. 32.) He argues that the political usefulness of freedom then ceases, for it can be no defence against painless and covert controls. (Marcuse, by contrast, tries to re-awaken vigilance against such controls in the name of freedom.) Two (of many) objections to Skinner are that his position logically commits him to agree that any amount of nonaversive control is acceptable, and also that, being a behaviourist, he can only conceive of the idea of freedom as some kind of entity operational instrumentally in the social context, and cannot view it as a powerful idea whose leverage is in the mind. Hence, he ignores its aspirational value.

In fact, as he correctly argues, feelings of freedom bear only a tenuous relation to the existence of freedom, which must therefore be defined in non-subjective terms, as in the three conditions given in the text (Ch.6). Either feeling or existence may be present without the other, and people may be deluded into feeling free when they are really constrained. The correspondence between Diagram 3(1) and (2b) suggests that the subjectively-felt happiness which relates to social control is largely co-extensive with *feelings* of freedom, which may be delusive. Thus, feeling free may become a good in itself, but a good bearing no relation to the actual state of control (See J. P. Plamenatz, *Consent, Freedom and Political Obligation*, 2nd edn., (Oxford U.P., 1968), Ch. VI). So it could be argued that the illusion of freedom should be maintained even in an unfree society, to promote short-term happiness.

It is hard to substantiate that the happiness born of the illusion of freedom is necessarily inferior to that generated by a truly free existence, but it can be argued that the illusion without the reality thwarts the development of the human character, despite subjective happiness. Methods of control such as ideology and conditioning are especially dangerous because they preserve the illusion of freedon while reducing the scope for action and self-control. It may therefore be thought acceptable to destroy both the illusion and the happiness, as Godwin would. In order to get beyond the illusion and maximise freedom, the three conditions must be fulfilled to the utmost.

SELECT BIBLIOGRAPHY

1. Fourier

Oeuvres Complètes (Paris, 1841-8), vols. I-VI.

Oeuvres Complètes (Paris, 1967-8), vols. VII-XII. Ed. S. Debout-Oleskiewicz.

The Passions of the Human Soul (London, 1850), trans. J. R. Morrell.

The Utopian Vision of Charles Fourier (Cape, 1971), ed. J. Beecher and R. Bienvenu.

Barthes, R. *Sade, Fourier, Loyola* (Paris, 1971).

Bourgin, H. *Fourier: Contribution à l'Étude du socialisme francaise* (Paris, 1905).

Bowles, R. C. 'Fourier and the French Revolution', *French Historical Studies,* I (1960), pp. 348-56.

Breton, A. *Ode to Charles Fourier* (Cape Goliard, 1969) trans. K. White.

Chevalier, J. le. *Études sur la Science Sociale* (Paris, 1834).

Considérant, V. *Destinée Sociale* (Paris, 1835), 2 vols.

Dautry, J. 'La Notion de Travail chez Saint-Simon et Fourier', *Journal de Psychologie,* LII (1955), pp. 59-76.

Friedberg, M. *L'Influence de Charles Fourier sur le Mouvement Sociale* (Paris, 1926).

Goret, J. *La Pensée de Fourier* (Paris, 1974).

Gide, C. *Précurseur de la Coopération* (Paris, 1924).

Lansac, N. M. *Les Conceptions Methodologiques et Sociales de Charles Fourier* (Paris, 1926).

Lehouck, E. *Fourier Aujourd'hui* (Paris, 1966).

Mason, E. 'Fourier and Anarchism', *Quarterly Journal of Economics,* 42 (1928), pp. 228-62.

Pellarin, C. *Life of Charles Fourier* (New York, 1848), trans. F. G. Shaw.

Revue Internationale de Philosophie XVI (1962). Articles by Debout-Oleskiewicz, Zilberfarb, Desroche, Poulat and Dautry.

Riasanovsky, N. V. *The Teaching of Charles Fourier* (California U.P., 1969).

Schérer, R. *Charles Fourier, L'Attraction Passionée* (Paris, 1967).

2. Godwin.

An Enquiry concerning Political Justice (London, 1798), 3rd edn. 1st edn. also consulted (Dublin, 1793).

The Enquirer (London, 1797).

Caleb Williams (London, 1816), 3rd edn.

Thoughts on Man (London, 1831).

Uncollected Writings, 1785-1822 (Gainesville, 1968), ed. J. Marken and B. Pollin.

Boulton, J. T. *The Language of Politics* (Routledge & Kegan Paul, 1963), Ch. XI.

Brailsford, H. N. *Shelley, Godwin and their Circle* (Oxford U.P., 1951), 2nd edn.

Carter, A. *The Political Theory of Anarchism* (Routledge & Kegan Paul, 1971).

J. P. Clark 'On Anarchism in an Unreal World', *American Political Science Review,* 69 (1975) pp. 162-7.

'Godwin: Apostle of Universal Benevolence', *Times Literary Supplement* (4.4.1936), pp. 285-6.

Monro, D. H. *Godwin's Moral Philosophy* (Oxford U.P., 1953).

Plamenatz, J. P. *The English Utilitarians* (Blackwell, 1949), pp. 88-96.

Pollin, B. R. *Education and Enlightenment in the Works of William Godwin* (Las Americanas, 1962).

Peru, J. 'Swift's Influence on Godwin' *Journal of the History of Ideas,* 15 (1954), pp. 371-383.

Rodway, A. E. *Godwin and the Age of Transition* (Harrap, 1952).

Werkmeister, L. 'Coleridge and Godwin on the Communication of Truth', *Modern Philology* LV (1958), pp. 170-77.

Willey, B. *The Eighteenth-Century Background* (Chatto & Windus, 1940), Ch. XI.

Woodcock, G. *Anarchism* (Penguin, 1963), Part I.

3. *Owen*

A New View of Society (Penguin, 1970).

Report to the County of Lanark (Penguin, 1970).

Observations on the Effect of the Manufacturing System (London, 1815).

Address to the Inhabitants of New Lanark (London, 1816).

Catechism of the New Society (London, 1817).

Book of the New Moral World, Parts I-VI, (Repr. A. Kelley, 1970).

Six Lectures Delivered in Manchester (Manchester, 1837).

Lectures on the Marriages of the Priesthood of the Old Immoral World (Leeds, 1840).

A Development of the Principles and Plans on which to establish Self-Supporting Home Colonies (London, 1841).

The Revolution in the Mind and Practice of the Human Race (London, 1849).

Millenial Gazette (London, 1841).

Butt, J. *Robert Owen: Prince of Cotton Spinners* (David & Charles, 1971).

Cole, G. D. H. *Robert Owen* (F. Cass, 1925).

Cole, M. *Robert Owen* (Batchworth, 1953).

Dolléans, E. *Robert Owen* (Paris, 1907).

Harrison, J. F. C. *Robert Owen and the Owenites in Britain and America* Routledge & Kegan Paul, 1966).

Miliband, R. 'The Politics of Robert Owen', *J. History of Ideas,* 15 (1954), pp. 233-45.

Podmore, F. *Robert Owen* (London, 1906).

Pollard, S. and Salt, J. (eds). *Robert Owen* (Macmillan, 1971).

Sargent, W. L. *Robert Owen and his Social Philosophy* (London, 1860).

4. *Saint-Simon.*

Oeuvres de Claude-Henri de Saint-Simon (Paris, 1966), 6 vols.

These comprise:

I *Lettre d'un Habitant de Génève à ses Contemporains:*
De La Réorganisation de la Société Européene
L'Industrie, t.i.
II. *L'Industrie,* t.ii.
Sur la Querelle des Abeilles et des Frelons
L'Organisateur
III. *Du Système Industriel*
Le Nouveau Christianisme
IV. *Catéchisme des Industriels*
V. *Catéchisme* (suite)
Quelques opinions philosophiques à l'usage du XIXe
siècle
De l'Organisation Sociale
De la Physiologie Sociale
Memoires sur la Science de l'Homme
Travail sur la Gravitation Universelle
VI. *Introduction aux Travaux Scientifique du XIXe siècle*
Des Bourbons et des Stuarts

Saint-Simon: Selected Political Writings (Blackwell, 1952), ed. F. Markham

La Physiologie Sociale: Oeuvres Choisies (Paris, 1965), ed. G. Gurvitch.

Henri de Saint-Simon (Croome Helm, 1975) trans. and ed. K. Taylor.

Political Thought of Saint-Simon, (Oxford U.P., 1976) ed. G. Ionescu.

Ansart, P. *Sociologie de Saint-Simon* (Paris, 1970).

Durkheim, É. *Socialism and Saint-Simon* (Antioch Press, 1958) trans. C. Sattler.

Fakkâr, R. *Sociologie, socialisme et internationalisme prémarxistes,* (Neuchâtel, 1968).

Gouhier, H. *La Jeunesse d'Auguste Comte* (Paris, 1936), vol. 2.

Halévy, É. *The Era of Tyrannies* (Allen Lane, 1967), trans. R. K. Webb, Ch. 2.

Leroy, M. *Le Socialisme des Producteurs:* Henri Saint-Simon (Paris, 1924).

Lyon, P. V. *The Social and Political Thought of Saint-Simon*. (Unpublished D. Phil Thesis, Bodleian Library, Oxford).

Manuel, F. E. *The New World of Henri Saint-Simon* (Harvard U.P., 1956)

Mason, E. 'Saint-Simonism and the Rationalisation of Industry,' *Quarterly Journal of Economics* XLV (1913), pp. 640-83.

Perroux, F. and Schuhl, P-M. *Saint-Simonisme et pari pour l'industrie XIX-XXe siècles* (Geneva, 1970).

Perroux, F. *Industrie et Creation Collective* (Paris, 1964), Part I.

Stark, W. 'The Realism of Saint-Simon's Spiritual Program', *Journal of Economic History*, 3 (1943), pp. 42-55 and Vol. 5 (1945) pp. 24-43.

Witt, E.de *Saint-Simon et le Système Industriel* (Paris, 1902).

5. *General*

Abrams, P. and McCulloch, A. *Communes, Sociology and Society* (Cambridge U.P., 1976).

Arblaster, A. and Lukes, S. (eds) *The Good Society* (Methuen, 1971).

Barry B. *Political Argument* (Routledge & Kegan Paul, 1965).

Becker, C. *The Heavenly City of the Eighteenth-Century Philosopher* (Yale U.P., 1932).

Benn, S. and Mortimore, G. W. (eds). *Rationality and the Social Sciences* (Routledge & Kegan Paul, 1976).

Berki, R. N. *Socialism* (Dent, 1975).

Buber, M. *Paths in Utopia* (Routledge & Kegan Paul, 1949).

Burrows, J. W. *Evolution and Society* (Cambridge U.P., 1966).

Burry J. *The Idea of Progress* (Macmillan, 1932).

Cassirer, E. *Philosophy of the Enlightenment* (Princeton U.P., 1951).

Cole, G. D. H. *Socialist Thought: The Forerunners 1789-1850* (Macmillan, 1953).

Crocker, L. G. *An Age of Crisis* (John Hopkins, 1959).

——————————*Nature and Culture* (John Hopkins, 1963).

——————————*The Age of Enlightenment* (Macmillan, 1969).

Dubois, C. G. *Problèmes de l'Utopie* (Paris, 1968).

Durkheim, É. *Division of Labour in Society* (Free Press, 1933) trans. G. Simpson.

Duveau, G. *Sociologie de l'Utopie* (Paris, 1961).

Engels, F. *Socialism: Utopian and Scientific* in K. Marx and F. Engels, *Selected Works* (Moscow, 1970), vol. 3.

Gay, P. *The Enlightenment* (Weidenfeld & Nicholson, 1967-70), 2 vols.

Halévy, É. *Growth of Philosophical Radicalism* (Faber, 1972).

Hollis, M. *Models of Man* (Cambridge U.P., 1977).

Kanter, R. M. *Commitment and Community* (Harvard U.P., 1972)

Kateb, G. *Utopia and its Enemies* (Collier-Macmillan, 1963).

Keat, R. and Urry, J. *Social Theory as Science* (Routledge & Kegan Paul, 1975).

Leroy, M. *Histoire des Idées Sociales en France* (Paris, 1950), 4th edn, t.ii.

Lichtheim, G. *The Origins of Socialism* (Weidenfeld & Nicolson, 1969), Part I.

Louvaincour, H. *De Saint-Simon à Fourier* (Chartres, 1913).

Lukes, S. *Individualism* (Blackwells, 1974).

Mannheim, K. *Ideology and Utopia* (Routledge & Kegan Paul, 1936).

Manuel, F. E. 'From Equality to Organicism', *J. History of Ideas, 17 (1956), pp. 54-69.*

——————————— *The Prophets of Paris* (Harvard U.P., 1962).

——————————— & F.P. *French Utopias* (Free Press, 1966).

——————————— (eds.) *Utopias and Utopian Thought* (Souvenir Press, 1973).

Marcuse, H. *Eros and Civilisation* (Sphere, 1969).

Morton, A. L. *The English Utopia* (Lawrence & Wishart, 1969).

Nozick, R. *Anarchy, State and Utopia* (Blackwell, 1975).

O'Neill, J. (ed). *Modes of Individualism and Collectivism* (Heinemann, 1973).

Passmore, J. *The Perfectibility of Man* (Duckworth, 1970).

Pennock, J. and Chapman, J. W. (eds) *Human Nature in Politics* (New York U.P., 1977).

Royal Institute of Philosophy, *The Proper Study* (Macmillan, 1970).

Servier, J. *Histoire de l'Utopie* (Paris, 1967).

Shklar, J. *After Utopia* (Princeton U.P., 1957).

Skinner, B. F. *Walden Two* (Macmillan, 1962).

———————— *Contingencies of Reinforcement* (Appleton-Century, 1969).

———————— *Beyond Freedom and Dignity* (Cape, 1972)

Snook, I. A. (ed.) *Concepts of Indoctrination* (Routledge & Kegan Paul, 1972).

Talmon, J. L. *Political Messianism, The Romantic Phase* (Secker & Warburg, 1960).

Thompson, E. P. *The Making of the English Working Class* (Gollancz, 1963).

Venturi, F. *Utopia and Reform* (Cambridge U.P., 1971).

Vereker, C. *Eighteenth-century Optimism* (Liverpool U.P., 1967).

Wilson, B. (ed). *Rationality* (Blackwell, 1970).

Zeitlin, I. M. *Ideology and the Development of Sociological Theory* (Prentice-Hall, 1968).

INDEX